TRUTH AND TOLERANCE

JOSEPH CARDINAL RATZINGER

TRUTH
AND
TOLERANCE

Christian Belief and World Religions

Translated by Henry Taylor

IGNATIUS PRESS   SAN FRANCISCO

Original German title:
Glaube—Wahrheit—Toleranz: Das Christentum und die Weltreligionen
© 2003 Herder Verlag Herder, Freiburg im Breisgau
Third printing 2004

Original Italian title:
Fede Verità Tolleranza: Il cristianesimo e le religioni del mondo
© 2003 Edizioni Cantagalli, Siena, Italy

Cover design by Roxanne Mei Lum

Central cover image: Altar cross (Christ on the Cross). Mosan. Late 12th c.
Victoria and Albert Museum, London, Great Britain
© Victoria & Albert Museum, London / Art Resource, New York

Dedicated to
Professor Horst Bürkle
in friendship and affection

CONTENTS

PREFACE

In a world that is drawing ever closer together, the question about the meeting of religions and cultures has become a most important subject, and one that is certainly not just the business of theology. The question of the peaceableness of cultures, of peace in matters of religion, has also moved up to become a political theme of the first rank. Yet it is nonetheless first of all a question directed to the religions themselves, how they relate to one another peacefully and how they can contribute to the "education of the human race" in the direction of peace. This complex of problems applies especially to the Christian faith, in that from its very origin, and in its essential nature, it claims to know and to proclaim the one true God and the one Savior of all mankind: "There is salvation in no one else, for there is no other name under heaven given among men by which we must be saved", said Peter to the rulers and the elders of the people of Israel (Acts 4:12). Can this absolute claim still be maintained today? How does it relate to the search for peace among religions and cultures? When the Congregation for the Doctrine of the Faith published the declaration *Dominus Iesus, On the Unicity and Salvific Universality of Jesus Christ and the Church*, in 2000, a cry of outrage arose from modern society, but also from great non-Christian cultures such as that of India: this was said to be a document of intolerance and of a religious arrogance that should have no more place in the world of today. The Catholic Christian could only, in all humility, put the

9

question that Martin Buber once formulated to an atheist:
But what if it is true? Thus it becomes apparent that, beyond
all particular questions, the real problem lies in the question
about truth. Can truth be recognized? Or, is the question
about truth simply inappropriate in the realm of religion and
belief? But what meaning does belief then have, what positive meaning does religion have, if it cannot be connected
with truth?

Thus, various levels of argument have emerged in the dispute, into the midst of which I have in the past decade been
drawn for a variety of reasons. We have first to try to understand what culture is and how cultures may relate to one
another. In the same way we have to get a view of the phenomenon of religion as such and cannot simply start from an
undifferentiated mass of "religions" in general. We first have
to try to understand them as they are, in their historical
dynamic, in their essential structures and types, as also in
their possible relations with one another or as possible threats
to each other, before we try to arrive at any judgments. In
the end, the question of man is up for discussion here, what
he is and how he can become himself or can squander the
opportunity to do so. And finally, we have inevitably to face
up to the question of whether man is made for the truth and
in what way he can, and even must, put the question of truth.

All of this describes a large program, toward which a small
book, which has grown rather by chance, can certainly make
only a modest contribution. As I looked through my lectures on this subject area from the past decade, it emerged
that these approaches from various starting points had nevertheless amounted to something like a single whole—quite
fragmentary and unfinished, of course, but, as a contribution to a major theme that affects us all, perhaps not entirely
unhelpful. I have therefore decided to present as a whole in

this book those texts whose themes are directed to questions concerning faith, religion, culture, truth, and tolerance and that—with the exception of the first piece, published as early as 1964—were all written in the past decade and to put them up for discussion. I hope that a book that has thus been put together, with all its insufficiencies, may yet be of help in the struggle for what concerns us all.

Joseph Cardinal Ratzinger
Rome
Feast of the Transfiguration of Christ
2002

PART ONE

THE CHRISTIAN FAITH IN ITS ENCOUNTER
WITH CULTURES AND RELIGIONS

THE UNITY AND DIVERSITY OF RELIGIONS:
THE PLACE OF CHRISTIANITY
IN THE HISTORY OF RELIGIONS

Preliminary Remarks

I wrote this piece in 1963, for the *Festschrift* published in 1964 on the occasion of Karl Rahner's sixtieth birthday;[1] it was then reprinted in the volume published by my former students for my seventieth birthday, which offered a representative selection from my work.[2] From 1955 to 1963, in the context of my lectures on fundamental theology at Freising and at Bonn, I had also taught about the philosophy of religion and the history of religions and had thereby discovered the importance of the subject of world religions. When this piece appeared in 1964, the Council was at its height; the great debates about the Church, about revelation, about Church and world, dominated theological literature. The subject of world religions was still somewhat marginal; in the work of the Council, it just happened to find a place in the decree *Nostra aetate* of October 28, 1965,

---

[1] *Gott in Welt: Festgabe für Karl Rahner zum 60. Geburtstag* [God in world: Essays presented to Karl Rahner on his sixtieth birthday], ed. H. Vorgrimler (Freiburg: Herder, 1964), 2:287–305.

[2] Joseph Cardinal Ratzinger, *Vom Wiederauffinden der Mitte: Grundorientierungen* [Rediscovering the center: Basic outlines] (Freiburg: Herder, 1997), pp. 60–82.

and to judge from the space allotted, it was not a central theme. Originally, if I recall things correctly, only a declaration on the relation between the Church and the Jews had been planned, which was seen as necessary because of the dramatic events during the Nazis' time in power. A rethinking of the relationship between Christians and the Jewish people had to be one of the themes of the Council. Eastern Christians, who could not regard the historical experience of the West as their own, held that such a declaration could only be made if at the same time something was said about Islam. After this broadening of the theme, it was an almost self-evident development to try to say something about the world of non-Christian religions as a whole. A decree that took shape more or less by chance proved later to be particularly forward-looking.

It seemed appropriate to honor Karl Rahner on his birthday with a paper on this theme, which was just beginning to come to the notice of theologians, inasmuch as this great theologian had included in the fifth volume of his collected works (1962) an essay on "Christianity and the Non-Christian Religions", which had been published in 1961 and in which he pointed out that, in a situation in which "each and every people and culture is becoming an element of inner motivation to every other people and every other culture", every religion that exists in the world has become something that raises questions and opens up possibilities for every other person in the world. This paper, in which Rahner developed the concept of the "anonymous Christian" as a keyword in his response to the challenge of other religions, later became the starting point for arguments that were at times heated. Toward the end of his article, he summed up what he meant by this concept: "It may appear presumptuous to non-Christians for the Christian to reckon the healthy element, that which has been healed and made holy, in every man as a fruit of the grace of Christ and as anonymously Christian and for him to regard the non-Christian as a Christian who has not yet become consciously aware of himself. But the Christian cannot renounce this 'presumption'" (p. 158).

I did not agree with this theory, but it would have seemed to me impertinent for me to take a critical attitude toward it in a *Festschrift* dedicated to him.[3] It seemed better to me first of all to widen the field of inquiry to questions that could be the basis for a dialogue with other religions. Rahner had, quite naturally, regarded the question concerning the salvation of the non-Christian as being really the only question for the Christian who is thinking about the phenomenon of the multiplicity of religions in the world. A second preliminary decision had been involved in this. In the face of the question concerning salvation, the distinction between one religion and another appears to be ultimately irrelevant. These two assumptions have remained determinative for the whole ensuing debate. Even the three basic lines of response in the present discussions about Christendom and world religions—exclusivism, inclusivism, pluralism—are all determined by this way of putting the question: the other religions are always treated as being ultimately of more or less equal value, always looked at from the point of view of their value for salvation. My view, after the years I had devoted to the study of the history of

---

[3] I later made up for this—in response to Rahner's *Grundkurs des Glaubens: Einführung in den Begriff des Christentums* (Freiburg: Herder, 1976) [English trans., *Foundations of Christian Faith: An Introduction to the Idea of Christianity*, trans. William V. Dych (New York: Seabury Press, 1978)]—in my book *Theologische Prinzipienlehre* (Munich: Wewel, 1982), pp. 169–79 [English trans., *Principles of Catholic Theology: Building Stones for a Fundamental Theology*, trans. Mary Frances McCarthy (San Francisco: Ignatius Press, 1987)].

religions, was that a phenomenological investigation, which would not straightaway concern itself with the value of these religions for eternity—thus imposing upon itself the burden of a question that can in fact be decided only by him who shall judge the world—needed to precede such theological judgments about other religions. I was of the opinion that we ought first of all to seek an overall view of the whole panorama of religions, with its inner development and spiritual structure. We should, it seemed to me, not just be discussing an undefined entity of "religion" en masse, which we did not examine closely, in practice, at all; rather, we should first of all try to see whether there was any kind of continuous historical development here and whether any basic types of religion could recognized, which we could then more easily evaluate; and finally we should have to ask how these basic types relate to one another and whether they present us with any basic alternatives, which could then be the subject of philosophical and theological reflections and verdicts.

Even at that time, there was a whole pile of literature on this question, since beyond the sphere of theology, people in religious studies had been working intensively at it since the nineteenth century; I have mentioned in the footnotes here what was of direct help to me in thinking about it. It did not seem right to me to bring these references up to date, which today strike us as rather obsolete, since bibliographies can easily be provided. It was only, and is only, a matter of specifying those writers from whom I learned something; only in a few places, where it really seemed useful, have I made some slight additions. In the introduction with which I had prefaced my article at the time, I described its purpose and its limits as follows: this piece could not provide anything like a "theology of the history of religions"; rather, it was simply intended as preparatory work, to show more clearly the place of Christianity in the history of religions and thereby to reinvest with some concrete and particular meaning theological statements about the uniqueness and the absolute value of Christianity, or perhaps to suggest a reworking of their theological content on the basis of their concrete significance. Because this purpose still seems to me to be worthwhile, and because the greater part of this work is still waiting to be done, it seemed to be appropriate to include the piece in this volume.

1. *The Problem*

The position that Christianity assigns itself in the history of religions is one that was basically expressed long ago: it sees in Christ the only real salvation of man and, thus, his final salvation. In accordance with this, two attitudes are possible (so it seems) with regard to other religions: one may address them as being provisional and, in this respect, as preparatory to Christianity and, thus, in a certain sense attribute to them a positive value, insofar as they allow themselves to be regarded as precursors. They can of course also be understood as insufficient, anti-Christian, contrary to the truth, as leading people to believe they are saved without ever truly being able to offer salvation. The first of these attitudes was shown by Christ himself with respect to the faith of Israel, that is to say, the religion of the Old Testament. That this may also, in a way, be done with regard to all other religions has been clearly shown and emphasized only in recent times. We may in fact perfectly well say that the story of the covenant with Noah (Gen 8:20—9:17) establishes that there is a kernel of truth hidden in the mythical religions: it is in the regular "dying away and coming into existence" of the cosmos that the

God who is faithful, who stands in a covenant relationship, not merely with Abraham and his people, but with *all* men,[4] exercises his providential rule. And did not the Magi find their way to Christ (even if they did so only by a round-about way, by way of Jerusalem, and by the Scriptures of the Old Testament) by means of the star, that is, by means of their "superstition", by *their* religious beliefs and practices (Mt 2:1–23)? Did not their religion, then, kneel before Christ, as it were, in their persons, recognizing itself as provisional, or rather as proceeding toward Christ?

It would seem to be almost a commonplace, in such a connection as this, to refer also to the speech on the Areopagus (Acts 17:22–32), particularly since the reaction of the audience, with their unfriendly attitude toward the message about the Risen One, appears to belie the optimistic theology of this speech: quite obviously, the religion of those people who were being flattered in this manner was not convergent upon Jesus of Nazareth. The contradiction toward which it much rather points calls to mind thereby the other side of the way the religions "of the nations" are conceived in the Bible, a side that is in any case far more in evidence and that is alive in the tradition of the prophets from the very beginning: that sharp criticism of false gods that people make for themselves, a criticism that in its relentlessness can hardly be distinguished from the flat rationalism of an Enlightenment thinker (compare, for example, Is 44:6–20). An analysis of each and every relevant passage in the Bible would, however, go beyond the limits of this essay; the little we have said, however, should be sufficient to establish that two attitudes toward the religions of

<hr>

[4] Cf. J. Daniélou, *Essai sur le mystère de l'histoire* (Paris, Éd. du Seuil) [English trans., *The Lord of History: Reflections on the Inner Meaning of History*, trans. Nigel Abercrombie [London: Longmans; Chicago, H. Regnery, 1958)]; in the German trans., *Vom Geheimnis der Geschichte*, pp. 25ff.

the nations can be found in the Scriptures: a partial recognition, under the heading of preparation, as well as a decided rejection.

The theology of our own day, as we said, has particularly brought to light the positive aspect and, in so doing, has in particular elucidated the extension of the concept of being provisional, preparatory: the fact that even hundreds of years "after Christ", from the point of view of history, people may still be living in the historical state "before Christ" and, thus, legitimately in the provisional, preparatory stage.[5] To sum up, we may say that, according to its own understanding of itself, Christianity stands at one and the same time in both a positive and a negative relation to the religions of the world: it recognizes itself as being linked with them in the unity of the concept of a covenant relationship and lives out of the conviction that the cosmos and its myth, just like history and its mystery, speak of God and can lead men to God; but it is equally aware of a decided No to other religions and sees in them a means by which man seeks to shield himself from God instead of leaving himself open to his demands.[6] In its theology of the history of religions, Christianity does not simply *take the side* of the religious person, *take the side* of the conservative who keeps to the rules of play of his inherited institution; the Christian rejection of the gods signifies much rather a choice to be on the side of the rebel, who for

---

[5] K. Rahner, *Schriften* [Works], 5:140ff.

[6] It was above all the so-called "dialectical theology", following the lead of Karl Barth, that most decidedly emphasized this; with regard to world religions, it was probably H. Kraemer who developed this position with the greatest logic and consistency. His last work of some size (*Religion and Christian Faith* [London: Lutterworth Press, 1956]) is certainly substantially more cautious and more nuanced than the earlier books. Cf. the well-considered account by H. Fries, in *Religion: Handbuch theologischer Grundbegriffe* [Religion: Handbook of basic theological concepts] 2:428–41, especially 438ff.

the sake of his conscience dares to break free from what is accustomed: this revolutionary trait in Christianity has perhaps far too long been hidden beneath various conservative models.[7] There are no doubt a whole series of conclusions waiting to be drawn from this; we will leave them aside for now to go into this question step by step.

If we put before the man of today Christianity's conception of other religions, as we have just outlined it, then he will not for the most part be particularly impressed. He will easily conclude that the recognition of other religions as having a provisional and preparatory character is a sign of arrogance. Christianity's rejection of these other religions, on the other hand, will seem to him an expression of the partisan and disputatious attitude of the various religions, each of which tries to assert itself at the expense of the others and is so incredibly blind as to be unable to see that in reality they are all one and the same. The dominant impression of most people today is that all religions, with a varied multiplicity of forms and manifestations, in the end are and mean one and the same thing; which is something everyone can see, except for them.[8] The man of today will for the most part scarcely respond with an abrupt No to a particular religion's claim to be true; he will

[7] In my little book *Die Einheit der Nationen: Eine Vision der Kirchenväter* [The unity of the nations: A vision of the Church Fathers] (Salzburg: Pustet, 1971), especially pp. 41–57, I have tried to show how clear an awareness of the revolutionary aspect of Christianity there was in patristic literature.

[8] The idea of all religions being one in the end can be seen as a background most clearly in the various books by F. Heiler; see, most recently, *Die Religionen der Menschheit* [The religions of mankind] (Stuttgart: P. Reclam, 1959), p. 52: "Because the reality experienced in religion is always one and the same, then basically there can be only one religion" (see also pp. 877–89); Heiler, *Erscheinsungsformen und Wesen der Religion* [The manifestations and the essence of religion] (Stuttgart: W. Kohlhammer, 1961). A similar view may be found in H. N. Spalding, *The Divine Universe* (Oxford: Basil Blackwell, 1958).

simply relativize that claim by saying "There are many religions." [9] And behind his response will probably be the opinion, in some form or other, that beneath varying forms they are in essence all the same; each person has his own.

If we were to try to extract, from a current intellectual view of that kind, a couple of characteristic opinions, then we might well say: the concept of religion held by "the man of today" (if you will permit me to continue using this fictional means of particularizing) is static; he usually does not foresee any development from one religion to another; rather, he expects each person to remain in his own and to experience it with an awareness that it is, in its basic spiritual core, identical with all the others. There is thus a kind of "worldwide religious citizenship", which does not exclude but rather includes belonging to a given "province" of religion, which finds any change of religious "nationality" undesirable, except just in certain exemplary instances, and in any case takes a very reserved attitude toward the idea of any mission and is basically inclined to reject it. There is a second factor always involved in what we have been saying. Today's man has a concept of religion that is always very much a matter of symbols, heavily spiritualized. Religion appears as a world of symbols, which despite the ultimate unity of the language of human symbols (as is increasingly demonstrated today by psychology and religious anthropology), [10] vary in many details but nonetheless mean just the

---

[9] This is the title of a little book by J. Thomé, dealing with the problem of the absolutist nature of Christianity.

[10] Most impressive on this point are the works collected in the *Eranos-Jahrbuch* and, besides that, the various particular investigations of M. Éliade, especially *Traité d'histoire des religions* (Paris: Payot, 1948) [English trans., *Patterns in Comparative Religion*, trans. Rosemary Sheed (New York: Sheed and Ward, 1958)]; also his enormous late work *Histoire des croyances et des idées*

same thing and really ought to begin to discover their deep, underlying unity. Once this comes about, then the unity of religions will be achieved without doing away with any of their variety—that is the most attractive illusion that particularly those people with religious awareness see before them today as a genuine hope for the future.

No one, to date, has been able to offer our generation a more impressive, warmer, or more persuasive picture of a religion of the future, which in its turn would be able to bring about a "future for religion", than the President of India, Radhakrishnan, whose written works ever and again lead up to a vista of the coming religion of the spirit, which will be able to unite fundamental unity with the most varied differentiation.[11] Over against such prophetic utterances, with their unmistakable weight of human and religious authority, the Christian theologian looks like a dogmatic stick-in-the-mud, who cannot get away from his know-it-all attitude,

---

religieuses, 3 vols. (Paris: Payot, 1976–1983) [English trans., *A History of Religious Ideas*, trans. Willard R. Trask, 3 vols. (Chicago: University of Chicago Press, 1978–1985)]; also the volume of source texts edited by G. Lanczkowski (Herder, 1981). The large book by P. Rech *Inbild des Kosmos: Eine Symbolik der Schöpfung* [Vision of the cosmos: A symbolic interpretation of creation], 2 vols. (Salzburg: O. Müller, 1966), is important. In this connection, Daniélou (*Essai sur le mystère*; in the German ed., pp. 144–52, with relevant material at pp. 153–70), brings to our attention the work of René Guénon, which is dominated by the concept of the symbol.

[11] See especially his books *The Hindu View of Life* (1926); *Eastern Religions and Western Thought* (1939); *Religion and Society* (1947); *Recovery of Faith* (1956). For a critical examination of Radhakrishnan, especially P. Hacker, "Ein Prasthnatraya-Kommentar des Neuhinduismus: Bemerkungen zum Werk Radhakrishnans" [A neo-Hindu Prasth-Natraya commentary: Observations on the work of Radakrishnan], *Orientalische Literatur-Zeitung* 56 (1961): 565–76; for a popular view: J. Neuner, "Gespräch mit Radhakrishnan" [Conversation with Radhakrishnan], *Stimme der Zeit* 87 (1962): 241–54. See also Kraemer, *Religions and Christian Faith* (in German trans., *Religion und christlicher Glaube* [Göttingen, 1959], pp. 95–134).

whether he expresses it in the swaggering manner of apologists in past times or whether in the friendly manner of contemporary theologians, who acknowledge to the other person to what extent he is already a Christian without being aware of it. Nevertheless, if the future of religion is something close to his heart, if he is convinced that Christianity, and not some vague religion of the spirit, is the religion of the future, then he will feel compelled to ask further questions and to conduct further research in order to gain a clearer idea of the meaning and direction of the history of religion and the place of Christianity within it.

2. *The Place of Christianity in the History of Religion*

The very first impression someone will receive when, in matters of religion, he begins to look beyond the limits of his own is that of a limitless plurality, an absolutely overwhelming multiplicity and variety, which makes the question about truth seem illusory from the very start. Yet, as we have already mentioned, this first impression does not last long; it soon gives way to another: that of the hidden identity of the religious worlds, which are distinguished from one another in name and superficial images but not in the great fundamental symbols or in what these ultimately stand for. This impression is very largely correct. There is in fact a wide sphere of religion in which commonly shared "religious experience" (to use Radhakrishnan's words) is more decisive than differences between the outward forms. There are many religions that, whether explicitly or unconsciously, are in a profound spiritual relationship with each other, which in ancient times was seen in the ease with which divine figures were exchanged or "translated" from one religion to another and could be identified as standing for the same thing: the multiplicity of religions resembles in this area the multiplicity of languages, which can be translated from one into another because they relate to the same structure of thought. A similar sense, though not exactly the same, is expressed whenever Asiatic religions are able to exist within each other: whenever a person can be, for example, at the same time a Buddhist and a Confucian, or a Buddhist and a Shintoist.

Thus, as we have already seen, out of the impression of complete plurality, which represents, so to speak, the first stage of perception, there develops an impression of all being ultimately the same. Modern philosophers of religion are convinced that they can even specify the basis of this hidden identity. In the way they conceive it, any religion that exists originates—so far as it is "genuine"—in that form of inner experience of the divine that is experienced in its final common form by mystics of all times and all places. All religion is said to be based in the final analysis on the experience of the mystic, who alone is able to make contact directly with the divine and who passes something of this on to the many, who are not capable of having such experience.[12] In this view, religion would exist among mankind in two (and only two) forms: in the direct form of mysticism as "firsthand" religion and, then, in the indirect form of knowledge only "passed on" from the mystic, that is to say, as faith and, thus, as "secondhand" religion. The articulate and formally expressed religion of the many would thus be secondhand religion, a mere sharing in a mystical experience that is in itself formless; it would be a secondary translation of this into a multifarious and changing

[12] This is particularly clear in O. Spann, *Religionsphilosophie auf geschichtlicher Grundlage* [Philosophy of religion on a historical basis] (Vienna: Gallus-Verlag, 1947). Compare with that the criticism of A. Brunner, *Die Religion* (Freiburg im Breisgau: Herder, 1956), pp. 57ff.

language of forms, but without any real significance of its own.[13] It is clear that this mystical interpretation of religion forms the background for the idea of religion of man today, which we have already outlined, and that the significance and correctness of this idea stands or falls with this reduction of religion to mysticism.

Thus, the starting point for a further theological investigation at last becomes clearer, and we can now formulate it in the quite concrete question of whether the mystical interpretation of religion is correct. It is beyond doubt that a large part of the phenomenon of religion is quite correctly thus conceived—that, as we have said, there is a hidden element of identity in the multiform world of religions. Yet it is equally clear that the whole phenomenon cannot be thus conceived; rather, any attempt to do so would result in a false simplification. If we look at the history of religion as a whole (so far as it is known to us), we get a far less static impression; we meet with a far greater element of genuine historical dynamic (history progresses; it is not merely a constant symbolic recurrence of the same thing); the simple identification of everything with a single thing, to which we are led by the notion of mysticism, breaks down and gives way to a certain structure that has become quite visible today, and the mystical way crystallizes out as one particular element among several, one that appears at a given point in the history of religion and that presupposes a series of developments that are independent of it.

---

[13] The widespread distinction between firsthand and secondhand religion seems to have been first used by American psychologists of religion; cf. E. Brunner, *Offenbarung und Vernunft: Die Lehre von der christlichen Glaubenserkenntnis*, 2nd ed. (Darmstadt: Wissenschaftliche Buchgesellschaft, 1961), p. 280 [English trans., *Revelation and Reason: The Christian Doctrine of Faith and Knowledge*, trans. Olive Wyon (Philadelphia: Westminster Press, 1946)].

There is first of all the stage of early (so-called primitive) religion, which passes over into the stage of mythical religion, in which the most varied experiences of the early stage are brought into a coherent overall view of things. Neither stage has anything to do with mysticism in the more limited sense, but both together constitute the broad preliminary field in the history of religion, which continues to remain significant as an underlying current beneath it all. If, accordingly, the first great step in the history of a religion lies in the transition from the scattered experiences of the primitive stage to large-scale myth, then the second and decisive step, determinative for present-day religion, lies in leaving the confines of myth. This step has historically occurred in three different ways:

1.   In the form of *mysticism*, in which the myth, as a merely symbolic form, is stripped of its illusion and the *absolute value* of an unnameable *experience* is set up. In fact, then, mysticism proves to be conservative of myth, providing a new foundation for the myth, which is now interpreted as a symbol of the reality.

2.   The second form is that of *monotheistic revolution*, which is seen in its classic form in Israel. Here the myth is rejected as man-made and lacking authority. The *absolute* nature of the *divine call* that is issued through the prophet is maintained.

3.   Then thirdly there is *enlightenment*, which first happened properly on a large scale in Greece: here, the myth is outgrown as a prescientific form of knowledge, and *rational knowledge* is set up as the *absolute value*. Religion and religious values become meaningless; at best they continue to perform a purely formal function as political ceremonial (that is, relating to the *polis*, the civic unit of society).

This third way did not gain full force until modern times, indeed, not really until the present day, and it still seems to have its real future before it. What is remarkable about it is that it does not represent a path within the history of religion but rather seeks to bring that to an end and to lead us beyond it, as something now obsolete. Nonetheless (or rather, therefore) it is not unrelated to the history of religion; on the contrary, we would have to say that how religion is able to establish its relationship to this "third way" will be of decisive importance for the future of religion and its prospects with mankind. It is well known that in the time of the early Church, Christianity (the "second way" in our scheme) succeeded in forging a fairly close relationship with the forces of enlightenment. Today, the effectiveness of Radhakrishnan and his way of conceiving things depends, not only on their religious power, but also on the remarkable alliance with what, *mutatis mutandis*, we may call the forces of enlightenment.

Summarizing what has been said, we find that there is no more an identity of religions in general than there is an unrelated plurality among them; rather, we find that a structural formula emerges that encompasses the dynamic aspect of history (of becoming, development), the aspect of constant relationship, and that of concrete and irreducible variety and differentiation. This historical development could be represented in outline thus:

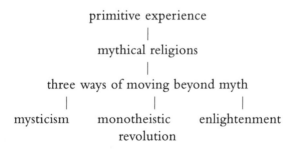

primitive experience
|
mythical religions
|
three ways of moving beyond myth
| | |
mysticism   monotheistic   enlightenment
             revolution

We could include within this basic scheme the result to which a "critique of historical reason" might lead in religious matters. It is located, as we have said, between the idea of unlimited plurality and that of an unlimited identity, so as to refer us instead to a limited number of patterns that have their place in a certain process of spiritual development. We have further found that setting up an absolute value is not, as is usually assumed, peculiar to the "monotheistic" way alone but is characteristic of all three ways in which man has left myths behind him. Just as "monotheism" maintains the absolute value of the divine call that it hears, so mysticism starts from the absolute value of the "spiritual experience", as being the only real thing in religion, beside which it sets down everything that can be said and formulated as being secondary and replaceable symbolic forms. This is where the actual point of misunderstanding lies between Christianity and those people caught up today by the theology of identity of spiritualizing mysticism. The man of today (let us for the sake of simplicity retain this collective label) feels repelled by Christianity's claim to absolute validity, which, in view of so many historical relativizations that are well known to him, seems to him little worthy of credence; and he feels much better understood and more attracted by the symbolism and spiritualism of someone like Radhakrishnan, who teaches the relativity of all religious expression that can be articulated and the ultimate validity of that spiritual experience alone which can never be adequately expressed, an experience that (though, indeed, coming in stages) is everywhere one and the same.

As obvious as such a choice may appear, it depends on drawing a premature conclusion. For it is only in appearance that Radhakrishnan stands, in contrast to the partisan position of the Christian, for an openness to all religion that is above any partisanship; the truth is that, like the Christian, he takes as his starting point the doctrine of an absolute value, to be precise, the one that holds a key place in *his* religious system and that seems for Christianity (for any kind of genuine monotheism whatever) no less an arrogant assumption than does the absolute claim of the Christian for his own way. For he teaches the absolute value of imageless spiritual experience, to which all else is relative; the Christian denies that mystical experience has sole validity and teaches the absolute value of the divine call that has been made audible in Christ. To force upon him the absolute value of mysticism as the only element ultimately valid is no less arrogant an imposition than offering the absolute value of Christ to the non-Christian.

Finally, we would have to add that even the third of the entities we found, which we called "enlightenment", referring to the move to an attitude based on a strictly rationalistic conception of reality, has its own absolute value: the absolute value of rational ("scientific") knowledge. When science becomes the dominant element in a view of the world (and this is just what we mean by "enlightenment" here), this absolute value becomes exclusive; it develops into the theory that scientific knowledge is the only valid knowledge and becomes a denial of the absolute value of religion, which is in itself on a different level of reality. In that case, the believer, or even someone who practices religion, will have to point to the limitations of this absolute claim. It moves within the limits of certain categories, within which it is strictly valid; but to maintain that it is only within these categories that man can know anything at all is an unfounded presupposition, which in any case is shown by experience to be untrue.[14] But we must bear in mind that

---

[14] K. Hübner, *Glaube und Denken: Dimensionen der Wirklichkeit* [Faith and thought: Dimensions of reality] (Tübingen: Mohr Siebeck, 2001), offers some important considerations on this question.

this third way is only indirectly involved in a decision about religion; the real questions concerning relations between religions arise between the first and the second way ("mysticism" and "monotheistic revolution"). Hence, we now have to go further into these questions.

3. Mysticism and Belief

After what we have just said, it is clear that as between the two ways we have called "mysticism" and "monotheistic revolution", no choice can be made in favor of one or the other on rational grounds. That would presuppose the straightforward absolute validity of the rational way, which we have just disputed. This choice is, rather, in the final analysis a matter of faith, albeit of a faith that makes use of rational standards. What can be done in the scientific field is simply this, to try to acquire a more detailed knowledge of the structure of the two ways and of the relationship between them.

At this point a more precise explanation of what is meant in this context by "mysticism" is no doubt required. It should have become clear, in what has already been said, that we are not referring simply to a form of religious practice that can also find its place in the Christian faith. "Mysticism" is here understood in a more radical sense, as one path in the history of religion, as an attitude that does not tolerate any other element superior to itself; rather, it regards the imageless, unmetaphorical, and mysterious experience of the mystic as the only determinative and ultimate reality in the realm of religion.[15] This

[15] Obviously, even a Christian's mysticism can pass over into this attitude, the temptation of which does in a certain sense lie in the very nature of mysticism. But it then ceases to be "Christian"; its being Christian depends on its accepting a subordinate position. In this respect, one could virtually define the nature of Christian mysticism on this basis.

attitude is just as characteristic of Buddha as of the great religious thinkers of the Hindu group of religions, even if they hold to positions so firmly opposed to each other as that of Shankara on one side and Ramanuja on the other.[16] This is the way that constitutes, amid multifarious derivations, the unified background to Asiatic higher religion. What is characteristic for this mysticism is the experience of identity: the mystic sinks down into the ocean of the all-one, irrespective of whether this is portrayed, with emphatic *theologia negativa*, as "nothingness" or, in a positive sense, as "everything". In the final stage of such an experience, the "mystic" will no longer be able to say to his God, "I am Thine"; the expression he uses is "I am Thee".[17] The difference has been left behind in what is provisional, preparatory, and what is ultimately valid is fusion, unity.

"Absolute monotheism is the perfection of dualism, which is where religious consciousness begins", says Radhakrishnan.[18] This experience of inner identification, in which all distinctions fall away and appear as an unreal veil over the hidden unity with the ground of all things, forms the basis

---

[16] See textbooks on the history of religions, and also H. Losch, "Ramanuja", in *Die Religion in Geschichte und Gegenwart* (Religion in history and today; hereafter abbreviated RGG), 2nd ed. (Tübingen: Mohr, 1927–31), 5:733f.; and his "Shankara", in RGG, 3rd ed. (Tübingen: Mohr, 1957–1965), 6:6f., with further literature cited. See also T. Ohm, *Die Liebe zu Gott in den nichtchristlichen Religionen* [Love for God in the non-Christian religions], 2nd ed. (Freiburg im Breisgau: Wewel, 1957), pp. 230ff.

[17] Cf. J. A. Cuttat, "Vergeistigungs-'Technik' und Umgestaltung in Christus" [Spiritualizing technique and transformation in Christ], *Kairos* 1 (1959): 18–30; Cuttat, "Östlicher Advent und gnostischer Versuchung" [Easter coming and gnostic temptation], *Kairos* 2 (1960): 145–63; H. W. Gensichen, "Die biblische Botschaft gegenüber dem Hinduismus" [The biblical message contrasted with Hinduism], in RGG, 3rd ed., 3:349–52, with detailed bibliography; in Gensichen, "Biblische Botschaft", 3:350, we find the contrast made between "I am Thee" and "I am Thine".

[18] As quoted by Gensichen, "Biblische Botschaft", 3:351.

for the secondary theology of identity, which we have discussed in detail, in which all the different religions, precisely because they are different, are relegated to the sphere of what is provisional and preparatory, the sphere in which the veil of distinction still hides the secret of identity. The dogmatic presupposition of the assertion that all religions are equal, with which the Western man of today has so much sympathy, is revealed here as the claim that God and the world, the Divinity and the depths of the soul, are identical. At the same time it becomes clear why, for Asian religious sensibility, the person is not an ultimate reality, and hence God is not conceived of in personal terms: the person, the contrast between I and Thou, belongs to the sphere of distinctions; in the all-is-one experience of the mystic, these boundaries that separate I from Thou are absorbed, are revealed as provisional.

The model in which the monotheistic revolution is embodied, on the contrary, is not the mystic but the prophet. For him, the decisive thing is, not identifying with, but standing over against the God who calls and who commands. Thereby we can finally explain why we have thus far continually talked about a monotheistic "revolution" whenever we wished to contrast this with the way of mysticism in terms of the history of religions. Not every form of so-called monotheism can be contrasted with mysticism as belonging to an independent stepping forth from the confines of myth. We have rather at this point, from the start, to exclude two forms of monotheism: on one hand, the various forms of belief in a single god that may be found in the primitive sphere and that are not part of the historical dynamic of higher religion; and, on the other, that kind of evolutionary monotheism that has, for instance, developed more and more strongly in India since the Middle

Ages.[19] Monotheism in India is different from that of Israel in two ways: firstly, it is directed toward mysticism, that is to say, it is open to monistic development and thus may appear as a mere preliminary stage to something of more permanence, that is, the experiencing of identity. Secondly, it arose, not through a revolution, as in Israel, but through an evolution; in consequence, the gods were never overthrown; rather a peaceful balance between varying forms came about, as between God and the gods, between monotheistic and polytheistic beliefs.[20] In contrast to that, the monotheism of Israel (and that of Zoroaster) had its origin by way of a revolution, the revolution of a few people who were filled with a new religious awareness and who shattered the myths and overthrew the gods of whom the myths spoke. Solely because of this completely independent departure from the myths monotheism, in the proper sense, represents a separate development in the history of religion. This is what took place in Israel and, springing from the root of Israel in Christianity and in Islam, also—but with far lesser historical effect—in the figure of Zoroaster.[21]

[19] On "monotheism" in India, see H. von Glasenapp, *Die fünf großen Religionen* [The five great religions] (Düsseldorf, 1952), 1:34ff. Concerning the problem of monotheism as such, see R. Pettazzoni, *Der allwissende Gott* (Frankfurt, 1957) (the German trans. of *L'onniscienza di Dio* [Torino: Einaudi, 1955]; English trans., *The All-Knowing God: Researches into Early Religion and Culture* [London: Methuen, 1956]).

[20] Pettazzoni, *Allwissende Gott*, pp. 109–18, has best made the distinction, in terms of the history of religions, between evolutionary and revolutionary monotheism. Cf. also H. de Lubac, "Der Ursprung der Religion", in *Gott, Mensch, Universum*, ed. J. Bivort de la Saudée (Graz: Verlag Styria, 1956), pp. 313–46, especially pp. 339ff.; a German trans. of de Lubac's "L'Origine de la religion" in *Essai sur Dieu, l'homme et l'univers* [Essay on God, man, and the universe], ed. J. Bivort de la Saudée (Tournai and Paris: Casterman, 1951).

[21] Concerning the enigmatic figure of Zoroaster, see especially R. C. Zaehner, *The Dawn and Twilight of Zoroastrianism* (London: Weidenfeld and Nicolson,

These brief indications should already suffice to show that in "monotheism" and "mysticism" we have before us two structures that right from the start are built up in quite different ways. In mysticism, inwardness holds the first place; spiritual experience is posited as an absolute. That includes the view that God is purely passive in relation to man and that the content of religion can only consist of man plunging into God. God does not act; there is only the "mysticism" of men, the gradual ascent to union. The monotheistic way starts from a conviction that is the opposite of this: here man is the passive element upon whom God acts; here it is man who can do nothing of himself, but instead we have here an activity on the part of God, a call from God, and man opens himself to salvation through obedience in response to the call. To that extent, we could choose, instead of the opposites "mysticism—monotheistic revolution", the opposites "mysticism—revelation", purely as a phenomenological criterion, without bringing monotheistic faith into play at all. For the one way, it is characteristic for "mysticism" to occur as a spiritual experience of man and for this occurrence to be regarded as the ultimate and, in truth, only reality in the history of religion and, hence, as being absolute. If this is our starting point, then there can ultimately be no "revelation" of God whatever; it would be illogical to speak of it in this context, whereas it is equally characteristic of the other way for "revelation" to exist, for there to be a call from God, and for this call to be what is absolute among mankind, for it to be from it that salvation comes to man.[22]

1961); W. Eilers, in RGG, 3rd ed., 6:1866ff. (with literature); G. Widengren, *Die Religionen Irans* [The religions of Iran] (Stuttgart: W. Kohlhammer, 1965), pp. 60–93, 98–102.

[22] This distinction—between the passivity of the divine and the activity of men, on one hand, and, on the other, the primary activity of God and the

What we have said has also dealt with the objection that monotheism is basically only an arrested form of mysticism[23] or an arrested form of enlightenment, in which people have forgotten to include one figure in the overthrow of the myths: the figure of the one and only God. In reality (and also in the phenomenology of religion) "God" is something different from the gods,[24] and in reality, as we have shown, there is a completely different structure of concepts from that of "mysticism": the experience of the activity and the personal nature of God is based on a quite different overall relationship to reality from the mystic's concept of identity and the reduction of the person to the impersonal state that is bound up with it. The "monotheist" holds that the absolutely contrary reduction is correct: the reduction of everything impersonal to persons. As we said, we will not discuss here which of these positions is right; it has just been a matter of demonstrating that they are quite independent of

---

passivity, or merely derivative activity, of man—though little attention is paid to it, represents in my view the principal difference between biblical and Greek thought. This is where the central difficulty lay in the synthesis of the two systems of thought that was achieved in the patristic era. The seams of this synthesis may still be clearly detected in dogmatic theology relating to the nature of God, and in theology as a whole, and seem today to be pulling apart again, so to speak. For the main biblical statements about God are those of creation and revelation (incarnation); both of these assume God's external activity and relationships outside himself, both of which are impossible on the basis of Greek metaphysics. One feels that, basically, the patristic attempt at synthesis was confronted by the same difficulties as those imposed on us with renewed urgency today by the encounter with the history of religions.

[23] That is, no doubt, the notion behind the theory of Radhakrishnan about dualism as the beginning of religious awareness.

[24] I tried to demonstrate this in my reception lecture at Bonn: "Der Gott des Glaubens und der Gott der Philosophen" [The God of faith and the God of the philosophers] (Munich and Zürich, 1960); republished in Ratzinger, *Vom Wiederauffinden der Mitte*, pp. 40–59.

one another and quite different. Recent analyses of mystical experience, of course, believe they are able to show the exact opposite of the previous objection (that monotheism is arrested mysticism): that the experience of identity is only the first stage on the way of mysticism, although of course few get beyond it, so that that becomes the real temptation in mysticism; not until that stage is past comes the far more painful step of separating from oneself and of passing beyond into real transcendence. This step demands of man the crucifixion of being torn free from himself and being left without a place, the state in which no earthly support remains, yet only this can bring man before the true face of God, so that when it is given him to journey forth into this mystery of darkness and of faith, all the previous mystery of light and of vision seems to him but an insignificant prelude, which he—not suspecting the depth of God—was earlier tempted to take for the ultimate reality, for the whole.[25] It should be clear that the best way forward for a fruitful dialogue between the two ways is opened up by reflections of this kind, a dialogue that would make it possible to get beyond the unsatisfactory duality of "monotheism" and "mysticism" without monotheism being absorbed into an unfruitful mystical syncretism or, contrariwise, making the religions devoted to mysticism subject to a false and petty absolutism on the part of

[25] R. C. Zaehner, "Zwei Strömungen der muslimischen Mystik" [Two currents in Muslim mysticism], *Kairos* 1 (1959): 92–99. From a different starting point, P. Hacker comes to similar conclusions in "Die Idee der Person im Denken von Vedanta-Philosophen" [The idea of the person in the thought of Vedanta philosophers], *Studia Missionalia* 13 (1963): 30–52. Further important points of view on this question are found in H. U. von Balthasar, "Fides Christi", trans. Edward T. Oakes, S.J., in Balthasar, *Explorations in Theology*, vol. 2: *Spouse of the Word* (San Francisco: Ignatius Press, 1991), pp. 43–79. I have tried to say something more detailed about light and darkness in mysticism in my article "Licht", in *Handbuch theologischer Grundbegriffe*, 2:44–54, especially 49 and 52f.

Western historical forms. But for that, a great deal of patience, tact, and integrity in their religious seeking will be needed on both sides.

4. *The Structure of the Great Ways of Religion*

Just for the moment, let us forgo any attempt to pursue this question farther, since it is still far too large, and instead draw a few more conclusions from the beginnings we have made about the structure of these two great ways, so that we can learn to understand more clearly the place of Christianity in the religious movement of mankind as a whole.

a.   As we have come to know from the foregoing, the real difference between the mystical and monotheistic ways is that, in the first case, "God" remains entirely passive and the decisive element is in man's experience, his discovery of his identity with the being of all that is; whereas in the second case there is belief in the activity of God, who calls man. This state of things results in a far more evident difference, particularly striking from the point of view of the phenomenology of religion, which brings a further series of consequences in its train. What results is the historical character of the beliefs based on the prophetic revolution and the unhistorical character of the mystical way. The experience upon which all else depends in mysticism expresses itself only in symbols: the heart of it is the same in all ages. It is not the exact time of the experience that matters but its content, which signifies a transcending and relativizing of everything temporal. But the divine calling that the prophet knows has come to him can be dated; there is a here-and-now about it, a story is beginning from it: a relationship has been established, and relationships between persons have a historical character—they *are* what we call history. Jean Daniélou in particular has shown this fact with great emphasis, stressing again and again that Christianity "is essentially faith in an event", whereas the great non-Christian religions maintain the existence of an eternal world "that stands in opposition to the world of time. The fact of the eternal breaking into time, which gives it duration and turns it into history, is unknown to them." [26] This trait of being unhistorical is something mysticism shares as well with myth and with primitive religions, which according to Mircea Éliade are characterized by "their revolt against concrete time, their nostalgia for a periodical return to the mythic time of origins".[27] Conversely, this would be the point at which to bring out what is special about Christianity within the monotheistic way, insofar as one might show how it is only here that the historical basis has been developed to its full strength, so that the monotheistic way attains here to the full force of its particularity.[28]

b. Furthermore, the obvious difference between the patriarchs and prophets of Israel and the great founders of East Asian religions becomes comprehensible on the basis of the principle outlined here. If we set the principal actors in the covenant-event of Israel against the religious personalities of

[26] Daniélou, *Vom Geheimnis der Geschichte*, p. 128.

[27] Ibid. Cf. M. Éliade, *Der Mythos der ewigen Wiederkehr* [German trans. of *Le Mythe de l'éternel retour*] (Düsseldorf, 1953), p. 5 [English trans., *The Myth of the Eternal Return; or, Cosmos and History*, trans. Willard R. Trask (New York: Princeton Univ. Press, 1974)].

[28] There is a detailed account of this in E. Brunner, *Offenbarung und Vernunft*, pp. 242–61, especially pp. 250–61; cf. also, with regard to Islam, the references in Daniélou, *Vom Geheimnis der Geschichte*, p. 130, where he quotes J. Moubarac: "Mohammedan thinking knows nothing of an eternal duration but contemplates only atoms of time, moments (anat)."

Asia, then first of all we feel remarkably uncomfortable. Abraham, Isaac, Jacob, and Moses, with all their wiles and tricks, with their ill-temper and their inclination to violence, seem at least quite mediocre and pathetic next to someone like Buddha, Confucius, or Lao-tzu,[29] but even such great prophetic characters as Hosea, Jeremiah, and Ezekiel are not entirely persuasive in such a comparison. That was a perception that concerned the Church Fathers in the meeting between the Bible and Hellenism. If Augustine, who had discovered and learned to love the beauty of truth in Cicero's *Hortensius*, found the Bible, which he picked up afterward, unworthy to be set by the side of the "Tullian dignity", the shock of such a comparison is carefully hidden: before the sublimity of mythical thought, the actors in the history of faith appear practically uncouth.[30] It was not much different for other Church Fathers: Marius Victorinus had difficulty here, and similarly Synesius of Cyrene, and if you read the circumstantial attempts at whitewashing by Saint Ambrose, in his *Apologia David*, then you feel the same question arise and, with it, a certain helplessness, which certainly cannot be overcome with such reflections as those. Disputing about the "scandal" makes no sense here; it merely opens the way to the real question. From the

---

[29] Cf. the way these figures are portrayed in K. Jaspers, *Die großen Philosophen*, vol. 1 (Munich, 1957), pp. 128–85; 898–933 [English trans., *The Great Philosophers*, 4 vols. (New York: Harcourt, Brace and World, 1962–1995)]. It is of course often disputed that the figure of Lao-tzu was historical (e.g., in H. Ringgren and A. Ström, *Die Religionen der Völker* [The religions of the peoples] [Stuttgart: Alfred Kröner, 1959], p. 425); but this question does not affect the comparison being made here.

[30] It is well known that this was the term by which Nietzsche referred to Augustine; see F. van der Meer, *Augustinus der Seelsorger* [Augustine the pastor] (Cologne: Bachem, 1951), pp. 306f.; it is interesting that Jaspers' judgment, *Großen Philosophen*, pp. 394ff., though more politely expressed, is not much different in essentials.

point of view of the history of religions, Abraham, Isaac, and Jacob really are not "great religious personalities".[31] Interpreting that away means here precisely interpreting away what impels us toward what is peculiar to and particular in the biblical revelation.

This particular and wholly other element lies in the fact that the God of the Bible is not seen, as by the great mystics, but is experienced as one who acts and who remains (for the inner as for the outer eye) in the dark. And this in turn is because man does not, here, make his own attempts to rise, passing through the various levels of being to the innermost and most spiritual level, thus to seek out the divine in its own place, but the opposite happens: God seeks out man in the midst of his worldly and earthly connections and relationships; God, whom no one, not even the purest of men, can discover for himself, comes to man of his own volition and enters into relationship with him. We could say that biblical "mysticism" is not a mysticism of images but of words and that its revelation is not a contemplation by man but the word and the act of God. It is not primarily the discovery of some truth; rather, it is the activity of God himself making history. Its meaning is, not that divine reality becomes visible to man, but that it makes the person who receives the revelation into an actor in divine history. For here, in contrast to mysticism, God is the one who acts, and it is *he* who brings salvation to man. Once again, it was Jean Daniélou who astutely perceived this. What he has to say about this deserves to be quoted at length. "For syncretism," he says (and we can say, instead of this, "for the various ways of religion outside the revolution started by the prophets"),

---

[31] See the following note.

Those who are saved are the inward-looking souls, whatever the religion they profess. For Christianity, they are the believers, whatever level of inwardness they may have achieved. A little child, an overworked workman, if they believe, stand at a higher level than the greatest ascetics. "We are not great religious personalities", Guardini once said; "we are servants of the Word." Christ himself had said that Saint John the Baptist might well be "the greatest among the children of men", but that "the least among the sons of the kingdom is greater than he" (see Lk 7:28). It is possible for there to be great religious personalities in the world even outside of Christianity; it is indeed very possible for the greatest religious personalities to be found outside Christianity; but that means nothing; what counts is obedience to the Word of Christ.[32]

c.   Finally, on this basis we can understand why the distinction between firsthand and secondhand religion, mentioned at the start (heading 2), which from the point of view of mysticism represents the only real distinction in the sphere of religion, is not recognized by Christianity, that is, it has no validity within Christianity. It could at once be objected that in Christianity, too, there is a distinction between the saint and the ordinary worshipper, between the mystic and the ordinary believer, for whom the direct experience of God is inaccessible. There is no doubt that this distinction exists, but it is secondary. It does not distinguish between two kinds of religion, between the possession of religious *reality* and mere borrowed piety that has to make do with symbols because the power of mystical absorption is lacking. If I regard mysticism as the essential thing in religion and see everything else merely as a secondary expression of what has taken place in the sanctuary of mystical experience, then the mystic is indeed the true

[32] Daniélou, *Vom Geheimnis der Geschichte*, pp. 133f.

possessor of religion; everyone else then has to be satisfied with the mere outer shell; theirs is "secondhand". But if the decisive thing is, not one's own religious experience, but the divine call, then in the last resort everyone who believes in that call is in the same situation: each is being called in the same way. While in mystical religion the mystic has "firsthand" and the believer "secondhand" religion, here just God alone deals at "first hand". All men without exception are dealing at second hand: servants of the divine call.

All that we have said cannot and should not serve to fashion a handy rational justification of Christian faith in the controversy between religions. We have been far more concerned to determine more clearly (and this is still rather inexact) the place of Christian faith and practice in the history of religions as a whole, by looking at the others to see ourselves and our own way more clearly. If, in looking at this question, what divides us from others has been emphasized, what unites us with them should not be forgotten: that we are all a part of a single history that is in many different fashions on the way toward God. For that was what turned out to be the critical insight: for Christian faith, the history of religions is not a circle of what is endlessly the same, never touching the essential thing, which itself ever remains outside of history; rather, the Christian holds the history of religions to be a genuine *history*, to be a path whose direction we call progress and whose attitude we call hope. And thus he should serve: as someone who hopes, who infallibly knows that, through every failure and all human discord, the end of history is being fulfilled—the transformation of the chaos with which the world began into the eternal city of Jerusalem, in which God, the one eternal God, dwells among men and enlightens them as the light forevermore (see Rev 21:23; 22:5).

INTERLUDE

I

The essential understanding that we gain from this investigation lies in the perception that the whole panorama of the history of religions sets before us a basic choice between two ways, which I described at the time—unsatisfactorily enough—as "mysticism" and "monotheism". Today I would prefer to talk instead about "a mysticism of identity" and "a personal understanding of God". Ultimately it is a question of whether the divine "God" stands over against us, so that religion, being human, is in the last resort a relationship—love—that becomes a union ("God is all in all": 1 Cor 15:28) but that does not do away with the opposition of I and Thou; or, whether the divine lies beyond personality, and the final aim of man is to become one with, and dissolve in, the All-One.[1] This choice of alternatives is going to accompany us throughout the book. At this point I should like to mention the way that J. Sudbrack, in his recent book about Dionysius the Areopagite and his influence, has expounded the insights underlying this. In the mysterious sixth-century thinker who concealed his identity behind

---

[1] H. Bürkle, *Der Mensch auf der Suche nach Gott—Die Frage der Religionen* [Man in search of God—The question concerning the religions], Amateca, no. 3 (Paderborn: Bonifatius, 1996), p. 127: "The overcoming of the attitude, tragic for the individual, of having to exist entirely for himself comes about through the discovery of his own hidden character, consistent with his being as Brahman. His breathing then appears to him as being one with the ground of being, the 'World-Soul'. It is experienced, no longer as a separate self, but as an integrated part of a mysterious whole."

the pseudonym of "Dionysius the Areopagite", Sudbrack sees the author of the most significant attempt at bridge-building between West and East, between Christian personalism and Asiatic mysticism. This is how he formulates the choice before which we stand: "Is it a question of dissolving into the unity of the whole or of the most basic trust in an endless 'Thou', in God, or whatever name one may give him or it?" [2]

In analyzing this question, he follows in the spiritual path of Martin Buber. In 1909, in his book *Ekstatische Konfessionen*, this great Jewish thinker had talked about a kind of mysticism of identity of the Word. After his conversion, "he rejected this so totally that he refused to allow any reprint of his book." His new view was that "It is not merging into unity but encounter that is the basic constituent of the human experience of existence." He had come to realize that, in understanding mysticism, two things that happen are often confused: "The one is the soul's becoming one, which enables [man] to undertake spiritual work. The other thing that happens is that unfathomable kind of act of relating in which we imagine that two are becoming one." Sudbrack then points out how Lévinas, in his philosophy of the "other", further developed these insights of Buber's. Lévinas regards the resolution of multiplicity into an all-absorbing unity as a confusion of thinking and as a form of spiritual experience that does not get to the bottom of things. For him, Hegel's "infinity" represents the most dreadful example of such a view of unity. He objects that in the philosophy and mysticism of identity the "face of the other", whose freedom can never become my possession, is eliminated in a nameless "totality".

[2] J. Sudbrack, *Trunken vom hell-lichten Dunkel des Absoluten: Dionysius der Areopagite und die Poesie der Gotteserfahrung* [Intoxicated with the utterly bright darkness of the absolute: Dionysius the Areopagite and the poetry of experiencing God] (Einsiedeln: Johannes Verlag, 2001), p. 72.

In reality, however, true eternity is only experienced in trust-
fully putting one's hopes in the freedom of the other to remain
other. Over against the unity of merging, with its tendency
to eliminate identity, should be set personal experience: unity
of love is higher than formless identity.

H. Bürkle has shown again from another angle, that of
actual practice in the life of society, how the idea of a person
is irreplaceable, an ultimate value.

> The development of modern Hinduism shows that for the
> idea of man in India today, also, this concept of personhood
> has become indispensable.... The experience of identity as
> found in the Upanishads, *tat tvam así*, offers no adequate basis
> for the enduring validity and dignity of the uniqueness, as an
> individual, of every single person. This cannot be reconciled
> with the notion that this life is merely a transitory phase in
> the rhythm of changing levels of reincarnation. It is impos-
> sible to maintain the individual value and dignity of the per-
> son if this is merely a passing phase and subject to variation....
> The modern reforms of Hinduism are thus quite logically
> committed to asking about the dignity of man. The Chris-
> tian concept of the person is taken over by them in the Hindu
> context as a whole, without its foundation in the concept of
> God."[3]

It would not be difficult to show, however, that the concept
of the individual as a person, and thus the defense of the
individual value and dignity of each person, cannot in the
end itself be maintained without its foundation in the idea
of God.

Finally, in the course of his reflections, Sudbrack draws our
attention to a criterion that is no less fundamental and by which
the difficulties in the mysticism-of-universal-identity position

---

[3] Bürkle, *Mensch auf der Suche nach Gott*, pp. 130f.

become glaringly obvious: "The problem of evil, as a turning against the absolute goodness of God, most clearly reveals the difference in the conceptions of being." [4] In a philosophy of the unity of everything, the distinction between good and evil is necessarily relativized. We can find some important clarifications of this question in the thinking of Guardini. In his philosophy of opposition, Guardini thought out the basic distinction between "opposition" and "contradiction", which is what it finally comes down to here. Oppositions are complementary; they constitute the richness of reality. In his most important philosophical work, he made "opposition" the central principle of the way he looked at reality, in which he saw in the many tensions of life the wealth of existence. Oppositions refer us to one another; each needs the other; and only between them do they produce the harmony of the whole. But contradiction breaks out of this harmony and destroys it. Evil is not even—as Hegel thought and as Goethe tries to show us in *Faust*—one side of the whole, and thus necessary to us, but is the destruction of being.[5] It is in fact unable to say of itself, as does *Faust*'s Mephistopheles, I am "a part of that power which always seeks evil and always works good." Good would then have need of evil, and evil would not really be evil at all but would just be a necessary part of the world's dialectical process. The sacrifice of countless thousands of victims by Communism was justified with this philosophy, building upon the dialectic of Hegel, which Marx then turned into a political

---

[4] Sudbrack, *Trunken vom hell-lichten Dunkel*, p. 77.

[5] Cf. R. Guardini, *Der Gegensatz: Versuche zu einer Philosophie des Lebendig-Konkreten* [Opposition: Essays for a philosophy of life in its particularity], 3rd ed. (Mainz: Matthias-Grünewald-Verlag, 1985). Some important clarifications of this are found in H. Kuhn, *Romano Guardini: Philosoph der Sorge* [Romano Guardini: Philosopher of care] (St. Ottilien: EOS-Verlag, 1987), e.g., pp. 42, 71f.

system. No, evil is not a part of the "dialectic" of being; rather, it attacks it at its very roots. God, who as a threefold unity represents, in multiplicity, the very highest unity, is pure light and pure goodness (see Jas 1:17), whereas in the mysticism of identity there is in the end no distinction between good and evil. "Good and evil, according to Buddhism, stand from the beginning in mutual interdependence. Neither has priority over the other. 'Enlightenment' is the realization of my being as it was before good and evil", is what Sudbrack says about this.[6] The choice between a personal God or the mysticism of identity is most certainly not a merely theoretical one—from the inmost depth of the question of being, it reaches out into practical living.

2

As I have briefly indicated in the preliminary remarks to this study, in the theology of religions today people distinguish between three basic positions, which are in fact seen as being the only real possibilities: exclusivism, inclusivism, and personalism. In the way this is usually portrayed, Karl Barth stands for the exclusivist position. This position is said to be that the Christian faith alone saves people and that other religions do not lead to salvation. But we have to bear in mind here that Barth did not simply regard Christianity as a kind of absolute religion, as opposed to all other religions, but distinguished between faith, on the one hand, and religion, on the other. He sees "religion" as being the opposite of faith: for him, religion is a network of human attitudes by which man tries to climb up to God; in contrast to that,

---

[6] Sudbrack, *Trunken vom hell-lichten Dunkel*, p. 78.

faith is a gift from God, who reaches out his hand to man: it is not our activity that saves us but God's kindly power alone. Everything in Christianity that is "religion" falls likewise under Barth's condemnation. On this basis, D. Bonhoeffer sketched out a program for religionless Christianity, which was very influential in the fifties and sixties. The Italian theologian and philosopher of religion G. Baget Bozzo recently published a book with the title *Profezia: Il Cristianesimo non è una religione*.[7] In any case, R. Guardini also emphasized the essential difference between faith and religion, even though he did not wish to share the radical position of Barth.[8]

To me, the concept of Christianity without religion is contradictory and illusory. Faith has to express itself as a religion and through religion, though of course it cannot be reduced to religion. The tradition of these two concepts should be studied anew with this consideration in mind. For Thomas Aquinas, for instance, "religion" is a subdivision of the virtue of righteousness and is, as such, necessary, but it is of course quite different from the "infused virtue" of faith. It seems to me that a postulate of the first order for any carefully differentiated theology of religions would be the precise clarification of the concepts of faith and religion, which are mostly used so as to pass vaguely into each other, and both are equally used in generalized fashion. Thus, people talk of "faiths" in the plural and intend thereby to designate all religions, although the idea of faith is by no means present in all religions, is certainly not a constitutive element for all

---

[7] G. Baget Bozzo, *Profezia: Il Cristianesimo non è una religione* [Prophecy: Christianity is not a religion] (Milan: Mondadori, 2002).

[8] Cf. R. Guardini, *Die Offenbarung: Ihr Wesen und ihre Formen* [Revelation: Its essence and its forms] (Würzburg: Werkbund, 1940); Guardini, *Religion und Offenbarung* [Religion and revelation], vol. 1 (Würzburg: Werkbund, 1958).

of them, and—insofar as it does occur—means very different things in them. The broadening of the concept of religion as an overall designation for the relationship of man to the transcendent, on the other hand, has only happened in the second part of the modern period.[9] Such a clarification is urgently needed, especially for Christianity to have a proper understanding of itself and for the way it relates to other world religions. We will come back to this problem later.

Just as Barth is seen as the chief representative of the exclusivist position, so Rahner is reckoned to be the classical advocate of inclusivism: that Christianity is present in all religions, or (putting it the other way around) that all religions, without knowing this, are moving toward Christianity. It is from this inner direction that they derive their power to save: they lead to salvation insofar as they carry the mystery of Christ hidden within them. In this view of things, on the one hand, it remains true that only Christ, and the relationship with him, has any saving power; on the other, we can ascribe a salvific value—albeit on loan, as it were—to other religions and thus explain the saving of men outside the "ark of salvation" of which the Fathers speak. At the same time, missionary work is still—even though in less radical fashion than on the exclusivist basis—explained as being necessary: What all religions offer only vaguely, beneath obscure symbols and even in part distorted or misrepresented, has become visible in faith in Jesus Christ. He alone purifies religions and leads them toward their proper essence, toward their most profound inner longing.

---

[9] Cf. U. Dierse, "Religion", in *Historisches Wörterbuch der Philosophie* [Historical dictionary of philosophy], ed. J. Ritter and K. Gründer (Basel: Schwabe, 1971–), 8:632f. Above all, the various pieces published by E. Feil are important for our theme, e.g., *Religio* (1986); *Religio zwischen Reformation und Rationalismus* [Religio from the Reformation to Rationalism] (1997).

Finally, a third position, the pluralistic one, has appeared, with the writings of the English theologian J. Hick, who is active in America, together with P. Knitter; and P. Schmidt-Leukel has gained publicity as its most committed supporter in the German-speaking world.[10] Pluralism makes a clear break with the belief that salvation comes from Christ alone and that his Church belongs to Christ. People in the plural-ist position are of the opinion that the plurality of religions is God's own will and that all of them are paths to salvation, or at least can be so, while an especially important, but by no means exclusive, position can be assigned to Christ in par-ticular. There are here, as with the so-called inclusivist posi-tion, many variations, so that here and there the two positions seem almost to merge into one another.

That is why there is no lack of attempts to reconcile these positions, among which may be numbered B. Stubenrauch's brilliant book *Dialogisches Dogma*.[11] But above all we must mention J. Dupuis as eminent advocate of an attempt at rec-onciliation, though of course the pluralists reckon him none-theless as being clearly an "inclusivist".[12] The Congregation for the Doctrine of the Faith also concerned itself with his

---

[10] Cf. especially P. Schmidt-Leukel, *Grundkurs Fundamentaltheologie: Eine Ein-führung in die Grundfragen des christlichen Glaubens* [A basic course in funda-mental theology: An introduction to the basic questions about the Christian faith] (Munich: Don Bosco, 1999). For all the questions merely raised here, one should consult W. Kern, H. J. Pottmeyer, and M. Seckler, *Handbuch der Fundamentaltheologie* [Handbook of fundamental theology], vol. 1: *Traktat Reli-gion* [Tractate on religion], 2nd ed. (Tübingen and Basel: Franke, 2000).

[11] B. Stubenrauch, *Dialogisches Dogma: Der christliche Auftrag zur interre-ligiösen Begegnung* [Dogma in dialogue: The Christian task of interreligious encounter], Quaestiones disputatae 158 (Freiburg im Breisgau: Herder, 1995).

[12] Jacques Dupuis, S.J., *Vers une théologie chrétienne du pluralisme religieux* (Paris: Cerf, 1997) [English trans., *Toward a Christian Theology of Religious Pluralism* (Maryknoll, N.Y.: Orbis Books, 1997)]; commenting on this, the Con-gregation for the Doctrine of the Faith, "Notification on the book *Toward a*

work, since the average reader—in all loyalty to the uniqueness of Jesus Christ—would nevertheless get an impression of a leaning toward pluralistic positions. The dialogue with the author led to a "Notification", in which all the theological points important to Fr. Dupuis were clarified by mutual agreement, and the boundary in the direction of pluralism was thus also clearly marked out.

The dispute between these three positions is not the subject of this book; the questions raised will nonetheless be with us all along, although faith in Jesus Christ as the only Savior and in the indivisibility of Christ and the Church is the foundation of this book. Certainly, I would thus far criticize the formulation of the questions that underlie these three positions, to the extent that I am persuaded that they are based on too hasty an identification of the problems associated with religion with the question of salvation and too indiscriminate a view of these religions as such, as I suggested to start with. How do we know that the theme of salvation should only be tied to religions? Do we not have to approach it, in a far more discriminating manner, from human existence as a whole? And should not the highest respect for the mystery of God's activity always be our guide? Do we necessarily have to invent a theory about how God can save people without abandoning the uniqueness of Christ? Besides that, there is the lack of discrimination in dealing with other religions, which by no means all lead men in the same direction but which above all do not, each in themselves, exist in one single form. Today, for example, we see before us quite clearly various ways in which Islam can be understood and lived out—destructive

Christian Theology of Religious Pluralism, by Father Jacques Dupuis, S.J." (Vatican City, 2001).

forms and forms in which we believe we can perceive a certain proximity to the mystery of Christ.

Can or must a man simply make the best of the religion that happens to fall to his share, in the form in which it is actually practiced around him? Or must he not, whatever happens, be one who seeks, who strives to purify his conscience and, thus, move toward—at the very least—the purer forms of his own religion? If we cannot assume as given such an inner attitude of moving onward, if we do not have to assume it, then the anthropological basis for mission disappears. The apostles, and the early Christian congregations as a whole, were only able to see in Jesus their Savior because they were looking for the "hope of Israel"—because they did not simply regard the inherited religious forms of their environment as being sufficient in themselves but were waiting and seeking people with open hearts. The Church of the Gentiles could develop only because there were "God-fearers", people who went beyond their traditional religion and looked for something greater. This dynamic imparted to "religion" is also in a certain sense the case—this is what is true about what Barth and Bonhoeffer say—with Christianity itself. It is not simply a network of institutions and ideas we have to hand on but a seeking ever in faith for faith's inmost depth, for the real encounter with Christ. In that way—to say it again—in Judaism the "poor of Israel" developed; in that way they would have to develop, again and again, within the Church; and in that way they can and they should develop in other religions: it is the dynamic of the conscience and of the silent presence of God in it that is leading religions toward one another and guiding people onto the path to God, not the canonizing of what already exists, so that people are excused from any deeper searching.

2

FAITH, RELIGION, AND CULTURE

The final word of the Risen Lord to his disciples is a word
of mission to the ends of the earth: "Go therefore and make
disciples of all nations, baptizing them ... [and] teaching
them to observe all that I have commanded you" (Mt 28:19f.;
cf. Acts 1:8). Christianity entered the world in the consciousness of a universal commission. The believers in Jesus
Christ knew, from the first moment on, that they had the
duty of handing on their faith to all men; they saw in their
faith something that did not belong to them alone, something to which, rather, everyone could lay claim. It would
have been utterly faithless not to carry what they had received
to the farthest corner of the earth. It was not the drive to
power that launched Christian universalism but the certi-
tude of having received the saving knowledge and the
redeeming love to which all people have a claim and for
which, in the inmost depths of their being, they are waiting. The mission was regarded, not as the acquisition of
people for their own sphere of domination, but as the

Differing variants of this text were read at the Salzburg Higher Education
week in 1992, at a meeting of the (Roman) Congregation for the Doctrine of
the Faith with the Commission for the Faith of the Asian Bishops' Conference
in Hong Kong in 1993, and at an educational function in Sassari (Sardinia).
The "Variations" were written especially for this book; the original text from
Salzburg has remained substantially unchanged.

passing on, as a matter of obligation, of something meant for everyone and of which everyone stood in need.

Today doubts have arisen about the universality of the Christian faith. The history of the worldwide mission is seen by many, not as the history of the spread of liberating truth and love, but to a great extent as the history of a process of alienation and of domination by force. The strongest expression within the Church of this new consciousness was perhaps in the text for the "European Procession of Penitence '92", in which we read:

> 1492–1992 are dates that in the perspective of native and black South Americans mark out a way of the cross, with countless stations of suffering and a Good Friday that has now lasted for five hundred years. The European Christians . . . conquered bodies with the sword and dominated souls with the cross. . . . For the natives and for the enslaved Africans, Christianity appeared as the religion of the enemy who subjugated and killed people. For them, the gospel could not be a message of joy; rather, it was bad news, which brought misfortune. . . . 1992 could be the year that represents the resumption of their religions, which were just and worthy, the coming of God to his peoples through these religions, and the peoples starting on their way to God through them.[1]

The protest that breaks out in these words goes far beyond the problem of the gospel and culture; and it signifies far more than the justified complaint against all of Europe's sins in connection with the discovery of America: ultimately, it

[1] L. Boff, "I cinquecento anni della conquista dell'America Latina: Un 'venerdì santo' che dura ancora oggi" [The five hundredth anniversary of the conquest of America: A "Good Friday" that is still continuing today], quoted after the Italian version of the text, circulated by the Adista news agency on January 25, 1992.

raises the question of the truth of the Christian faith and of whether mission is justified at all.

To that extent, the new consciousness expressed here demands of Christians a radical process of reflection about what they are and what they are not, what they believe and what they do not believe, what they have to offer and what they cannot offer. Within the framework we have at present, we can only attempt a few steps toward part of this great process of reflection. In any case, we are not here concerned with judgments about the historical events involved in Europe's encounter with America in the centuries since 1492, or with a speech to celebrate "five hundred years of America", of which I do not feel capable and for which I was not asked. My intention is both more modest and, at the same time, more demanding: a reflection on whether the Christian faith has the right, or the capacity, to share with other cultures, to take them into itself and to give itself to them. When you come down to it, this includes all the questions about the basis of Christian existence: Why believe? Is there any truth for men, truth that is accessible as such for all men and belongs to all men, or are we only ever, in differing symbols, just touching on the mystery that never unveils itself to us? Is it a presumption to talk about the truth of faith, or is it a duty? These questions, too, cannot be addressed directly at this point or discussed in their full dimensions; we will have to deal with them at greater length in other parts of this book. Here they have to remain as a conscious backdrop to our problems with faith and culture.

In this chapter, we are directly dealing only with the question of how the one faith relates to the multiplicity of cultures and how true universality is possible in this multiplicity of cultures, without one culture setting itself up as

the only valid one and repressing the others. We hardly
need to make a point of saying that this question applies to
the whole extent of history and right across all the continents. Five hundred years have passed since Columbus'
epoch-making journey, but the first direct contact between
Christianity and black Africa, too, in the then kingdom of
the Congo, present-day Angola, takes us back to the same
period; and likewise the beginning of the Portuguese mission in India, which of course already had a long Christian
history behind it, which goes back perhaps as far as the
time of the apostles. America, Africa, Asia are the three
great cultural spheres that brought to the saying about "the
ends of the earth" and "all nations" an entirely new meaning and brought new dimensions to the task of mission.
But perhaps the consciousness of the inadequacy of previous attempts at Christian universality has become so urgent
today because there is meanwhile another kind of universality that has truly reached to the farthest corners of the
earth: the unity of technical culture, which imposes itself
by the power of its capacities and its successes and yet, at
the same time, through its method of centralizing power
and through its exploitation of the earth, has brought about
that division of the world into north and south, into rich
and poor, which represents the real emergency of our time.
It is therefore ever more strongly emphasized today that in
order to survive, faith must inculturate itself into the modern technical/rational culture. But then the question naturally arises: Can we refer to the civilization of technical
unity as a "culture" in the same sense as the great cultures
that have grown up at different times and places in the life
of mankind? Can faith be inculturated in one and in the
other at the same time? What identity could it then still
have at all?

1. *Culture—Inculturation—The Meeting of Cultures*

We shall come back to these questions, at least indirectly; for the moment, what we have said is only intended to indicate the size of the problem we finally have to face up to: What in fact is culture? How does it relate to religion, and in what way can it forge links with religious entities that were originally alien to it? We should say straightaway that only in modern Europe has a concept of culture been developed that portrays it as a sphere separate from religion, or even in opposition to it. In all known historical cultures, religion is an essential element of culture, is indeed its determinative center; it is religion that determines the scale of values and, thereby, the inner cohesion and hierarchy of all these cultures. But if that is how things are, the inculturation of the Christian faith in other cultures only looks that much more difficult. For one cannot see how a culture that is interwoven with religion, that lives in it and intertwines with it, could be transplanted into a different religion, so to speak, without both being destroyed in the process. If one takes from a culture its own religion, which has begotten it, one is robbing it of its very heart; if one plants a new heart into it—the Christian one—then it seems inevitable that this organism, which is not adapted to it, will reject it. A positive outcome to this operation seems hard to envisage.

It can only really make sense if the relationship between the Christian faith and the respective other religion together with its living culture is not one of absolute foreignness, if there is, rather, a certain inner openness, each to the other, within them; or, to put it another way, if the tendency to move toward each other and to unite is in any case a part of their nature. Inculturation thus assumes the potential universality of every culture. It assumes that the same human nature is at work in all of them and that there is a common truth of humanity alive within that human nature that aims toward union. To put it yet another way, the intention of inculturating makes sense only if no harm is being done to the culture by the way that, through the common direction imparted by the truth of humanity, it is opened up and further developed by a new cultural force. Whatever elements in any culture exclude such opening up and such cultural exchange represent what is inadequate in that culture, because exclusion of what is different is contrary to human nature. The height of development of a culture is shown in its openness, in its capacity to give and to receive, in its power to develop further, to let itself be purified and thus to become better adapted to the truth and to man.

At this point we can try to give something like a definition of culture. We could say: Culture is the social form of expression, as it has grown up in history, of those experiences and evaluations that have left their mark on a community and have shaped it. Let us now try to consider a little more closely the individual elements of this definition, so that we may better be able to understand those possible exchanges between cultures to which the term "inculturation" must refer.

a.   In the first place, culture has to do with perceptions and values. It is an attempt to understand the world and the existence of man within it; an attempt, however, not of a purely theoretical nature, but rather guided by the fundamental interest of our existence. This understanding is meant to show us how to go about being human, how a man takes his proper place in this world and responds to it, so as to improve himself, to live his life successfully and happily. This question, in turn, does not in the great cultures refer to the individual alone, as if each person could work out for himself a pattern of coping with the world and with living. Each can do this only with the help of others; the question of correct perception is thus also a question concerning the proper shaping of the community. This in turn is the prerequisite for each individual's life being successful. Culture is concerned with understanding, which is a perception that opens the way for practical action, that is, a perception of which the dimension of values, of morality, is an indispensable part. We should just add one thing, which would have been self-evident for the old world: In any question concerning man and the world, the question about the Divinity is always included as the preliminary and really basic question. No one can understand the world at all, no one can live his life rightly, so long as the question about the Divinity remains unanswered. Indeed, the very heart of the great cultures is that they interpret the world by setting in order their relationship to the Divinity.

b.   Culture in the classical sense thus includes going beyond what is visible and apparent to the real basis of things and, at its heart, opens the door to the Divinity. Bound up with that (as we have seen) is the other feature, of the individual transcending his own self and finding mutual support for himself in a greater social agency, whose perceptions he can, as it were, borrow and then, of course, also carry farther and develop for himself. Culture is always associated with a social agent, which accepts into itself the experiences of the individuals and, on the other hand, also molds them. This social agent preserves and develops perceptions that go beyond what any individual is capable of—insights we may describe as prerational and suprarational. In doing this, cultures refer to the wisdom of the "elders", who were closer to the gods;

to traditions from the beginnings, which have the character
of revelation, that is, they are the result, not simply of human
questioning and reflection, but of aboriginal contact with
the ground of all things; to communications from the Divinity.[2] The point of crisis for a cultural agent is when it can no
longer succeed in relating this given suprarational element
with new critical perceptions in a persuasive fashion. The
truth of the element already given is then placed in doubt;
from being true it becomes merely usual and loses its living
power.

c.   This already hints at something further: society progresses through time, and culture therefore has to do with history. Culture develops along the way, through the encounter
with new realities and the assimilation of new perceptions. It
is not closed up in itself but is affected by the impetus of time's
onward flow, in which the confluence of different currents, the
processes of union are important. The historical character of
culture signifies its capacity for progress, and that implies its
capacity to be open, to accept its being transformed by an
encounter. We do indeed distinguish between cosmic/static
cultures and historical cultures. In that view, the older, pre-
scriptive cultures would in essence represent the mystery of the
universe, which remains always the same, while the Jewish and
Christian cultural paths, especially, are said to understand their
path with God as history and are therefore molded by a conception of history as a fundamental category. That is true to a
certain extent, but it does not cover everything, since the cosmic cultures, too, point to death and rebirth and to human existence as a path. As Christians, we would say that they carry

---

[2] Cf. on this point J. Pieper, *Überlieferung: Begriff und Anspruch* [Tradition: Its
concept and its claim] (Munich: Kösel, 1970); Pieper, *Über die platonischen Mythen*
(Munich: Kösel, 1965).

within themselves the dynamic of advent, and we are going to have to talk about this in more detail.[3]

This little attempt to clarify some of the basic categories of the concept of culture will now help us better to understand the question of their contact with one another and their merging together. We can now say that what is special about cultures lies in the association of culture with a cultural individuality, with a certain cultural agent, giving the multiplicity of cultures and also the particular nature of each one. We can see, on the other hand, that their historical nature, their movement with time and in time, includes an openness. Each particular culture not only lives out its own experience of God, the world, and man, but on its path it necessarily encounters other cultural agencies and has to react to their quite different experiences. This results, depending always on the degree to which the cultural agent may be closed or open, inwardly narrow or broad in outlook, in that culture's own perceptions and values being deepened and purified. That may lead to a profound reshaping of that culture's previous form, yet this does not necessarily involve any kind of violation or alienation. In a positive case, it may be explained by the potentially universal nature of all cultures, which is concretized in the acceptance of what is other and the change of what is its own. A process of this kind can in fact lead to a breaking open of the silent alienation of man from the truth and from himself that exists within that culture. This can represent the healing Pasch for a culture, which through an apparent death comes to new life and becomes then for the first time truly itself.

[3] The concept of "advent" within pre-Christian paganism is one that T. Haecker introduced in this area with some emphasis; see T. Haecker, *Vergil: Vater des Abendlandes* [Virgil: Father of the West], 5th ed. (Munich: Kösel, 1947).

With this in mind, we should talk, no longer about "inculturation", but about a meeting of cultures, or—if we have to use a technical term—about "interculturality". For "inculturation" presupposes that, as it were, a culturally naked faith is transferred into a culture that is indifferent from the religious point of view, so that two agents that were hitherto alien to each other meet and now engage in a synthesis together. But this depiction is first of all artificial and unreal, because there is no such thing as a culture-free faith and because—outside of modern technical civilization—there is no such thing as religion-free culture. But above all one cannot see how two organisms that are in themselves totally alien to each other should, through a transplantation that starts by mutilating them both, suddenly become a single living whole. Only if it is true that all cultures are potentially universal and have an inner capacity to be open to others can interculturality lead to new and fruitful forms.

With everything we have said thus far, we have remained in the phenomenological sphere, that is, we have recorded how cultures function and how they develop, and we have established the potential universality of every culture as an essential concept for a history leading toward cultural unions. But the question now arises: Why is that so? Why are all cultures, on the one hand, just particular cultures and, thus, differentiated one from another, and why are they at the same time open toward each other, capable of mutually purifying each other and of merging with each other? There are also, of course, positivistic answers, and I do not want to go into them here. It seems to me that at this point in particular one cannot avoid reference to the metaphysical dimension. A meeting of cultures is possible because man, in all the variety of his history and of his social structures and customs, is a single being, one and the same. This one being, man, is however touched and affected in the very depth of his existence by truth itself. The fundamental openness of all men to others, and the agreement in essentials to be found even between those cultures farthest removed from each other, can only be explained by the hidden way our souls have been touched by truth. But the variety, which can even lead to a closed attitude, comes in the first instance from the limitation of the human mind: no one can grasp the whole of anything, but many and varied perceptions and forms come together in a sort of mosaic, suggested by the way that each is complementary with regard to the others: in order to form the whole, each needs all the others. Only in the interrelating of all great works of culture can man approach the unity and wholeness of his true nature.

Yet we can certainly not rest content with this optimistic diagnosis, for the potential universality of cultures is often blocked by quite insurmountable obstacles that prevent it from turning into an actual universality. Not only a communal dynamic exists, but equally communal divisions, barriers against others, contradictions that exclude, an impossibility of transition because the waters between are far too deep. We have been talking just now about the unity of the human being and about his being secretly touched by the truth spoken by God. We are now brought to recognize that there must be in opposition to this a negative factor in human existence: an alienation that hinders our perceiving things and that, at least partially, cuts men off from the truth and thus also from each other. In this undeniable factor of alienation lies the real difficulty in all the struggle to bring about any meeting of cultures. That is why anyone who sees in the religions of the world only reprehensible superstition is wrong; but also why anyone who wants only to give a positive evaluation of all religions, and who has suddenly forgotten the criticism of religions that has been burned into our souls not only by Feuerbach and Marx but also by such great theologians as Karl Barth and Bonhoeffer, is equally wrong.

2. *Faith and Culture*

All this has brought us to the second part of our consideration. Up to now we have set out the essence of culture and, on that basis, the conditions for a meeting of cultures and for their merging into new cultural entities. Now we must venture forth from the sphere of principles into that of facts. First we have once more to sum up our essential findings and to ask what is it that can bind cultures so closely together that they are not just externally tied to each other but, through their encounter, are inwardly fertilized and purified? The medium by which they encounter each other can only be their shared truth concerning man, within which the truth about God and about reality as a whole is always involved. The more human a culture is, the higher it is, the more it can lay claim to truth that was hitherto hidden from it; and the more it will be capable of assimilating that truth and of adjusting itself to that truth. At this point, what is special about the self-understanding of Christian faith can be seen. It knows very well, if it is aware and uncorrupted, that there is a great deal of what is human in its particular cultural forms, a great deal that needs purifying and opening up. But it is also certain that it is at heart the self-revelation of truth itself and, therefore, redemption. For the real problem of mankind is the darkening of truth. This distorts our action and sets us against one another, because we bear our own evil within ourselves, are alienated from ourselves, cut off from the ground of our being, from God. If truth is offered, this means a leading out of alienation and thus out of the state of division; it means the vision of a common standard that does no violence to any culture but that guides each one to its own heart, because each exists ultimately as an expectation of truth. That does not mean reduction to uniformity; quite the opposite: only when this happens can things in opposition become complementary, because they can all, each in its own way, unfold and be fruitful in relation to that central standard.

That is the high claim with which the Christian faith entered the world. From this claim there follows the inner obligation to send all peoples to the school of Jesus, because he is the truth in person and, thereby, the way to be human. We do not, for the moment, want to enter into the argument about the truth of this claim, although we will naturally have to come back to it later. Right now we are asking: What follows from that claim, for the concrete relationship of the Christian faith to the cultures of the world?

A first point we should note is that faith itself is cultural. It does not exist in a naked state, as sheer religion. Simply by telling man who he is and how he should go about being human, faith is creating culture and is culture. This message of faith is not an abstract message; it is one that has matured through a long history and through manifold intercultural fusions, in the course of which it has shaped an entire way of life, a way of man's dealing with himself, with his neighbor, with the world, and with God. Faith itself exists as culture. But that also means that it exists as an independent agent: a social and cultural community that we call "the people of God". It is probably in this concept that the nature of faith as a historical agent is most clearly expressed. Does faith, therefore, stand as *one* cultural agent among others, so that one would have to choose to belong either to it—to this people, as a cultural community—or to

another people? No. At this point, what is quite particular
and peculiar to the culture of faith becomes apparent. The
people of God, as a cultural agent, differs from the classic
cultural agents, which are defined by the boundaries of a
communal life as a tribe, as a nation, or otherwise, in that
it subsists within various different cultural entities, which
for their part do not thereby cease, even for the individual
Christian, to be the primary and immediate agent of his
culture. Even as a Christian, one remains a Frenchman or a
German, an American or an Indian, and so on. In the pre-
Christian world, even in the high cultures of India, China,
and Japan, the cultural agent is one and indivisible. Belonging to two cultural entities is impossible in general, although
of course Buddhism represents an exception, in the way it
is able to combine itself with other cultural entities as an
inner dimension of them, so to speak. But the full development of this double cultural identity first appears with
Christian culture, so that man now lives within two cultural entities: in his historical culture and in the new one of
faith, which meet and mingle in him. This existing together
will never be a complete synthesis; it brings with it a need
for continuing processes of reconciliation and purification.
Again and again there must be a going beyond into wholeness and universality, into the sphere, not of an empirical
people, but of those who are indeed the people of God
and, from there, the sphere of all mankind. And, contrariwise, again and again this shared entity has to be brought
into our own territory and has to be lived out and even
struggled for in the concrete historical place.

From what we have said there follows a most important
point. One might think that culture is always the business
of an individual cultural entity (Germany, France, America,
and so on), while faith is simply in search of a cultural

expression. The various cultures would thus, so to speak, provide faith with a cultural body. Faith, in that case, would live only through borrowed cultures, which would, however, all remain somehow exterior to it and could be stripped off again. Above all, none of these borrowed cultural forms would mean anything to or for people living in any of the others. Universality would, thereby, become ultimately a fiction. Thinking like this is basically Manichaean: it reduces culture to a mere interchangeable embodiment; faith is dematerialized into a mere spirit, ultimately lacking in reality. Such a conception is of course typical of post-Enlightenment spirituality. Culture is relegated to mere outward form, and religion to mere inexpressible feeling or into pure thought. Thus the productive tension, which ought normally to arise from the coexistence of two cultural entities, disappears. If culture is more than mere form or mere aesthetics, if it is much more a way of ordering values within a historic form of life, and if it cannot ignore the question concerning the divine, then there is no way of getting around the fact that, for believers, the Church is a separate cultural entity in her own right. This cultural entity or agency, the Church, the people of God, does not—even in periods when particular peoples seem to have been fully christianized, as people used to believe was the case in Europe—coincide with any of these other historic cultural entities; rather, she retains her own overarching form and is indeed on that account significant.

If that is how things are, then in the encounter between faith and its culture and another hitherto foreign culture, it cannot be a matter of dispensing with this duality of cultural entities on either one side or the other. The sacrifice of one's own cultural heritage in favor of a Christianity with no particular human coloring or the disappearance of the cultural features of faith in the new culture would both be equally mistaken. It is the tension itself that is productive, renewing faith and healing the culture. It would accordingly be nonsense to offer a Christianity that was, so to speak, precultural or deculturalized, as such a Christianity would be deprived of its own historical power and reduced to an empty collection of ideas. We should not forget that Christianity, as early as the period of the New Testament, carries within itself the fruit of a whole history of cultural development, a history of acceptance and rejection, of encounter and of change. Israel's history of faith, which was taken up into itself, was shaped in struggles with Egyptian, Hittite, Sumerian, Babylonian, Persian, and Greek culture. All these cultures were at the same time religions, all-embracing historical ways of life that in the course of God's struggle with Israel, of the struggles of its great prophetic figures, were assumed and transformed in a passionate endeavor to provide an ever more pure vessel for the new cultural element, the revelation of the one God; yet it was in this very process that those cultures found their lasting fulfilment. They would otherwise all have sunk into the distant past had they not remained present as purified and uplifted in the faith of the Bible. Israel's history of faith begins, of course, with the call to Abraham: "Go from your country and your kindred and your father's house" (Gen 12:1); it begins with a cultural break. There will always be such a break with one's own prehistory, such a setting forth, at the beginning of a new moment in the history of faith. Yet this new beginning then proves to be a force for healing, creating a new center with the ability to draw to itself all that is true to the measure of humanity, all that is true to the measure of divinity. "I, when I am lifted up from the earth, will draw all men to myself" (Jn 12:32)—this saying of the ascended Lord also has a place in our context here: the Cross is, first, a break, the being cast forth, the being lifted up from the earth, but in that very way it becomes a new center of gravity, a point of gravitation drawing things up from the history of the world, for the bringing together of what is divided.

Anyone entering the Church has to be aware that he is entering a separate, active cultural entity with her own many-layered intercultural character that has grown up in the course of history. Without a certain exodus, a breaking off with one's life in all its aspects, one cannot become a Christian. Faith is no private path to God; it leads into the people of God and into its history. God has linked himself to a history, which is now also his history and which we cannot simply erase. Christ remains man to eternity, retains a body to eternity; but being a man, having a body, includes having a history and a culture, this particular history with its culture, whether we like it or not. We cannot repeat the process of the Incarnation at will, in the sense of repeatedly taking Christ's flesh away from him, so to speak, and offering him some other flesh instead. Christ remains the same, even according to his body. But he is drawing us to him. That means that because the people of God is, not just a single cultural entity, but is gathered together from all peoples, therefore the first cultural identity, rising again from the break that was made, has its place therein; and not only that, but it is needed in order to allow the Incarnation of Christ, of the Word, to attain its whole fullness. The tension of many active entities within a single entity is an essential part of the unfinished drama of the Son's Incarnation. This is the real inner dynamic of history, and of course it stands always beneath the sign of the Cross; that is to say that it must always be struggling against the opposing weight of shutting off, of isolation and refusal.

3. Faith, Religion, and Culture in the Technological World

That is all quite correct if Jesus of Nazareth is truly the meaning of history, the Logos who has become man, the self-revelation of truth itself. It is then clear that this truth is the sphere within which everyone can find and relate to one another and, in so doing, lose nothing of his own value or his own dignity. This is the point at which criticisms are made today. To lay claim to truth for one religion's particular expressions of faith appears today, not merely presumptuous, but an indication of insufficient enlightenment. Hans Kelsen was expressing the spirit of our age when he represented the question of Pilate, "What is truth?" as being the sole appropriate attitude for determining the structure of society within the state, in the face of the great religious and moral difficulties of mankind. Truth is replaced by the decision of the majority, he says, precisely because there can be no truth, in the sense of a binding and generally accessible entity for man.[4] Thus the multiplicity of cultures serves to demonstrate the relativism of all cultures. Culture is set against truth. This relativism, which is nowadays to be found, as a basic attitude of enlightened people, penetrating far into the realm of theology, is the most profound difficulty of our age. This is also the reason why practice is now substituted for truth and why the whole axis of religions is thereby displaced: we do not know what is true, but we do know what we should do: raise up and introduce a better society, the "kingdom", as people like to say, using a term taken from the Bible and applied to the profane and utopian sphere. Ecclesiocentricity, christocentricity, theocentricity—all these

---

[4] Cf. V. Possenti, *Le società liberali al bivio: Lineamenti di filosofia della società* [The liberal society in life: Outlines of a social philosophy] (Genoa: Marietti, 1991), pp. 315–45, especially 345f.; W. Waldstein, *Teoria generale del diritto* [General theory of law] (Pont. Univ. Lat., 2001).

now seem to be rendered obsolete by regnocentricity, the centering of things around the kingdom as the common task of all religions; and it is held that they should meet only from this point of view and according to this standard.[5] There is thus no longer any reason to move them closer to one another in their essentials, in their moral and religious teaching; but they will certainly all be reshaped at the deepest level, insofar as they are now to serve as instruments for the construction of the future, in a way that was not hitherto their task and that ultimately deprives their content of any object or point of reference.

The dogma of relativism has, however, yet another effect: Christian universalism, which is carried out concretely in mission, is no longer the obligatory handing on of a good meant for everyone, that is, of truth and love; with this presupposition, mission becomes the mere presumptuous attitude of a culture that imagines itself to be superior, that tramples upon a whole multitude of religious cultures in the most shameful fashion, thus, it is held, depriving those peoples of what is best: their own heritage. Thence comes the imperative: Give us back our religions, as the right ways for the various peoples severally to come to God and God to them; where these religions still exist, do not touch them! Is this demand appropriate? It is at any rate here that the good sense, or nonsense, of the dogma of relativism in the sphere of cultures and religions must be demonstrated.[6]

---

[5] Cf. the literature referred to by J. Dupuis, "The Kingdom of God and World Religions", *Vidyajyoti: Journal of Theological Reflection* 51 (1987): 530–44; Dupuis, *Vers une théologie chrétienne du pluralisme religieux* (Paris: Cerf, 1997) [English trans., *Toward a Christian Theology of Religious Pluralism* (Maryknoll, N.Y.: Orbis Books, 1997)].

[6] A most significant contribution to this discussion is to be found in C. Gnilka, "La conversione della cultura antica vista dai Padri della chiesa" [The conversion of classical culture as seen by the Church Fathers], *Cristianesimo nella storia* 11 (1990): 593–615, where he expounds the important insights of

At least, in the face of such demands, one ought to look carefully at each religion to see whether its restoration would really be desirable. When we think, for instance, of how on the occasion of the most recent rebuilding of the main Aztec temple, in the year 1487, "at the very lowest estimate, twenty thousand people" bled to death, "over four days, on the altars of Tenochtitlán" (the capital city of the Aztecs, in the upper Mexico valley) as human sacrifices to the sun god, it will be difficult for us to encourage the restoration of this

---

the Fathers on the question of inculturation in the struggle with the relativism of late antiquity. We can see here that contemporary relativism is merely a return to the theory of religion of late antiquity. This is reflected, for instance, in the dialogue *Octavius*, by Minucius Felix (around A.D. 200), in which the pagan participant says that everything is uncertain in human existence, probable rather than true, and one should therefore stick to the old religious traditions. The Christians are ironically referred to as "champions of the truth" (*antistites veritatis*). The classic formulation of this religious pluralism, based on the obscurity concerning truth, is to be found in the famous reflection of Symmachus (d. 402): "Uno itinere non potest perveniri ad tam grande secretum [It is not by a single way that one can attain to such a great mystery]." Julian the Apostate takes a similar philosophy as his starting point and emphasizes that one should respect the variety of national cultures and ways of life and likewise, accordingly, the multiplicity of divinities and religions. The principal reproach he makes against Christianity, and his sole objection to Judaism, lies in his rejection of the First Commandment: he sees in monotheism, in the denial of other gods, the original sin of Christian and Jewish religion. To this theory of the many ways, the Christians oppose the teaching about the two ways (Mt 7:13): the way of life and the way of destruction; the many ways of the pagan religions are in reality only a *single* way—the wide path that the Gospel talks about. Gnilka then shows how the Fathers quite consciously talk about the conversion of cultures; conversion—they say—is a reshaping (transformation), not destruction. As a process of transformation this always includes preservation—an idea that is also worked out in practice in dealing with temples and idols just as in dealing with the renewal and continuity of languages and of thought. C. Gnilka has described this whole area in his book *Chrēsis: Die Methode der Kirchenväter im Umgang mit der antiken Kultur* [Chrēsis: The Church Fathers' method in dealing with classical culture], vol. 2: *Kultur und Conversion* (Basel: Schwabe, 1993).

religion.[7] Such a sacrifice took place because the sun lived on the blood of human hearts, and the end of the world could only be prevented through human sacrifice. Thus, the wars in which captives were taken who served as sacrificial victims were undertaken by divine command. To the earth gods and the vegetation gods, the Aztecs offered "men and women, who were for the most part flayed alive"; to the gods of rain, who were thought of as being like dwarfs, they offered up little children, who were drowned in springs, in water holes, and in certain parts of the Lake of Tetzcoco. There were rituals, a part of which was the slaughter of human beings. All of this derived, as W. Krickeberg has established, not from some inborn "inclination to bloodthirstiness", but from a fanatical belief in the duty of men to provide in this fashion for the continuation of the world.[8] This is, of course, an extreme instance, but it none-theless shows that one cannot simply see in any and every religion the way for God to come to man and man to God.

But we have to tackle the question at a more basic level. Can one, in any circumstances, simply allow religions to remain as they are, stopping history right there, so to speak? It is obvious that one cannot declare some people to be living in a kind of "nature conservation park" for religious and cultural history, into which the modern age would not be allowed to come. Any such attempts are not merely undignified and, ultimately, lacking in respect for people, they are also completely unrealistic. The meeting of cultures and the gradual growing together of the separate geographical areas

[7] Cf. W. Krickeberg, H. Trimborn, W. Müller, and O. Zerries, *Die Religionen des alten Amerika* (Stuttgart: Kohlhammer, 1961), p. 49 [English trans., *Pre-Columbian American Religions*, trans. Stanley Davis (London, Weidenfeld and Nicolson, 1968)].

[8] Ibid., pp. 50f.

of history into one common history of mankind are grounded in the nature of man himself. Likewise, one cannot make use oneself of the possibilities offered by technological civilization, while at the same time forcing upon other people one's own dream of a pretechnological world. It is in fact quite undisputed nowadays, not only that the spread of modern civilization is in fact incapable of being prevented, but that making its instruments available to those cultures as yet untouched by it is a question of justice. That one must proceed with more caution and show more respect for these people's own traditions than was the case hitherto is quite a different question. It is not the spread of technological capabilities themselves that is bad but rather the presumption, typical of the Enlightenment, with which people very often destroyed structures that had grown up over time and trampled upon men's spirits, carelessly sweeping aside their religious and ethical traditions. This tearing up of people's spiritual roots and the destruction of the network of social relationships that happened in such cases are certainly one of the main reasons why development aid has so far brought positive results only in very rare instances. People thought it was enough to develop technological capabilities; that man also needs traditions and inner values to sustain him was—and still is—widely disregarded.

But we could now ask, ought we not now to proceed by handing on the technology, cautiously, but leaving the religion untouched? This idea, at first sight such an obvious one, is nonetheless misleading. For in situations that are quite different, one cannot preserve fully developed religions as such, shutting them up in a kind of religious nature reserve, and at the same time superimpose the technological view of the world. Technological civilization is not in fact religiously and morally neutral, even if it believes it is. It changes people's standards and their attitudes and behavior. It changes the way people interpret the world, from the very bottom up. The religious cosmos inevitably starts to shift on account of technology. The arrival of these new opportunities in life is like an earthquake that shakes the spiritual landscape to its foundations. What takes place with increasing frequency, at any rate, is that the Christian faith is shaken off for the sake of people's own authenticity, and in the realm of religion the pagan religions are restored, while at the same time technology, although it is no less Western, is passionately received and applied. This division of the Western heritage into what is useful, which is accepted, and what is foreign, which is left aside, most certainly does not lead to the saving of ancient cultures. For it now becomes evident that what is great in the old religions, the elements that point the way forward, I would say, their advent dimension, drops out, because it seems impossible to reconcile with the new knowledge about the world and is no longer of interest to people, while the element that is (in the widest sense of the word) magical—everything that offers some power over the world, is preserved and becomes really decisive in people's lives. These religions are thus losing their real value, because what is best in them is pruned off, and the only thing left is what represented the danger in them.

That could be clearly shown in the instance of Voodoo. In its original form, it was in the last analysis shaped by an anticipation of the Paschal Mystery, of death and resurrection; the business of initiation into being a man, of the marriage of the two sexes, of the forgiveness of sins—all these basic sacramental forms were determinative in its essential structure.[9]

---

[9] Cf. on this point B. Adoukonou, *Jalons pour une théologie africaine: Essai d'une herméneutique chrétienne du Vodun dahoméen* [Blazing the trail for an African

But this mythological form stands in need of a new rational means of communication, of a new center, which Voodoo itself is unable to offer. From within its historical moment, it reaches out toward the unknown. Yet where technology and Voodoo are superimposed, these forward-looking gestures break down, and what is left are the magical powers, which now constitute an irrational second world alongside the technological world and its one-sided rationalism. More and more Europeans, whose Christian faith has collapsed, are taking up these irrational forces, and that brings a real paganizing process: man being cut off from God; man is now just looking for various systems of power, and in doing so he is destroying both himself and the world. This, however, is precisely the wrong way for cultures to encounter one another, basically a non-meeting in which rational and irrational attitudes combine with each other in a fatal manner. In a world that is moving with history, religions cannot simply stand still, just as they were or as they now are. Yet the Christian faith, which carries within itself the great heritage of the religions and which opens up this heritage to the Logos, to true reason, could offer a new basis to them at the deepest level and could at the same time make possible a real synthesis of technological rationality and religion, something that can only come about, not by a flight into the irrational, but by opening up reason to its true height and breadth.

Here lie the great tasks of our contemporary historical moment. Christian mission will doubtless have to understand other religions far more profoundly and accept them at a deeper level than has been the case hitherto, but these

---

theology: An attempt at a Christian hermeneutic of Dahomian Voodoo], 2 vols. (Paris: Namur 1980); Y. K. Bamunoba and B. Adoukonou, *La Mort dans la vie africaine* [Death in African life] (Paris: UNESCO, Préserce africaine, 1979).

religions, on the other hand, in order for their best elements to survive, need to recognize their own adventual character, the way they point forward to Christ. If in this sense we proceed on an intercultural search for traces of a path toward a common truth, then something unexpected will appear: Christianity has more in common with the ancient cultures of mankind than with the relativistic and rationalistic world that has cut loose from the fundamental insights of mankind and is thus leading man into a vacuum, devoid of meaning, which risks being fatal for him unless the answer to it comes to him in time. For the knowledge that man must turn toward God, and toward what is eternal, is found right across all the cultures; the knowledge about sin, repentance, and forgiveness; the knowledge concerning communion with God and eternal life; and finally the knowledge of the basic rules of morality, as they are found in the form of the Ten Commandments. It is not relativism that is confirmed; rather, it is the unity of the human condition and its common experience of contact with a truth that is greater than we are.

VARIATIONS ON THE THEME OF FAITH, RELIGION, AND CULTURE

1. INCLUSIVISM AND PLURALISM

Following these reflections on the relations between religion, faith, and culture, we can again take up the classification of possible solutions to the problem of religions, which we met before in the three concepts of exclusivism, inclusivism, and pluralism. Probably no one today takes the position of exclusivism in the sense of denying salvation to all non-Christians—which, by the way, was not even Karl Barth's view. I have already tried to indicate that his "exclusivism" related to the phenomenon of "religion" as such, and not at all specifically to "other religions", and to that extent it did not directly touch upon the question of salvation for non-Christians. In that sense, his position relates to another question, which is probably too much forgotten today. Essentially, then, in response to the question of the relation between Christian faith and the religions of the world, there remain the two possible positions of inclusivism and pluralism.

It has meanwhile become common to reject "inclusivism", too, as a kind of Christian imperialism, as presumptive in relation to other religions: it is said to be not our business to see other religions as directed toward an end in Christ and, thus, to take them over in a Christian sense. Now, Karl Rahner, as we heard, said that as Christians we "cannot renounce this presumption". Anyone who wants to deprive us of this is disputing the right of Christians to their faith and to the belief that everything is created in relation to Christ and that he, as the "Son", as the true God who has come down into flesh, is the heir of the universe—and this simply because he, as God's creative Word, is the truth of all things and all men. The truth, however, takes no one by force. If we develop this idea more profoundly, the concept of "presumption" can probably be exploded from within. We had been talking about the potential universality of cultures: the cultures of mankind, each of which together with its religion forms a whole, are not just unrelated blocks standing side by side or in opposition to each other. The one being, man, is at work within them all, since there are differing historical experiences and paths, differing errors and dangers, yet everywhere it is in the end man who is expressing himself in them. Because the one being, man, is at work in all mankind, all men are capable of coming into communion with one another; indeed, all are called to this. No true culture is ultimately impenetrable for others; all are capable of coming into contact with one another and are related to each other. Always, therefore, in history—we were talking about this—there have been intercultural exchanges and the fusion of cultures. "Inclusivism" belongs to the essence of the cultural and religious history of mankind, which is certainly not structured as a strict pluralism. Pluralism in its radical form ultimately denies the unity of mankind and denies the dynamic of history, which is a process of various unions.

Up to this point we are still in the purely phenomenological realm; faith is not involved in these statements and remarks. It makes its first appearance in the statement that in this process of various unions the real point of reference is the revelation offered in Christ, for the very reason that faith in this revelation springs, not from any one single culture, but from an intervention from above and, hence, does not simply "absorb" anything. It allows room for all the great spiritual experiences of being human, in a many-toned harmony: this is exactly what the Christian sees as foreshadowed in the wonder of Pentecost, in which there is not one single language (single civilization) prescribed for all the others, as in Babylon (the type of cultures of achievement and of power), but unity comes to pass in multiplicity. The many languages (cultures) understand each other in the one Spirit. They are not abolished; rather, they are brought together in harmony. From a phenomenological point of view, what must be regarded as the new element peculiar to Christianity is the way that it has not simply taken its place in the history of religions as an "absolute religion" among "relative religions" (although one could even understand such a conceptual structure correctly).

In the first few centuries the Christian faith looked for its prehistory rather in enlightenment, that is, in the movement of reason criticizing religion's tendency to ritualism. Those patristic texts about the "sowing of the Word" (and similar concepts and images), which are nowadays taken as evidence for the power of salvation in other religions, did not originally refer to religions at all but to philosophy, to a "pious" enlightenment, which is what Socrates stands for, at the same time active both in enlightening people and in seeking after God. We will talk about all that at greater length. This "enlightenment" trait of early Christian preaching, critical of religion, is also the reason why it was classified by the state as atheism, as a rejection of *pietas* and of the rituals that upheld the state. We cannot of course lapse into a one-sided view here. Although Christianity, as we said, saw its prehistory in enlightenment and not in religions, it did connect with the religious search of men, and, in shaping its prayer and worship, it drew on the heritage of religion. Its inner prehistory—the Old Testament—consists accordingly in a constant struggle between becoming absorbed into the religious forms of the peoples and the prophetic enlightenment that sweeps the gods aside in order to discover the face of God. Thus Christianity has a quite singular position in the spiritual history of mankind. We could say that it lies in Christianity's not dividing enlightenment from religion but in combining them in a structure in which each has repeatedly to make the other purer and more profound. This desire for rationality, which still constantly pushes reason to go beyond itself in a way it would rather avoid, is part of the essence of Christianity. We could also say that the Christian faith, which grew out of the faith of Abraham, insists relentlessly on the question of truth and, thus, on what in all circumstances concerns all men and unites them all. For we have all to be pilgrims of truth.[1]

Mere pluralism of religions, as blocks standing forever side by side, cannot be the last word in the historical situation today. Perhaps we will have to replace "inclusivism"—which, by the way, until just recently was used in the history of religions with quite a different meaning—with some better concepts. It is certainly not the absorption of religions by one single one that is meant; but an encounter, in a unity that transforms pluralism into plurality, is something necessary. Today it is certainly desired. If I have rightly understood, there are currently three models for this: the spiritual monism of India—the mysticism of identity, to which Radhakrishnan first gave the classic formulation—regards itself as the overarching way: it can offer all other religions a place,

---

[1] Particularly relevant to this question is M. Fiedrowicz, *Apologie im frühen Christentum: Die Kontroverse um den christlichen Wahrheitsanspruch in den ersten Jahrhunderten* [The apology in early Christianity: The controversy about the Christians' claim to truth in the first centuries], 2nd ed. (Paderborn: Schöningh, 2001), especially pp. 227–315.

allow them to stand in their symbolic significance, as it seems, and at the same time it transcends them in an ultimate profundity. It "relativizes" all of them and, at the same time, lets them stand in its relativity; the absolute value with which it surrounds them lies beyond anything that can be named; it is strictly "non-categoric". It can thus equally well be called "being" as "nonbeing", "word" as "nonword"; it is obvious that this solution finds many supporters today, since in its own fashion it maintains that relativism which in certain respects has become the real religion of modern men.

Beside that stands the Christian version of universality, which regards as the ultimate value, not the unnamable, but that mysterious unity created by love and which is represented, beyond all our categories, in the Trinity and unity of God, which for its part is the highest picture of the reconciliation of unity and multiplicity. The last word about being is, no longer the unnamable absolute, but love, which then makes itself visible in the God who himself becomes a creature and thus unites the creature with the Creator. This form seems in many respects more complicated than the "Asiatic" one. Yet is it not the case that basically we all understand that love is the highest word, the truly last word to be said on anything real? All our reflections hitherto, and everything that follows, serve to make more clear how this Christian "model" is the true power for uniting, the inner goal of history.

Finally, Islam stands in the ring with the theory that it is the "final" religion, which takes us beyond Judaism and Christianity into the true simplicity of the one God, while Christianity, with its faith in the Godhead of Christ and in God the Trinity, has supposedly fallen back into heathen error. It is claimed that Islam, without cult or mystery, emerges as the universal religion, in which the religious development of mankind has reached its goal. There is no doubt that the question Islam poses for us deserves detailed attention. But it is not within the scope of this book, which is limited to the (to my mind) more fundamental choice between the mysticism of identity and the mysticism of personal love.

2. IS CHRISTIANITY A EUROPEAN RELIGION?

In the discussions about the history of Christian missions, it has become commonplace to say nowadays that through the missions Europe (the West) tried to force its religion on the rest of the world: it was just a matter of religious colonialism, as part of the colonial system as a whole. The renunciation of Eurocentrism must therefore include renunciation of missions. This theory can first of all be criticized historically. Christianity, as we know, originated, not in Europe, but in the Near East, in the geographical point at which the three continents of Asia, Africa, and Europe come into contact. This was never merely geographical contact; rather, it was a contact between the spiritual traditions of the three continents. In that sense, "interculturality" is part of the original shape of Christianity. And in the first centuries the missions, too, reached out just as much to the east as to the west. The heart of Christianity lay in Asia Minor, in the Near East, but Christianity soon pressed on to India; the Nestorian mission reached as far as China, and in terms of numbers Asiatic Christianity was more or less equal to European. Only the spread of Islam robbed Christianity in the Near East of much of its life and strength and, at the same time, cut off the Christian communities in India and Asia from the centers in Syria, Palestine, and Asia Minor and, thus, to a great extent brought about their disappearance.

Very well, someone might say, but from then on Christianity did become European. The response is both Yes and No. For the heritage of its origin, which developed outside Europe, remained as the taproot for the whole and, thus, remained as a standard and criticism of what was merely our own, European. And then again, what is "European" is not a monolithic mass. It is temporally and culturally extremely diverse. There is, first of all, the process of "inculturation" in the Greek and Roman world, followed by "inculturation" in the various cultural expressions of the German, Slavic, and Romance peoples. From classical times through the Middle Ages to modern times and the contemporary world, all these cultures have come a long way, in the course of which Christianity has had ever again to be reborn, so to speak, and was never simply there as a possession. It is a good thing to see that in one or two examples. For the Greeks, Christianity was, as Paul says, "foolishness", that is to say, barbarism, as compared with their own level of culture. The Greek mind bequeathed to Christianity important forms of thinking and speaking, yet not without encountering great resistance: the Christian way of understanding things had to be won from Greek thought at the cost of serious struggles, in which the Greek heritage was appropriated and extensively reshaped. That was a process of death and rebirth. Yes, there is a "Christian Plato", but there was always also an "anti-Christian Plato": from Plotinus down to its latest forms, Platonism opposed Christianity most strongly and saw itself as its opposite. We see similar things in the sphere of Latin. It is enough to recall the story of Augustine's conversion. Reading Cicero's book *Hortensius* had brought into the open for him a longing for eternal beauty, a longing for encounter and contact with God. It was clear to him, from his whole upbringing, that the answer to this longing that philosophy had aroused must lie in Christianity.

So he turned from *Hortensius* to the Bible and suffered culture shock. Cicero and the Bible, two worlds, crash together: two cultures collide. No, that cannot be right: that was what Augustine felt. The Bible appeared to him sheer barbarism, which could not come up to the level of the spiritual demands transmitted to him by Roman philosophy. We can take the culture shock experienced by Augustine as symptomatic of the novelty and strangeness of Christianity, which really was not coming from the area familiar to the Latin mind, though, on the other hand, there was indeed in that mind, too, an expectation of Christ. To become a Christian, Augustine—and the Graeco-Roman world—had to make an exodus, through which they were of course given back anew what they had lost.

Exodus, making a cultural break, with its death and regrowth, is a basic pattern in Christianity. The story of this begins with Abraham, with the command from God: "Go from your country and your kindred and your father's house" (Gen 12:1). The exodus of Israel out of Egypt, the event that really brought the peopie of Israel into existence, is anticipated in the exodus of Abraham, which as such was likewise a cultural break. We can say of the Christian faith, in line with the faith of Abraham, that no one simply finds it there as his possession. It never comes out of what we have ourselves. It breaks in from outside. That is still always the way. Nobody is born a Christian, not even in a Christian world and of Christian parents. Being Christian can only ever happen as a new birth. Being a Christian begins with baptism, which is death and resurrection (Rom 6), not with biological birth.

It was Romano Guardini, above all, who indicated an important aspect of this basic pattern of Christian—indeed, biblical—faith, which does not well up from within us but comes to us from outside: Christianity, the Christian faith, he tells us, is not the product of our own experiences; rather, it is an event that comes to us from without.[2] Faith is based on our meeting something (or someone) for which our capacity for experiencing things is inadequate. It is not our experience that is widened or deepened—that is the case in the strictly "mystical" models; but something *happens*. The categories of "encounter", "otherness" (*altérité*: Lévinas), "event", describe the inner origins of the Christian faith and indicate the limitations of the concept of "experience". Certainly, what touches us there effects an experience in us, but experience as the result of an event, not of reaching deeper into ourselves. This is exactly what is meant by the concept of

[2] It seems to me significant that the Evangelical writer Eva Zeller, in her autobiographical novel *Nein und Amen*, comes to talk about Guardini's lectures, which she had heard in Berlin before the war, and shares with us something that had been impressed on her memory: "From our inner experiences"— Guardini says it in a quiet voice—"we can never ever derive God; on the contrary, he can only break in despite all experiences, from some quite different starting point, which presupposes our capacity to be gripped by him." Cf. J. Sudbrack, *Trunken vom hell-lichten Dunkel des Absoluten: Dionysius der Areopagite und die Poesie der Gotteserfahrung* [Intoxicated with the utterly bright darkness of the absolute: Dionysius the Areopagite and the poetry of experiencing God] (Einsiedeln: Johannes Verlag, 2001), p. 222. Equally impressive is the final evaluation of religions and the religious experience of mankind in Guardini's book *Religion und Offenbarung* [Religion and revelation], vol. 1 (Würzburg: Werkbund, 1958), pp. 227f.: "Our final impression is one of a profound uselessness. What is sublime stands side by side with what is base, what is free with the expression of intimidation, what is noble with what is vulgar.... It is as if I am looking for something with no idea of how to go about it, almost find it, and then it slips from my hands again; I follow the wrong direction, start again. There is a great melancholy in the religious history of mankind; there is, of course, also a great longing and an expectation that is ever again looking forward." Also important on the theme of religious experience is R. Brague's article "Was heißt christliche Erfahrung?" [What is Christian experience?], *Internationale katholische Zeitschrift "Communio"* 5 (1976): 481–96, as also H. U. von Balthasar, "Gotteserfahrung biblisch und patristisch" [Experience of God in the Bible and the Fathers], *Internationale katholische Zeitschrift "Communio"* 5 (1976): 497–509.

revelation: something not ours, not to be found in what we have, comes to me and takes me out of myself, above myself, creates something new. That also determines the historical nature of Christianity, which is based on events and not on becoming aware of the depths of one's own inner self, what is called "illumination".[3] The Trinity is not the object of our experience but is something that has to be uttered from outside, that comes to me from outside as "revelation". The same is true of the Incarnation of the Word, which is indeed an event and cannot be discovered in one's inner experience. This coming to us from outside is scandalous for man, who is striving after autonomy and autarchy; for *every* culture it is a presumption: when Paul says that Christianity is a scandal for the Jews and foolishness for the "nations" (1 Cor 1:23), he is trying to express this feature peculiar to the Christian faith, which for *everyone* is something coming "from without". And yet this new intervention, intruding upon our sphere of experience and our consciousness of our identity, breaking them up, brings us out into the open spaces of a greater reality and, in so doing, opens for us the possibility of overcoming pluralism and coming together.

[3] The contrast drawn between Gnosis and Pseudo-Dionysius the Areopagite, as formulated by H. Ball in his well-known essay, is instructive on this point, e.g.: "It is characteristic of Gnosticism . . . that at the heart of the redemptive process lies, not the suffering and death of Christ, not the crucifixion, but the 'message concerning the holy path', the teaching. Illumination comes, not through pain, but through the communication of knowledge" (Dionysius the Areopagite, *Die Hierarchien der Engel und der Kirche*, with an introduction by Hugo Ball [Hierarchy of the angels and the Church] (Munich: O. W. Barth, 1955), p. 53. Cf. p. 59: "Paul came with his teaching about earthly redemption, yet more sharply contrasted to Gnosticism. . . . The wise and wonder-working, highly communicative Jesus of the Gnostics disappeared behind the obedient, the tormented Christ, the Christ who was done to death and had therefore risen again. Baptism is no longer a conjuring-up of fire and light. It is being immersed in the death of Christ."

3. HELLENIZATION?

The view that Catholic and Eastern Christianity is not the Christianity of the Bible but is based upon an amalgamation of the Bible with Greek philosophy and Roman law is a commonly held opinion today. The sixteenth-century Reform, with its principle of "Scripture alone", opened up a perspective of this kind, which was at any rate mitigated by the fact that early Christian dogma was retained, formulated as it was in the Greek language and with Greek intellectual tools. Since the Enlightenment, this distinction between biblical and historical Christianity has become more radical; this whole conception, gathered together, has found expression in the slogan about the "Hellenization" of Christianity. The great historian of dogma Adolf Harnack has most thoroughly and consistently worked out this idea in terms of history and concrete examples: according to him, Gnosis was the acutely Hellenized version of Christianity, and Catholic Christianity the more slowly developing form of the same process that became historically effective.[4] Historians today are unanimous in thinking that this interpretation of Gnosis and of Catholic Christianity is untenable. But the slogan of Hellenization has lost none of its fascination; it is more widely known and

---

[4] Cf. A. Harnack, *Lehrbuch der Dogmengeschichte*, 5th ed. (Tübingen: Mohr, 1931) [English trans., *History of dogma* (New York: Dover, 1961)]; see 1:243–90 for Gnosis as "an acute form of secularization of Christianity"; 1:496–796 for "the fixing and gradual Hellenization of Christianity as doctrine about faith". It is clear, in the most recent edition of a history of dogma from an Evangelical perspective, that scholars have turned away from this view: W. Bienert, *Dogmengeschichte* (Stuttgart: W. Kohlhammer, 1997), pp. 27–115. On the theme of Hellenization in general, see J. Drumm, "Hellenisierung", in *Lexikon für Theologie und Kirche*, ed. J. Höfer and K. Rahner, 2nd ed. (Freiburg im Breisgau: Herder, 1957–1967), 4:1407–9; and literature listed there. I would like to draw attention especially to the writings of Grillmeier, Scheffczyk, and Lutz-Bachmann referred to there.

accepted than ever before. From liberation theology to the pluralistic theology of religions, it is at work in varying oscillations.[5] The content of this slogan has now become very simple and obvious: the Bible is said to be the expression of religious experiences and to have worked out a practical teaching ["praxis"] for right living; the early Church, dominated by Greek culture, it is said, overlaid this practical teaching with a philosophical theory and developed it into a literalist orthodoxy that is no longer reasonable for anyone today. Even theologians who wish their work to remain within the consensus of the whole Church, and who try to understand the dogma of the early Church, still intimate that this may have had significance for a particular period and in given cultural situations and yet is not relevant to the Church as a whole, in her various cultures, toward which the faith is on its way. This, it is said, is just *one* cultural form—the Greek, or Graeco-Latin—of Christianity, but one to which other cultures could not be committed.

And now, of course, there is again the whole problem of culture and faith to be discussed, and we will not go into all that again. In this book we are going to meet the problem of Hellenization again and again, from various aspects, and various answers will be given from different points of view. So at this point two suggestions, which we will take up again in other chapters, may suffice.

1.   The first encounter between Greek thought and biblical faith took place, not in the early Church, but in the

[5] Fairly typical is the significance of belief in a process of Hellenization in the Christology of J. Sobrino, *La fe en Jesucristo: Ensayo desde las víctimas* (San Salvador: UCA Editores, 1999), pp. 437–65 [English trans., *Christ the Liberator: A View from the Victims*, trans. Paul Burns (Maryknoll, N.Y.: Orbis Books, 2001)], as in various articles in the periodical *Vidyajyoti* (Delhi, 1975–).

course of the biblical path itself. Moses and Plato, belief in the gods and enlightened criticism of polytheism, theological ethics and ethical teaching drawn from "nature" had already encountered each other within the Bible itself. The conclusive breakthrough to a clear monotheism during the Exile, the struggle to find a new basis for ethics, after the collapse of the connection between doing and letting happen (in Job, various psalms, and so on), and finally the criticism of the animal sacrifices in the Temple and the search for an understanding of worship and sacrifice appropriate to God were all processes that of themselves involved the encounter of the two worlds. The Greek translation of the Old Testament, the Septuagint, which was the Bible of the New Testament, is not—as we now know—to be regarded as a Hellenizing version of the Masora (the Hebrew Old Testament); rather, it represents an independent textual tradition; the two texts stand before us, each with its own value, as witnesses to the development of the biblical faith.[6] The early Church continued the consistent development of an intercultural encounter that was locked into the core of the biblical faith itself.

2.   The great fundamental decisions of the early councils, which were expressed in the creeds, do not bend the

---

[6] An important contribution on this comes from A. Schenker, "L'Écriture sainte subsiste en plusieurs formes canoniques simultanées" [Holy Scripture exists in several canonical forms simultaneously], in *L'interpretazione della Bibbia nella Chiesa: Atti del Simposio promosso dalla Congregazione per la dottrina della fede* [The interpretation of the Bible: Report of the symposium called by the Congregation for the Doctrine of the Faith] (Vatican City, 2001), pp. 178–86. The reflections of E. Lévinas about Hebrew as the first language and Greek as necessarily the second language of the Bible are worth consideration; cf. on that point J. Wohlmut, *Die Tora spricht die Sprache der Menschen* [The Law speaks the language of men] (Paderborn: Schöningh, 2002), pp. 28–35.

faith into a philosophical theory; rather, they give verbal expression to two essential, unchanging elements of the biblical faith: they assure the realism of the biblical faith and prevent a merely symbolic or mythological interpretation; they assure the rational nature of the biblical faith, which in fact goes beyond reason itself and any possible "experiences" it may have yet nonetheless appeals to the reason and comes forward with the claim to be telling the truth—to be opening up access for man to the very heart of reality. I should like to demonstrate this—as I have often done—with the help of a little example, the one purely philosophical and certainly not biblical word that found its way into the great Creed and has thus been held up as a prime example of the "Hellenization" of Christianity. What I mean is the statement that Jesus Christ, God's only-begotten Son, is *homoousios* with the Father—of one being with him. It is well known how much dispute there was about this word, how people tried toned-down versions, compromises—on political grounds, as in seeking to mediate between opposing groups, seeking peace in the Church—but in the end nevertheless stayed with this one word, as a guarantee of loyalty to the biblical faith.[7] Is a philosophy that is foreign to the faith being canonized? A metaphysical theory being elevated to the status of dogma, when it does after all belong to only *one* culture? In order to answer that, we have to recall the question that was at issue here.

[7] Cf. C. Kannengiesser, art. "Homoousios", in Höfer and Rahner, *Lexikon für Theologie und Kirche*, 5:252f. (with bibliography); M. Simonetti, "Homoousios", in *Dictionnaire encyclopédique du Christianisme ancien* [French trans. of *Dizionario patristico e di antichità cristiane*, ed. Angelo Di Berardino] (Paris: Cerf, 1990), 1:1190f. [English trans., *Encyclopedia of the Early Church*, trans. Adrian Walford (New York: Oxford University Press, 1992)].

The New Testament talked about Jesus as the Son of God. Well, the religions into whose world the Christian mission was making its way also talked about sons of God and sons of the gods. Was Jesus of Nazareth this kind of son of God? Was that, then, a poetical exaggeration, a "mythological" way of talking, of the kind perhaps usual between lovers, who set their beloved on a pedestal, as absolute for them, but of course have no intention of making a ruling about reality itself, as a whole? Was this just an image? Or what kind of realism was being claimed for it? This question determines what Christianity as such is—whether Jesus is to be numbered among the "avatars", the many and various forms of manifestation of the Divinity in the world, whether Christianity is just one variant of religion among others, or whether we have here a different degree of realism. *Homoousios* answers this question. It is saying: The word "Son" is not meant poetically or allegorically (or mythologically, symbolically), but quite realistically. That is what Jesus *is* in reality; that is not just what he is being called. The realism of biblical faith is being defended, that is all; the reality and seriousness of event, of what happens, of what comes in from outside. In this "is", there is the echo of the "I am" used in the burning bush (Ex 3:14), whatever its historical origin and significance may have been. Jesus said more than once, "I am" and thereby expressed all the realism of the biblical faith: the expression in the Creed, which seems to be advanced for no good reason, is just telling us in the end that we can take the Bible at its word, that in its ultimate assertions it is literally, and not just allegorically, true.[8] In deciding this the Fathers very clearly grasped that the Bible was not just meaning to intro-

[8] For a more detailed exposition, see J. Ratzinger, *Der Gott Jesu Christi* (Munich: Kösel, 1976), pp. 70–76 [English trans., *The God of Jesus Christ: Meditations on God in the Trinity*, trans. Robert J. Cunningham (Chicago: Franciscan Herald Press, 1979].

duce some kind of "orthopraxy". It lays claim to something more. It regards man as being able to recognize truth and means to confront him with truth itself, to open for him the truth that stands before men as a person in Jesus Christ. The distinguishing mark of Greek philosophy was that it did not rest content with traditional religions or with the images of the myths; rather, in all seriousness, it put the question about truth. So perhaps at this point we may be able to recognize the hand of providence—why the encounter between the faith of the Bible and Greek philosophy was truly "providential".

4. ABRAHAM AND MELCHIZEDEK

In the Roman Canon, in the First Eucharistic Prayer of the Missal as reformed by Pope Paul VI, the request is made to God that, with a gracious and tranquil countenance, he be pleased to look upon the offering of the Church, as once he did upon the offering of his just servant Abel, upon the sacrifice of our Patriarch Abraham, and upon the holy sacrifice, a spotless victim, offered by the high priest Melchizedek. This petition called forth Luther's anger and was also strongly criticized in the circles of the Liturgical Movement as a misunderstanding of Christian worship, as a "regression" into Old Testament, pre-Christian attitudes. The early Church, whose faith and prayer are expressed in this text, thought otherwise. For the early Church there was no clear break between the prayer of the nations, the prayer of Israel, and the prayer of the Church. Of course, the "novelty" of Christian worship and practice was a fundamental category of the Christian faith: the Lord has brought to pass something new, the new thing itself; but this new thing had been prepared for, and history, for all its confusion and errors, had been leading up to it. It was, of course, a matter of distinguishing between what led up to Christ and what was opposed to him. It was a matter of subjecting all this to a process of purification and renewal, but this would in fact mean, not destroying things and making an absolute break, but initiating renewal and healing. Faith makes its appearance in the history of religions as a crisis and a judgment, but not as a total condemnation of them.

The prayer "Supra quae", from which the quotations above are taken, is thus an introduction to the discernment of spirits, an interpretation, both critical and positive, of pre-Christian ways of worship. The choice of these figures is in many respects significant; Abel is the first martyr—someone who has not killed but who let himself be killed and thus himself became a "lamb", anticipating the fate of Christ, the true Paschal Lamb. Abraham is ready to sacrifice Isaac, his only son, and thus to give up his future, the meaning of the promise; the lamb, the ram, takes the place of the son—the light of Christ casts its rays ahead in multiple refractions. Melchizedek, the king of Salem, is priest of El Elyon—of "the most high God"; he offers bread and wine. This mysterious figure repeatedly drew the attention both of early Judaism and of the growing Church; the Letter to the Hebrews sees him as representing the priesthood of Jesus Christ as against the Aaronic priesthood. Let us note the two things that are predicated of him: *zedek* means righteousness, justice; *salem* refers to Jerusalem and is a variant form of *shalom*, peace. Justice and peace are his characteristics. He worships the "most high God"—not just any gods, but the one God who is over the gods. He sacrifices, not animals, but the purest offerings of the earth—bread and wine. Once again, Christ is manifested in many ways.

The Fathers were right to see "types" of Christ in the three figures who are mentioned. Nowadays it is the fashion to attack typology as doing violence to the text, and there certainly have been inappropriate applications of typology. But the central and quite justified significance, the essential message, of typology is absolutely clear right here: there is a line running right through the history of faith and worship. Inwardly, things correspond to this—there are deviations, but there is also a path in a particular direction; the inner harmony with the figure of Jesus Christ, with his message and his existence, simply cannot be ruled out, in spite of the variety of historical contexts and stages. The true meaning of what people call "inclusivism" becomes apparent here: it is a matter, not of absorbing other religions externally, on the basis of a dogmatic postulate, as would do violence to them as phenomena, but of an inner correspondence that we may certainly call finality: Christ is moving through history in these forms and figures, as (again, with the Fathers) we may express it.

There is something else we should notice about these figures: Abel and Melchizedek are, in the classical terminology, "heathen", that is, they are not directly a part of Israel's special history of faith. Abraham is the forefather of Israel—our father, the Canon therefore says of him, drawing on Pauline theology. To become a Christian means entering into the history of faith that began with Abraham and, thus, accepting him as father. The sacrifice of Abraham referred to by the Roman Canon epitomizes the transition from the "heathen" cults to the purified cult of Israel and, with the sacrifice of a lamb (which links Abraham with Abel), indicates the move toward the Christian cult, at the center of which stands the Lamb who was sacrificed (Rev 5:6)—Christ, who gave himself to God in the night of suffering and who in his love reconciles us and draws us up to God. In that sense, the whole of the history of religion is referred to in this text, first leading up to Abraham (Israel) and, thereby, to Christ, and interpreted from his standpoint—from that of him who also offers us the standard by which to make the requisite distinctions, who is indeed himself that standard.

Here we ought to refute yet another misunderstanding of the petition of the "Supra quae", which has repeatedly been influential in history. Our asking God to look graciously upon our gifts does not mean, as one might think, that we regard Christ, who was sacrificed, as a thing that we offer to God in much the same way as the sacrifice of a lamb, uncertain whether this sacrifice, Christ, will please him or not. Such an interpretation, the mistake people could make—and have made—through a mere external reading of the text, runs completely counter to its inner logic. It is much more a matter of our asking for the very same attitude as that of Abel, of Abraham, of Isaac, and thus asking to move toward Christ, to enter into his attitudes, his thoughts, to become one with him, just as Abel, Abraham, Isaac, and Melchizedek were his types, his anticipatory presence in history. And thus we ask that the gaze of reconciliation, which in the end has always been, and always is, directed toward Christ, may fall on us, because we have ourselves become one with his attitude, his mind (Phil 2:5).

In the Old Testament story, Melchizedek stands there, not just in himself, but as someone we know only through his meeting with Abraham. Abraham, when God called him, separated himself from the gods of his homeland and held himself apart from the Canaanite gods and their cults. He follows "his God", the God who called him. But he meets up with Melchizedek, the king who serves the most high God as priest and who is characterized by the attributes of justice and peace. Abraham recognizes this king's cult as his own cult; he joins in praying to his God, accepts a blessing from him, and gives him "a tenth of everything" (Gen 14:18–20), as one does only in the case of a legitimate priest. There is an encounter in faith. But that does not indeed mean that "religions" are bundled together and treated as one thing, all classified as similar to each other. Yes, there are encounters between religions, but distinction is also comprised in these encounters. The Roman Canon teaches us both things: the inward contact between religions and the necessity of making distinctions for which Christ—the Son of the most high God, the King of justice and of peace—is the criterion.

Even within the Old Testament we can find the view that in his relations with God, man is not entirely without a standard by which to judge; in all his alienation, he may have an inner knowledge to show him the way. Seen in this light, I find the story of Jonah particularly enlightening. Jonah proclaims destruction to the sinful city of Nineveh. "And the people of Nineveh believed God", the text of the Bible tells us (Jon 3:5). Nineveh was a heathen city, a city with many gods. But at the call of the prophet, they believe God. They know in their inmost hearts that he exists, the one God, and they recognize the voice of that God in the preaching of the foreign prophet. Even sin has not quite extinguished in the heart of man the capacity to recognize the voice of God.

5. DISTINGUISHING WHAT IS CHRISTIAN

In 1994, the Office of Inter-Religious Relations of the World Council of Churches and the Pontifical Council for Inter-religious Dialogue initiated a joint process of reflection on "interreligious prayer". A first stage was devoted to a survey of the religious experiences of various Churches with this question. A second stage, undertaken in 1996, consisted in a consultation in Bangalore, in India, and taking part in this were a limited number of people from "a variety of Christian traditions", who had in common some experience with interreligious prayer. Here individual theologians expounded their insights and opinions. The whole process closed with a "final statement": "Findings of an Exploratory Consultation on Interreligious Prayer".[9] Finally, in 1997 in Bose (Italy), a small group of theologians from various Churches elaborated a document on the theological basis of interreligious prayer.[10]

While the Bose document—in spite of many questions that need to be raised—may be regarded as a sound piece of work which really moves us ahead, the Bangalore text gives me an unfortunate impression of superficiality and dilettantism. I would just like to give one example:

Among other things, interreligious prayer is justified with the category of hospitality. The Bangalore statement tells us that interreligious prayer is not just an answer to the demands of certain situations but is "an expression of our loyalty to the gospel itself". Luke 10:7 is cited as biblical evidence for this: Jesus himself urges us, it says, to accept hospitality from others just as to offer it. This accepting of hospitality is not just restricted to eating and drinking, we are told, but includes what is precious to our neighbor: prayer and worship.[11] Anyone who opens his New Testament after hearing these assertions and reads Luke 10:1–12, about Jesus sending out the seventy-two disciples, can only rub his eyes

[9] "Findings of an Exploratory Consultation on Interreligious Prayer", Pontificium Consilium pro dialogo inter religiones, *Bulletin* 98, no. 2 (1998): 231–36.

[10] "Theological Reflections on Interreligious Prayer: Final Statement (Bose, Italy)", Pontificium Consilium pro dialogo inter religiones, *Bulletin* 98, no. 2 (1998): 237–43.

[11] "Findings", p. 233.

in amazement at such an exegesis. Jesus commissions the disciples to proclaim the imminence of the Kingdom of God by word and by deed (healings). While on this task they have the right to hospitality (10:5–7). "But whenever you enter a town and they do not receive you, go into its streets and say, 'Even the dust of your town that clings to our feet, we wipe off against you; nevertheless know this, that the kingdom of God has come near.' I tell you, it shall be more tolerable on that day for Sodom than for that town" (10:10–12). The sending out of the seventy-two (seventy, or seventy-two, was held to be the number of peoples on the earth) is an anticipatory representation of the post-Easter mission, in which the disciples are called to carry the gospel to all peoples—and after Easter it becomes clear that Jesus is the Kingdom in person, so that the good news of the Kingdom has to proclaim him. The refusal to accept the messengers and their message stands in danger of judgment. Making out that the hospitality demanded for the messengers involves cultural exchanges and sharing of prayer really has nothing further in common with the biblical text. We should be able to expect a little more by way of serious argument.

But apart from such difficulties with the way things are argued, the text is concerned with something more basic, the question: Who, or what, is God? How do we respond to him? Does he know us? The Bangalore text says that inter-religious prayer raises some important theological themes for discussion, "for example, what does it mean, when we say that God is one? Are we all praying to one and the same God, even if our images and our understandings of God are various and different? How shall we venture to teach about God in non-theistic contexts?" We must find new ways to articulate our faith, the text tells us, with a view to the place of other religions in the economy of salvation and, over and beyond the categories of exclusivism, inclusivism, and personalism, find other creative ways to perceive the work of the Spirit in other religions in theological terms.[12] Admittedly, these are, not theories, but questions that are being advanced. Yet these questions still insinuate that the boundaries between God and the gods, between a personal and an impersonal understanding of God should not be ultimately decisive—that behind all this, everybody in the end means to say the same thing. We are supposed to think that the distinction between God and gods, between an image of God as a person and an impersonal mysticism of identity, is a distinction between images and concepts, that is, a penultimate distinction that does not affect the essentials, because all concepts and images fall short of the ineffable reality of the absolute. The real distinction—one could then infer—would certainly be, not that between these various images and ways of understanding, but between all human discourse about God, of whatever kind, and the reality of the unknown beyond all the words, which is ultimately, in various ways, only ever distantly approached. This concept has in itself something fascinating for present-day man; it seems to express a greater reverence toward the mystery of God and a greater humility before the absolute on the part of man, and in its all-inclusive tolerance, it seems to be, in terms both of religion and of thought, greater than the insistence on the personal nature of God as being indispensable, an inalienable gift through revelation. It is undeniable that these conceptions are becoming widespread meanwhile, especially among Christians, and are being put into practice in "interreligious prayer".

[12] Ibid. p. 234.

Is this view really "more pious", and, above all, is it more true? Let us ask, in practical terms, What does it change? What happens in terms of our faith and prayer? First of all, if personal and impersonal concepts of God are equal, interchangeable, then prayer becomes merely a fiction, since if God is not a God who sees and hears, if he does not recognize me and stand over against me, then prayer is going out into the void. It is then merely a form of self-recollection, of conversing with myself, not a dialogue. It may be a preparation for the absolute, a deliberate foray out of the separation of the self into the infinite being with which I am myself at the deepest level to be identified and into which I wish to be absorbed. But it has no point of reference that sets me a standard and from which I may in any sense expect a response. And further: if I can leave behind the belief in God as a "person", as one possible conception side by side with the impersonal one, then not only is this God not a God who perceives me, hears me, speaks to me (a Logos)—then he certainly has no will of his own. Perceiving and willing are the two essential elements in the concept of person. Then there is no will of God. Neither, then, is there any ultimate distinction between good and evil: good and evil then (as we have already seen) stand no longer in contradiction but merely in relational opposition, in the sense that each is complementary to the other. Then the one, just as much as the other, is a mere surge of the waves of being, and I am then subject to no standard. But in that case it is not just some image or system of concepts that has been changed, but everything is profoundly different. Yet if God is a person, then the ultimate and very highest being is also the most concrete—in that case, I am standing under the eye of God, in the realm of his will, of his love.

Because this is how it is, the *Shema Israel* is for Israel, as
equally for the Church, the immutable basis of our existence: "Hear, O Israel: The LORD our God is one LORD; and
you shall love the LORD your God with all your heart, and
with all your soul, and with all your might" (Deut 6:4). The
martyrs of Israel died for this faith, as did the martyrs of Jesus
Christ. The First Commandment, "You shall have no other
gods before me" (Ex 20:3; Deut 5:7), is, not just numeri-
cally, but in accordance with its inner status the first commandment, upon which everything else is founded. In the
story of the temptation, Christ set it before us again, in lap-
idary terms, as the foundation of the Christian life: "You
shall worship the Lord your God and him only shall you
serve" (Mt 4:10). Between God and the gods, between a
personal and an impersonal concept of God, there is in the
end no middle way, however true it may be that truth is to
be found in polytheism, just as in the mysticism of identity,
truth that has its place in the Christian faith yet that can only
appear in its true significance if the distinction has been made
of what is Christian and if the "face of God" has thus not
been lost sight of, not been lost from our hearts.

Only from this standpoint, from belief in God, can the
Church's belief in Christ be properly understood. The uniqueness of Christ is directly related to the uniqueness of God
and to the concrete form of this. Christ is not an avatar of
God, perhaps an especially impressive one, one of the multifarious finite manifestations of the divine, in which we learn
to have some inkling of the divine. He is not a "manifestation" of the divine, but *is* God. In him, God has shown his
face. Anyone who sees him has seen the Father (Jn 14:9).
Here it is genuinely a matter of the "is"—this is the real
dividing line in the history of religions, and for that very
reason it is the effective force for uniting them. That is why

the encounter with the Greeks' ontology—with its question concerning "is"—is not a philosophical distortion of the Christian faith but has become its indispensable form of expression.

On that basis, finally, we should understand two other fundamental concepts of the Christian faith, which have become unmentionable nowadays: conversion (*conversio*) and mission. The opinion has become nearly general these days that conversion should be understood to mean a turning point in one's inner path but not a transition from one religion to another and, thus, not a transition to Christianity. The notion that all religions are ultimately equivalent appears as a commandment of tolerance and respect for others; if that is so, then one must respect the decision of another person who decides to change religions, but it is not permissible to call this conversion: that would assign a higher status to the Christian faith and thus contradict the idea of equality. The Christian has to resist this ideology of equality. Not as if he wanted to make himself out to be superior—no one achieves being a Christian for himself, as we were saying; each is only Christian through "conversion". But the Christian certainly does believe that in Christ the living God calls us in a unique way, which demands obedience and conversion. This presupposes that the question of truth plays a part in the relations between religions and that truth is a gift for everyone and alienates no one. The second part of this book will be devoted to this fundamental question.

And that says what is essential about the concept of "mission". If all religions are in principle equal, then mission can only be a kind of religious imperialism, which must be resisted. But if in Christ a new gift, the essential gift—truth—is being granted us, then it is our duty to offer this to others—freely, of course, for truth cannot operate otherwise, nor can love exist.

6. MULTIRELIGIOUS AND INTERRELIGIOUS PRAYER

In the age of dialogue and of the encounter between religions, the question has necessarily arisen as to whether we can pray with each other. Nowadays people make a distinction here between multireligious and interreligious prayer. The model for multireligious prayer is offered by the two World Days of Prayer for Peace in Assisi, in 1986 and 2002. People belonging to various religious affiliations meet together. They have in common an acute concern for the needs of the world and its lack of peace; they share a longing for help from above against the powers of evil, that peace and justice might enter into the world. Hence their intention to give a public sign of this longing, which might stir up all men and strengthen the goodwill that is a condition of peace. Those who meet also know that their understandings of the divine, and hence their way of turning to him, are so varied that shared prayer would be a fiction, far from the truth. They meet to give a sign of their shared longing; but they pray—albeit simultaneously—in separate places, each in his own fashion. "Praying" in the case of an impersonal understanding of God (often associated with polytheism) obviously means something quite different from praying in faith to the one personal God. The distinction is visibly represented, though in such a fashion as to become at the same time a cry for the healing of our divisions.

Following from Assisi—in 1986 as in 2002—the question was repeatedly and most seriously raised: Can one do this? Does this not give most people a false impression of common ground that does not exist in reality? Does this not promote relativism, the opinion that, fundamentally, the differences that divide "religions" are merely penultimate? And is not the seriousness of faith being undermined thereby and God set farther away from us, in the end, our forsak-enness intensified? We should not lightly set aside such ques-tions. There are undeniable dangers, and it is indisputable that the Assisi meetings, especially in 1986, were misinter-preted by many people. It would, on the other hand, be wrong to reject, completely and unconditionally, multireli-gious prayer of the kind I have described. To me, the right thing in this case seems to be, rather, to link it with con-ditions corresponding to the demands of inner truth and responsibility for such a great undertaking as the public appeal to God before all the world. I see two basic conditions:

1.   Such multireligious prayer cannot be the normal form of religious life but can only exist as a sign in unusual situ-ations, in which, as it were, a common cry for help rises up, stirring the hearts of men, to stir also the heart of God.

2.   Such a procedure almost inevitably leads to false inter-pretations, to indifference as to the content of what is believed or not believed, and thus to the dissolution of real faith. That is why—as was said in point 1—these procedures must remain exceptional and why a careful explanation, of what happens here and what does not happen, is most impor-tant. This explanation, which must make clear that there is no such thing as "the religions" altogether as such, no such thing as a common concept of God or belief in God, that difference not merely exists in the realm of changing images and concepts but involves ultimate decisions—this explana-tion is important, not only for those participating in the event itself, but for all who witness it or learn about it in some other way. What is happening must be so clear in itself, and to the world, that it does not become a demon-stration of that relativism through which it would nullify its own significance.

While in multireligious prayer this is done in fact within the same context, yet separately, interreligious prayer means people or groups of various religious allegiances praying together. Is that, in all truth and in all honesty, possible at all? I doubt it. In any case, three elementary conditions have to be set, without which such prayer would become a mere denial of faith:

1.   We can pray with each other only if we are agreed who or what God is and if there is therefore basic agreement as to what praying is: a process of dialogue in which I talk to a God who is able to hear and take notice. To put it another way: shared prayer presumes a shared understanding of the addressee and thus likewise of the inner action directed toward him. As in the case of Abraham and Melchizedek, of Job, and of Jonah, it must be clear that we are talking with a God above all gods, with the Creator of the heaven and the earth—with my Creator. It must then be clear that God is a "person", that is, that he can perceive and love; that he has power to hear me and to respond; that he is good and is the standard of all good, and that evil has no part in him. On the basis of Melchizedek we can say that it must be clear that he is the God of peace and justice. Any confusion of a personal and an impersonal understanding, of God and the gods, must be excluded. The First Commandment is true, particularly in any possible interreligious prayer.

2.   Yet there must also be fundamental agreement—on the basis of the concept of God—about what is worth praying about and what might be the content of prayer. I see the petitions of the Lord's Prayer as a measure of what we may rightly ask of God, in order to pray in a manner worthy of God: it becomes manifest in them who and how God is and who we ourselves are. They purify our will and show us

with what kind of willing we are on our way to God and what sort of wishing keeps us far from God, sets us against him. Petitions contrary to those of the Lord's Prayer cannot be for the Christian the subject of interreligious prayer or of any kind of prayer at all.

3. The whole thing must be so arranged that the relativistic misinterpretation of faith and prayer can find no foothold in it. This criterion relates not only to Christians, who should not be led astray, but equally well to non-Christians, to whom no impression should be given that "religions" are interchangeable, that the basics of Christian belief are not of ultimate significance and thus replaceable. To avoid misleading people in such ways demands that the Christian's faith in the uniqueness of God and the uniqueness of Jesus Christ the Savior of all mankind be not obscured for the non-Christian. The Bose document we have referred to says quite rightly that participation in interreligious prayer must not be allowed to put in question our commitment to the preaching of Christ to all men.[13] If the non-Christian should be able to see the participation of a Christian as the relativizing of faith in Jesus Christ, the Savior of all, or be bound to see it thus, then such participation cannot take place. For it would then be pointing in the wrong direction, backward instead of forward, in the history of the way of God.

[13] "Theological Reflections", p. 241.

PART TWO

RELIGIONS AND THE QUESTION OF TRUTH

FOREWORD

The first part of this book was devoted to the question of the relation between Christian faith and the cultures and religions of the world. We tried to understand what the word *religion* means, what religion is, what faith means, and what we mean, more exactly, by culture, so as to fathom what possibilities exist for a fruitful encounter of these three realities. It became steadily more clear that the whole area of encounters, of dialogue, and likewise of mission leads us inevitably to the question concerning truth: there is no way around it, however unmodern it may seem to be. The individual sections of this second part, in which I try to tackle this question, arose from the demands of my office and from reflections upon its basis; they approach the theme from various sides and thus attempt to illuminate the individual aspects of the problem.

The first chapter is a paper I prepared for the meeting between the Congregation for the Doctrine of the Faith and the presidents of the commissions of faith of the various bishops' conferences of Latin America, in 1996 in Guadalajara, Mexico, and which I read there; it was intended as an introduction to the new complex of problems that had developed since the turnaround of 1989. The second chapter tried to respond directly to the question of whether we can talk of truth in the realm of faith, in what way, and in what sense of the word. The first section ("Faith between Reason and Feeling") I read in Hamburg in 1998, the second in Paris in 1999.

The third section originated simply as an introduction to the encyclical *Fides et Ratio* (Faith and reason) and then gradually developed to its present form through lectures in Paderborn, San Francisco, Cracow, and Madrid.

Because the claim to know the truth is widely regarded nowadays as a threat to tolerance and freedom, this whole question had to be taken up. I put up the first section of the third chapter for discussion by a wider public in 2002, in Lugano and Naples; and in response to an invitation from Padua, I read the second section there in 1995.

THE NEW QUESTIONS THAT AROSE
IN THE NINETIES: THE POSITION
OF FAITH AND THEOLOGY TODAY

The Crisis for Liberation Theology

In the eighties, the theology of liberation, in its radical forms, appeared as the most urgent challenge facing the belief of the Church, demanding response and clarification. For it offered a new, plausible, and at the same time practical answer to the basic question of Christianity: the question of redemption. The word liberation was supposed to express, in another, more readily comprehensible way, what in the traditional language of the Church had been called redemption. In fact the same underlying question is always there: we experience a world that does not correspond to a good God. Poverty, oppression, unjust domination of every kind, the suffering of the righteous and of the innocent are the signs of the times—in every age. And each single person is suffering; no one can say about the world, or about his own life: Stay yet awhile, you are so lovely. Liberation theology said, in response to this experience of ours: This state of affairs, which cannot be allowed to continue, can only be overcome by a radical change in the structures of the world, which are sinful structures, evil structures. If, then, sin applies its power through structures, and if our reduction to misery is preprogramed through them, then sin cannot be overcome by individual conversion but only by a struggle against the structures of injustice. Yet this struggle, it was said, would have to be a political struggle, because the structures were strengthened and maintained by politics. Thus redemption became a political process, for which Marxist philosophy offered the essential directions. It became a task that men themselves could—indeed had to—take in hand and became, at the same time, the object of quite practical hopes: faith was changed from "theory" into practice, into concrete redeeming action in the liberation process.

The collapse of the Marxist-inspired governments of Europe was for this theology of redeeming political practice a kind of twilight of the gods: precisely there where the Marxist ideology of liberation had been consistently applied, a total lack of freedom had developed, whose horrors were now laid bare before the eyes of the entire world. Wherever politics tries to be redemptive, it is promising too much. Where it wishes to do the work of God, it becomes, not divine, but demonic. The political events of 1989 have thus also changed the theological landscape. Marxism had been the most recent attempt to formulate a universally valid code for determining the correct action to be taken in history. It believed it knew the fundamental structure by which the history of the world is built up and that it was therefore able to show how this history could finally be brought onto the right track. The fact that it underpinned all this with what seemed to be strictly scientific methods, and thus completely replaced belief by science and turned knowledge into practice, made it enormously, monstrously fascinating. It seemed as though all the unfulfilled promises of religion could be realized by means of a system of political practice with a scientific basis. The collapse of this hope inevitably brought with it an immense disillusionment that is still far from having been worked through. It seems to me quite conceivable that we will meet with new forms of the Marxist view of the world. At first people were at a loss. The failure of the one system incorporating a scientifically based solution to human problems could only favor nihilism or at any rate absolute relativism.

Relativism—The Dominant Philosophy

So in fact relativism has become the central problem for faith in our time. It by no means appears simply as resignation in the face of the unfathomable nature of truth, of course; rather, it defines itself positively on the basis of the concepts of tolerance, dialectic epistemology, and freedom, which would be limited by maintaining one truth as being valid for everyone. Relativism thus also appears as being the philosophical basis of democracy, which is said to be founded on no one's being able to claim to know the right way forward; and it draws life from all the ways acknowledging each other as fragmentary attempts at improvement and trying to agree in common through dialogue, although the advertising of perceptions that cannot be reconciled in a common form is also part of this. A free society is said to be a relativistic society; only on this condition can it remain free and open-ended.

In the realm of politics this view is to a great extent true. The one single correct political option does not exist. What is relative, the construction of a freely ordered common life for men, cannot be absolute—thinking that it could be was precisely the error of Marxism and of the political theologies. Even in the realm of politics, of course, one cannot always manage with absolute relativism: there are things that are wrong and can never become right (killing innocent people, for instance; denying individuals the right to be treated as humans and to a way of life appropriate to that); there are things that are right and can never become wrong. In the realm of politics and society, therefore, one cannot deny relativism a certain right. The problem is based on the fact that it sees itself as being unlimited. And now it is being quite consciously applied to the field of religion and ethics. I can only give a couple of brief references here to the developments that are determinative for theological intercourse today. The so-called pluralistic theology of religions had in fact been gradually developing since the fifties, but it did not occupy the center of attention for Christians until now.[1] With respect to the ramifications of the questions it raises, and likewise to its being present in the most various

---

[1] A survey of the most significant authors of the pluralistic theology of religions is offered by P. Schmidt-Leukel's "Das Pluralistische Modell in der Theologie der Religionen: Ein Literaturbericht" [The pluralist model in the theology of religions: An annotated bibliography], *Theologische Revue* 89 (1993): 353–70. For a discussion of it, see: M. von Brück and J. Werbick, *Der einzige Weg zum Heil? Die Herausforderung des christlichen Absolutheitsanspruchs durch pluralistische Religionstheologien* [The sole path to salvation? The challenge from pluralistic theologies of religion to the Christian claim to absolute validity], Quaestiones Disputatae 143 (Freiburg: Herder, 1993); K.-H. Menke, *Die Einzigkeit Jesu Christi im Horizont der Sinnfrage* [The uniqueness of Jesus Christ against the horizon of the question of meaning] (Einsiedeln: Johannes Verlag, 1995), especially pp. 75–176. Menke offers an excellent introduction to the ideas of two of the principal representatives of this tendency, J. Hick and P. F. Knitter, upon which much of what I say here is based. Menke's discussion of this question in the second part of his book includes much that is important and deserving of our attention, but as a whole, unfortunately, it remains unsatisfactory. An interesting systematic attempt at a new approach to the problem of other religions from the starting point of Christology is offered by B. Stubenrauch, *Dialogisches Dogma: Der christliche Auftrag zur interreligiösen Begegnung* [Dialectical dogma: The Christian task of interreligious encounter], Quaestiones Disputatae 158 (Freiburg: Herder, 1995). On the problem of the pluralistic theology of religions, cf. also the document published in 1996 by the International Theological Commission.

cultural spheres, it occupies much the same place as did liberation theology in the past decade; it is also frequently combined with the latter in an attempt to give it a new, updated form. It appears in widely varying forms, so that it is impossible to express it in a short formula and present its essential elements briefly. On the one hand, this is a typical product of the Western world and of its thought forms, yet, on the other hand, it is astonishingly close to the philosophical and religious intuitions of Asia, and especially of the Indian subcontinent, so that in the current historical situation the contact of these two worlds gives it a particular impact.

Relativism in Theology—The Revocation of Christology

That is clearly visible in the work of one of its founders and principal representatives, the English Presbyterian J. Hick, whose philosophical starting point is found in Kant's distinction between phenomenon and nouomenon: we can never know ultimate reality in itself but only ever its appearance in the way we perceive things, seeing it through various "lenses". Everything we perceive is, not actual reality as it is in itself, but a reflection corresponding to our capacities. This approach, which Hick first tried to apply in a context that was still christocentric, he transformed after a year's stay in India, in what he himself calls a Copernican turning point in his thinking, into a new form of theocentrism. The identification of one single historical figure, Jesus of Nazareth, with "reality" itself, with the living God, was now rejected as a relapse into myth; Jesus was consciously relativized, reduced to one religious genius among others. There can be no absolute entity in itself, or absolute person in himself, within history, only patterns, only ideal figures, which direct our attention toward the wholly other, which in history cannot in fact be comprehended in itself. It is clear that by the same token Church, dogma, and sacraments must thereby lose their unconditional status. To regard such finite mediations as absolute, or even as real encounters with the universally valid truth of the God who reveals himself, amounts to setting up one's own experience as absolute and thus failing to perceive the infinity of the God who is wholly other.

From such a standpoint, which dominates thinking far beyond the scope of Hick's theories, the belief that there is indeed truth, valid and binding truth, within history itself, in the figure of Jesus Christ and in the faith of the Church, is referred to as fundamentalism, which appears as the real assault upon the spirit of the modern age and, manifested in many forms, as the fundamental threat to the highest good of that age, freedom and tolerance. Thus to a great extent the concept of dialogue, which certainly held an important place in the Platonic and in the Christian tradition, has acquired a different meaning. It has become the very epitome of the relativist credo, the concept opposed to that of "conversion" and mission: dialogue in the relativist sense means setting one's own position or belief on the same level with what the other person believes, ascribing to it, on principle, no more of the truth than to the position of the other person. Only if my fundamental presupposition is that the other person may be just as much in the right as I am, or even more so, can any dialogue take place at all. Dialogue, it is said, has to be an exchange between positions that are fundamentally of equal status and thus mutually relative, with the aim of achieving a maximum of cooperation and integration between various religious bodies and entities.[2] The

---

[2] Cf. on this point the most illuminating editorial in *Civiltà Cattolica* 1 (1996): 107–20: "Il cristianesimo e le altre religioni" [Christianity and the other reli-

relativist elimination of Christology, and most certainly of ecclesiology, now becomes a central commandment of religion. To turn back to Hick: the belief in the divinity of an individual, he tells us, leads to fanaticism and particularism, to the dissociation of faith from love; and this is the thing that must be overcome.[3]

The Recourse to Asian Religions

In the thought of J. Hick, whom we have particularly in mind here as a prominent representative of religious relativism, the postmetaphysical philosophy of Europe converges in a remarkable way with the negative theology of Asia, for which the Divinity can never enter, in itself and undisguised, into the world of appearances in which we live: it only ever shows itself in relative reflections and in itself remains beyond all words and beyond all comprehension in absolute transcendence.[4] In their starting points, as in the direction they give to human existence, the two philosophies are in themselves fundamentally different. Yet they appear nonetheless to support one another in their metaphysical and

---

gions]. The editorial engages in discussion especially with Hick, Knitter, and R. Panikkar.

[3] Cf., for example, J. Hick, *An Interpretation of Religion: Human Responses to the Transcendent* (New Haven: Yale University Press, 1989); Menke, *Einzigkeit Jesu Christi*, p. 90.

[4] Cf. E. Frauwallner, *Geschichte der indischen Philosophie*, 2 vols. (Salzburg: O. Müller, 1953 and 1956) [English trans., *History of Indian Philosophy*, trans. V. M. Bedekar (New York: Humanities Press, 1974)]; H. von Glasenapp, *Die Philosophie der Inder* [The philosophy of the Indians], 4th ed. (Stuttgart: A. Kröner, 1985); S. N. Dasgupta, *History of Indian Philosophy*, 5 vols. (Cambridge: University Press, 1922–1955); K. B. Ramakrishna Rao, *Ontology of Advaita with Special Reference to Māyā* (Mulki: Research and Publication, Vijaya College, 1964).

religious relativism. The a-religious and pragmatic relativism of Europe and America can borrow a kind of consecration from India, which seems to give its renunciation of dogma the dignity of a heightened reverence for the mystery of God and of man. Conversely, the way that European and American thinking has turned back to India's philosophical and theological vision has the effect of further strengthening that relativizing of all religious figures which is part of India's heritage. Thus it now actually seems imperative in India, even for Christian theology, to extract from its particularity the figure of Christ, regarded as Western, and to set it beside Indian redemption myths as if it were of similar status: the historical Jesus, so people now think, is actually no more uniquely the Logos than any other savior figures from history are.[5] The fact that here, in the context of the encounter between cultures, relativism seems appropriate as the true philosophy of humanity gives it (as we have already suggested) such an appreciable impact, both in East and West, that it hardly seems possible to offer further resistance. Anyone who opposes it is not only setting himself against democracy and tolerance, that is, the fundamental rules of human intercourse; he is obstinately insisting on the preeminence of his own Western culture and thus refusing to share in that coexistence of cultures which is obviously the order of the day. Anyone who wants to stick with the Bible and the Church starts by finding himself thrust out into a cultural no-man's land; he has to come to terms again with the "folly" of God (1 Cor 1:18) in order to recognize true wisdom in it.

[5] F. Wilfrid, *Beyond Settled Foundations: The Journey of Indian Theology* (Madras: Department of Christian Studies, University of Madras, 1993), is clearly moving in this direction; Wilfrid, "*Some Tentative Reflections on the Language of Christian Uniqueness: An Indian Perspective*", in Pontificium Consilium pro Dialogo inter Religiones, Pro Dialogo, *Bulletin* 85–86, no. 1 (1994): 40–57.

Orthodoxy and Orthopraxy

In that kind of feeling one's way toward truth within the folly of faith, it helps if we can, at least to start with, try to make sure what purpose is served by Hick's relativist theory of religion, in what direction it is pointing man. What religion means in the end for Hick is that man passes from "self-centeredness", the life of the old Adam, to "reality-centeredness", the life of the new man, thus reaching out from within his own self, his "I", to the "Thou" of his neighbor.[6] That sounds fine, but in the cold light of day it is just as meaningless and void of content as Bultmann's call to authenticity, which he borrowed from Heidegger. You do not need religion for that. The former Catholic priest P. Knitter, clearly aware of this, has tried to overcome the emptiness of a theory of religion that is ultimately reduced to the categorical imperative with a new and more concrete synthesis between Asia and Europe, with a greater content.[7] His suggestion is to give religion a new concrete dimension by linking pluralist theology of religions with the liberation theologies. Interreligious dialogue was to be radically simplified, and at the same time made effective in practice, by basing it on one single premise: "on the primacy of orthopraxy over orthodoxy".[8] This giving practice superior rank over knowledge is also bequeathed from good Marxism, yet Marxism for its part puts into practice only

[6] J. Hick, *Evil and the God of Love*, 4th ed. (Norfolk, 1975), pp. 240f.; Hick, *Interpretation of Religion*, pp. 236–40; cf. Menke, *Einzigkeit Jesu Christi*, pp. 81f.

[7] P. F. Knitter's major book *No Other Name? A Critical Survey of Christian Attitudes toward the World Religions* (Maryknoll, N.Y.: Orbis Books, 1985) has been translated into many languages. Cf. on this Menke, *Einzigkeit Jesu Christi*, pp. 94–110. A careful critical evaluation is also offered by A. Kolping in his review in *Theologische Revue* 87 (1991): 234–40.

[8] Cf. Menke, *Einzigkeit Jesu Christi*, p. 95.

what is the logical result of the renunciation of metaphysics: when it is impossible to know, it only remains to act. Knitter says: One cannot comprehend the absolute, but one can do it. The question is: How, in fact? Whence do I derive right action if I have no idea what is right? The collapse of the Communist regimes resulted directly from the fact that they had changed the world without knowing what was good for the world and what was not; without knowing in what direction it must be changed so as to be better. Mere praxis gives no light.

This is the point at which the concept of orthopraxy must be critically investigated. The older history of religions had established that the religions of India knew nothing, in general, of any orthodoxy but that they did have an orthopraxy; it is probably from this that the concept crept into modern theology. But it has a quite specific meaning in describing the religions of India: people were trying to say that these religions had no generally binding teaching and that belonging to them is therefore not defined by acceptance of a given creed. Yet these religions do have a system of ritual actions that are regarded as being necessary for salvation and that distinguish the "believer" from the unbeliever. He will be recognized, not by any particular intellectual content, but by the conscientious following of a ritual that embraces the whole of life. What orthopraxy means, what "right action" is, is quite precisely determined: a whole code of rites. In any case, the word "orthodoxy" originally had almost the same meaning in the early Church and in the Eastern Churches. For in the "doxy" part of the word, *doxa* was of course not understood in the sense of "opinion" (correct opinion)—in the Greek view, opinions are always relative: *doxa* was understood rather in the sense of "glory", "glorifying". To be orthodox, therefore, meant: to know and to practice the right way in which God wishes to be glorified. It refers to worship and, on the basis of worship, to life. In that sense, there might well be a substantial bridge here for a fruitful dialogue between East and West.

But let us return to the use of the word orthopraxy in modern theology. No one any longer was thinking here about following ritual. The word thus acquired an entirely new significance, which had nothing to do with the genuine ideas of India. One thing does of course remain: if the demand for orthopraxy is to have some meaning, and is not merely to serve as a fig leaf for being indeterminate, then there must be a recognizable common practice for everyone that goes beyond all the generalized talk about being centered on the "I" or being related to the "Thou". If we exclude the ritual sense, which was what was signified in Asia, then "praxis" may be understood in terms of ethics or politics. In the first case, orthopraxy would presume the existence of an ethic with a clearly defined content. In the relativist discussion of ethics, that is of course absolutely excluded: there is no such thing as good in itself or evil in itself. Yet if orthopraxy is understood in terms of politics and society, the question once more arises as to what is correct political action. Liberation theologies, which were animated by the conviction that Marxism tells us clearly what correct political action is, were able to use the concept of orthopraxy in a way that made sense. There was no vagueness or indecisiveness here but a system of correct action laid down for everyone, that is, a true orthopraxy that united the community and distinguished it from those people who refused to act correctly. In that sense the Marxist-oriented liberation theologies were in their own way logically consistent.

Yet as we can see, this orthopraxy is entirely based upon a certain orthodoxy (in the modern sense)—a scaffolding of obligatory theories about the path to freedom. Knitter is staying close to this base when he says that that freedom is the criterion by which orthopraxy is to be distinguished from pseudopraxy.[9] But he fails to satisfy us with a practical and persuasive explanation of what freedom is and of what helps toward the true liberation of man: Marxist orthopraxy certainly does not help us, as we have seen. Yet one thing is clear: the relativist theories, without exception, lead to what is binding upon no one and thus render themselves superfluous; or, on the other hand, they suggest absolute standards in the realm of practice, where in fact absolutes can have no place. It is of course a fact that today, even in Asia, we can see how concepts drawn from liberation theology are being put forward as supposed forms of Christianity that more closely correspond to the Asian spirit, that transpose the essential elements of religious action into the realm of politics. When mystery no longer counts for anything, then politics necessarily becomes the religion. This, of all things, is of course profoundly opposed to the native conception of religion in Asia.

New Age

The relativism of Hick and Knitter and other related theories is ultimately based on a rationalism that holds that reason in Kant's sense is incapable of any metaphysical knowledge;[10] religion is then given a new basis along pragmatic lines, with either a more ethical or a more political coloration. There is, however, a consciously antirationalist response to the experience that "everything is relative", a complex reality that is lumped

[9] Cf. ibid., p. 109.

[10] Knitter, like Hick, claims the support of Kant for his denial that the absolute can exist in history; cf. Menke, *Einzigkeit Jesu Christi*, pp. 78 and 108.

together under the title of New Age.[11] The way out of the dilemma of relativism is now sought, not in a new encounter of the "I" with the "Thou" or the "We", but in overcoming subjective consciousness, in a re-entry into the dance of the cosmos through ecstasy. As in the case of Gnosis in the ancient world, this way believes itself to be fully in tune with all the teachings and the claims of science, making use of scientific knowledge of every kind (biology, psychology, sociology, physics). At the same time, however, it offers against this background a completely antirationalist pattern of religion, a modern "mysticism": the absolute is, not something to be believed in, but something to be experienced. God is not a person distinct from the world; rather, he is the spiritual energy that is at work throughout the universe. Religion means bringing my self into tune with the cosmic whole, the transcending of all divisions. K.-H. Menke epitomizes the turning point in the history of ideas that is taking place just precisely here when he says that: "That self, which hitherto wished to subject everything to itself, now wants to dissolve itself in 'the whole'."[12] Objectifying reason, New Age thinking tells us,

[11] The concept of "New Age", or "Age of Aquarius", was introduced toward the middle of the twentieth century by Raul Le Cour (1937) and by Alice Bailey (she talked about messages she said she had received in 1945 concerning a new world order and a new world religion). The Esalen Institute was set up in California between 1960 and 1970. Marilyn Ferguson is the best-known representative of New Age thinking today. Michael Fuß ("New Age: Supermarkt alternativer Spiritualität", *Communio* 20 [1991]: 148–57) sees New Age as the result of a conjunction of Judaeo-Christian elements with the process of secularization, with gnostic tendencies, and with elements of oriental religions. The 1990 pastoral letter of Cardinal G. Danneels, *Le Christ ou le Verseau* [Christ or Aquarius], which has been translated into many languages, offers some helpful guidelines. Cf. also Menke, *Einzigkeit Jesu Christi*, pp. 31–36; J. Le Bar (ed.), *Cults, Sects and the New Age* (Huntington, Ind.: Our Sunday Visitor, 1989).

[12] Menke, *Einzigkeit Jesu Christi*, p. 33.

closes our way to the mystery of reality; existing as the self shuts us out from the fullness of cosmic reality; it destroys the harmony of the whole and is the real reason for our being unredeemed. Redemption lies in breaking down the limits of the self, in plunging into the fullness of life and all that is living, in going back home to the universe. Ecstasy is being sought for, the intoxication of infinity, which can happen to people en masse in ecstatic music, in rhythm, in dance, in a mad whirl of lights and darkness. Here it is not merely the modern way of domination by the self that is renounced and abolished; here, man—in order to be free—must let himself be abolished. The gods are returning. They have become more credible than God. Aboriginal rites must be renewed in which the self is initiated into the mysteries of the universe and freed from its own self.

There are many reasons for the renewal of pre-Christian religions and cults that is being widely undertaken today. If there is no truth shared by everyone, a truth that is valid simply because it is true, then Christianity is merely a foreign import, a form of spiritual imperialism, which needs to be shaken off just as much as political imperialism. If what takes place in the sacraments is not the encounter with the one living God of all men, then they are empty rituals that mean nothing and give us nothing and, at best, allow us to sense the numinous element that is actively present in all religions. It then seems to make better sense to seek after what was originally our own than to permit alien and antiquated things to be imposed on us. But above all, if the "rational intoxication" of the Christian mystery cannot make us intoxicated with God, then we just have to conjure up the real, concrete intoxication of effective ecstasies, the passionate power of which catches us up and turns us, at least for a moment, into gods, helps us for a moment to sense the pleasure of infinity and to forget the misery of finite existence. The more the pointlessness of political absolutisms becomes obvious, the more powerful will be the attraction of irrationalism, the renunciation of everyday reality.[13]

Pragmatism in Everyday Church Life

Side by side with these radical solutions, and side by side also with the greater pragmatism of the liberation theologies, there is also the gray pragmatism at work in the everyday life of the Church, whereby everything is apparently being done right, yet in reality the faith is stale and declining into a shabby meanness. I am thinking of two phenomena that I regard with some concern. On one hand, there are attempts, some more determined than others, to extend the majority principle to matters of faith and morals and, thus, to "democratize" the Church in a decided fashion. What is not obvious to the majority cannot have any binding claim upon us, so it seems. Majority of whom, in fact? Will this majority be different tomorrow from what it is today? A faith we can decide for ourselves is no faith at all. And no minority has any reason to allow a majority to prescribe what it should believe. Either the faith and its practice come to us from the Lord by way of the Church and her sacramental services, or there is no such thing. The reason many people are abandoning the faith is that it seems to them that the faith can be decided by some officials or institutions, that it is a kind of party

[13] On this point, it must be noted that two different tendencies of New Age are increasingly being crystallized out: a gnostic, religious tendency, which seeks for transcendental and transpersonal being and looks to find the true self therein, and an ecological, monistic tendency, which worships material existence and mother earth and, in the eco-feminist movement, is linked with feminism.

program; whoever has the power is able to decide what should be believed, and so it is a matter of getting hold of power oneself within the Church or, on the other hand—more obviously and logically—just not believing.

The other point I would raise concerns the liturgy. The various phases of liturgical reform have allowed people to gain the impression that liturgy can be changed as and how you wish. If there is any unchanging element, people think, then this would in no instance be anything other than the words of consecration: everything else might be done differently. The next idea is quite logical: If a central authority can do that, then why not local decision-making bodies? And if local bodies, then why not the congregation itself? It ought to be expressing itself in the liturgy and should be able to see its own style recognizably present there. After the rationalist and puritan trend of the seventies, and even the eighties, people are tired of liturgies that are just words and would like liturgies they can experience; and these soon get close to New Age styles: a search for intoxication and ecstasy, not the λογικ← λατρεία, the *rationabilis oblatio* (the rationally directed worship conformed to the *logos*, "spiritual worship") that Paul, and the Roman liturgy with him, is talking about (Rom 12:1).

Now, I admit—and I say this with emphasis—that what I am saying does not apply to the normal situation of our congregations. But these tendencies are there. And that is why it is appropriate to be on our guard, lest some other gospel than that given us by our Lord is secretly substituted for this.

The Tasks Facing Theology

Thus, all in all, we are facing a remarkable situation: liberation theology had tried to give a new practice to a Christendom that was tired of dogma, a practice by means of which redemption was finally to become an actual event. This practice, however, instead of bringing freedom, left destruction in its wake. What was left was relativism and the attempt to come to terms with it. Yet what that offers is in its turn so empty that the relativist theories look for help from the liberation theology, so as thus to become of more practical use. Finally, New Age says, "Let's just leave Christianity as a failed experiment and go back to the gods—it's better that way." Many questions arise. Let us just take the most immediately practical one: Why has classic theology proved so impotent in the face of these developments? Where are the weak points at which it lost credibility?

I would like to mention two points suggested by what Hick and Knitter say. Both refer to exegesis for their revocation of faith in Christ: they say that exegesis has shown that Jesus himself certainly did not regard himself as the Son of God, as God incarnate, but that he was only subsequently transformed into that, gradually, by his followers.[14] Both, but Hick more clearly than Knitter, also refer to philosophical evidence. Hick assures us that Kant has irrefutably demonstrated that no one can perceive any absolute entity or person in history and that no such entity or person could, as such, be present in history.[15] On the basis of our ability to perceive and to know things, according to Kant, the things the Christian faith asserts cannot exist, cannot happen: it is crazy to believe in miracles, mysteries, and channels of grace, Kant explains to us in his book on "religion within the bounds of mere reason".[16] The question concerning exegesis and

[14] References for this in Menke, *Einzigkeit Jesu Christi*, pp. 90 and 97.

[15] See n. 10, above.

[16] B 302. The spiritual climate deriving from this philosophy, which is still widely influential to this day, is most graphically described, from his own experience, by M. Kriele, in *Anthroposophie und Kirche: Erfahrungen eines Grenzgängers*

that concerning the limits and possibilities of our reason, that is, about the philosophical premises of faith, seem to me in fact to indicate the real point of crisis of present-day theology, on account of which faith—and to an ever-increasing extent, even the faith of simple people—is reaching to a crisis.

I would just like here briefly to indicate the task facing us because of that. First, as concerns exegesis, it should first be remarked that Hick and Knitter certainly cannot call on the support of exegesis as a whole, as if what they are talking about were a clear and universally recognized conclusion. That is impossible in historical research, which does not deal in such certainties. It is still more impossible in the case of a question that is not purely historical or literary but involves value judgments that go beyond just establishing a sequence of events or interpreting a text. What is true is that a quick survey of modern exegesis may leave you with an impression that agrees with what Hick and Knitter say.

Yet how certain is that? Even supposing that a majority of exegetes think like that (which must be open to doubt), the question still remains: How well founded is that kind of majority opinion? I maintain that many exegetes think like Hick and Knitter and reconstruct the history of Jesus accordingly because they share the same philosophy. It is not a case of exegesis providing evidence that supports a philosophy; rather, it is a matter of a philosophy that produces the exegesis.[17] If

[Anthroposophy and the Church: The experiences of someone who went to the limits] (Freiburg: Herder, 1996); especially pp. 18ff.

[17] This can be very clearly seen in the encounter between A. Schlatter and A. Harnack, at the end of the last century, which is carefully portrayed, on the basis of the original sources, by W. Neuer in his book *Adolf Schlatter: Ein Leben für Theologie und Kirche* (Stuttgart: Calwer Verlag, 1996), pp. 301ff. [English trans., *Adolf Schlatter: A Biography of Germany's Premier Biblical Theologian*, trans. Robert W. Yarbrough (Grand Rapids, Mich.: Baker Books, 1996). Schlatter

(to speak in Kant's terms) I know a priori that Jesus cannot be God, that miracles, mysteries, and means of grace are three things it would be crazy to believe in, then I cannot discover in Holy Scriptures any fact that cannot exist as a fact. I can then only discover why and how people came to make such assertions, how these gradually came about.

Let us look a little closer. The historicocritical method is a marvelous instrument for reading historical sources and interpreting texts. But it does include its own philosophy, which generally—if, for instance, I want to learn about the medieval emperors—hardly affects anything. For in that case I want to learn about the past, that is all. Even that is not entirely free of values and value judgments, and to that extent the method has its limitations. If you apply it to the Bible, then two factors you would otherwise scarcely notice are clearly manifest: the method seeks to know about the past as something past. It seeks to know what happened then, in

commented on this in a letter: "We have defined the religious difference [between us]: he said that the prophet's cry, 'O, that thou wouldst rend the heavens' (Is 64:1), was in fact unfulfilled; that we were restricted to the psychological plane, to faith" (p. 306). When Harnack declared, in a meeting of their colleagues on the faculty, "Only the question of miracles separates me from my colleague Mr. Schlatter!" Schlatter interrupted, calling out: "No, the question of God!" Schlatter saw the basic point of difference as being embodied in Christology: "Whether Jesus was being shown to us as he is ... or whether the New Testament disappeared behind our 'scholarship', that was the question" (p. 307). Nothing has changed with regard to this question in a hundred years. Cf. also in Kriele, *Anthroposophie und Kirche*, the chapter on "Loss of Faith through Theology", pp. 21–28. I have tried to present my own view of the problem in *Schriftauslegung im Widerstreit* [Controversy concerning the interpretation of Scripture], ed. J. Ratzinger, Quaestiones Disputatae 117 (Freiburg im Breisgau: Herder, 1989), pp. 15–44. Cf. also the collective work by I. de la Potterie, R. Guardini, J. Ratzinger, G. Colombo, and E. Bianchi, *L'esegesi cristiana oggi* [Christian exegesis today] (Casale Monferrato: Piemme, 1991).

the form it took then, at the point at which things stood right then. And it assumes that all history is in principle the same kind of history: man, in all his different manifestations, the world in its manifold variety, are yet determined by the same laws and the same limitations, so that I can eliminate what is impossible. What cannot possibly happen could not have happened yesterday and, likewise, cannot be going to happen tomorrow.

If we apply this to the Bible, it means that a text, an event, or a person is strictly fixed in his or its place in the past. We are seeking to bring out what the writer said at the time and what he could have said or thought at the time. It is a matter of what is "historical", what was "current at the time". That is why historicocritical exegesis does not transmit the Bible to today, into my present-day life. That possibility has been excluded. On the contrary, it distances it from me and shows it as firmly set in the past. This is the point at which Drewermann was right in criticizing historicocritical exegesis, insofar as it aims to be all-sufficient. Of its nature, it does not speak about today, or about me, but about yesterday, about other people. Therefore it can never show Christ yesterday, today, and forever, but only (if it remains true to itself) Christ as he was yesterday.

Then there is the second presupposition, that history and the world are always the same, that is, what Bultmann called the modern view of the world. M. Waldstein has shown, by a careful analysis, that Bultmann's theory of epistemology was entirely determined by the neo-Kantian philosophy of Marburg.[18] It was on that basis that he knew what could happen and what could not. In the case of other exegetes, their philosophical consciousness will be less clearly determined, but the

---

[18] M. Waldstein, "The Foundations of Bultmann's Work", in *Communio* (American ed.) 1987: 115–45.

foundation in Kant's theory of epistemology is always silently present, as a self-evident hermeneutic entry to the path that criticism should follow. Since that is the case, the authority of the Church cannot simply impose from outside the obligation of arriving at a Christology of Jesus as the Son of God. But it certainly can and must challenge scholars, require them to look critically at the philosophy of their own method. In the revelation of God it is, in the end, precisely a matter of him, the Living and True One, breaking into our world and thus breaking open the prison of our theories, by means of whose iron bars we seek to protect ourselves against this coming of God into our lives. Today, praise God, in the crisis of philosophy and theology through which we are passing, a new consciousness of these fundamentals has come into play, not least on the basis of knowledge that has come to light through the careful historical interpretation of the texts.[19] This is helping to burst asunder the prison of philosophical presuppositions that was hindering interpretation: the wide realm of the Word is opening up again.

The problem concerning exegesis, as we have seen, to a great extent coincides with the problem of philosophy. The desperate situation of philosophy—that is to say, the desperate situation into which reason obsessed by positivism has maneuvered itself—has become the desperate situation of our faith. Faith cannot be set free unless reason itself opens up again. If the door to metaphysical knowledge remains barred, if we cannot pass beyond the limits to human perception set by Kant, then faith will necessarily atrophy, simply for lack of breathing space. Of course, the attempt to use a strictly

[19] Cf., e.g., the collection of essays edited by C. E. Braaten and R. W. Jensson: *Reclaiming the Bible for the Church* (Grand Rapids, Mich.: W. B. Eerdmans, 1995), and in it especially that by B. S. Childs, "On Reclaiming the Bible for Christian Theology", pp. 1–17.

autonomous reason that refuses to know about faith, to pull ourselves out of the slough of uncertainties by our own hair, so to speak, can hardly succeed in the end. For human reason is not autonomous at all. It is always living in one historical context or other. Any historical context, as we see, distorts the vision of reason; that is why reason needs the help of history in order to overcome these historical limitations. It is my view that the neoscholastic rationalism that was trying to reconstruct the *praeambula fidei*, the approach to faith, with pure rational certainty, by means of rational argument that was strictly independent of any faith, has failed; and it cannot be otherwise for any such attempts to do that kind of thing. In that sense, Karl Barth was right when he rejected philosophy as a basis for faith that is independent of faith itself: for in that case, our faith would in the end be based on changing philosophical theories. Yet Barth was mistaken in declaring faith on that account to be a sheer paradox, which can only ever exist contrary to reason and quite independent of it. By no means the least important practical function of faith is to offer healing for the reason as reason, not to overpower it or to remain outside it, but in fact to bring it to itself again. Faith, as a historical instrument, can set reason itself free again, so that—now that faith has set it on the right path again—reason can once more see properly for itself. We have to strive toward such a renewed process of dialogue between faith and philosophy, for each has need of the other. Without faith, philosophy cannot be whole, but faith without reason cannot be human.

Prospect

If we look at the current constellation in the history of ideas that I have been trying to sketch in outline, then it must seem like a real miracle that, despite all this, people still hold the Christian faith—not just in the substitute versions of Hick, Knitter, and others, but the full and joyful faith of the New Testament, of the Church down all the ages. Why has faith still any chance at all? I should say it is because it corresponds to the nature of man. For man is more generously proportioned than the way Kant and the various post-Kantian philosophies see him or will allow him to be. Kant himself ought to have found a place for this, somehow or other, among his postulates. The longing for the infinite is alive and unquenchable within man. None of the attempted answers will do; only the God who himself became finite in order to tear open our finitude and lead us out into the wide spaces of his infinity, only he corresponds to the question of our being. That is why, even today, Christian faith will come to man again. It is our task to serve this faith with humble courage, with all the strength of our heart and of our mind.

2

THE TRUTH OF CHRISTIANITY?

1. FAITH BETWEEN REASON AND FEELING

The Present-Day Crisis of Faith

In his conversations "around atomic physics", Werner Heisenberg tells of a dialogue with some younger physicists that took place in Brussels in the year 1927, in which, besides Heisenberg himself, both Wolfgang Pauli and Paul Dirac took part. They got to talking about the way Einstein often spoke about God and about the fact that Max Planck argued that there was no conflict between science and religion; the two could—and at that time, this was a somewhat surprising notion—perfectly well be reconciled with each other. Heisenberg interpreted this new openness of scientists to religion on the basis of his experience of his parents' home. This was based, he said, on the view that natural science and religion dealt with two completely different spheres, which were not in competition with each other: in natural science it was a matter of things being true or false; in religion, of their being good and bad, valuable or worthless. The two realms were quite separate, belonging to the objective and the subjective aspects of the world. "Natural science is to some extent the way we approach the objective aspect of reality. . . . Religious faith, on the contrary, is the expression

of a subjective decision, by means of which we determine
for ourselves the values by which we direct ourselves in life." [1]
This decision of faith had of course various preconditions in
history and culture, in one's education and environment, but
it was—Heisenberg was still talking about the view of the
world shared by his parents and Max Planck—ultimately subjective and thereby not amenable to the criterion of "true or
false". Planck, he said, had in this fashion made a subjective
decision in favor of the Christian value system; the two
realms—the objective and the subjective aspects of the
world—remained however narrowly yet clearly divided from
each other. At this point, Heisenberg added: "I have to admit,
that I do not feel happy about this division. I doubt whether
any human society can in the long term live with this sharp
division between knowledge and faith." [2] Then Wolfgang
Pauli took up the thread of the discussion and agreed with
Heisenberg's doubt, asserting in fact that this was quite certain: "The complete division between knowledge and faith
is surely just a temporary stopgap measure. In Western society and culture we could for instance, in the not-too-distant
future, come to the point at which the parables and images
that religion has used up to now are no longer convincing,
even for simple folk; and then, I fear, traditional morality
will also very rapidly break down, and things will happen
that are more frightful than anything we can yet imagine." [3]
At that time, in 1927, those taking part in the conversation
could have at most a vague suspicion that soon afterward the
unholy twelve years would begin, in the course of which

[1] W. Heisenberg, *Der Teil und das Ganze: Gespräche im Umkreis der Atom-
physik* (Munich: R. Piper, 1969), p. 117 [*Physics and Beyond: Encounters and
Conversations*, trans. Arnold J. Pomerans (New York: Harper and Row, 1971)].
   [2] Ibid.
   [3] Ibid., p. 118; cf. p. 295.

things did indeed happen that were "more frightful" than could previously have been thought possible. There were of course a good number of Christians, some of whose names we know and some who have remained nameless, who opposed the demonic forces with the power of their Christian conscience. But on the whole the power of temptation was stronger; those who just went along with things left a clear path for evil.

In the new start that was made after the war, there was real confidence that nothing like that could ever happen again. The fundamental legal structure that was decided upon, on the basis of "responsibility before God", was intended to express the connection of law and politics with the great moral imperatives of biblical faith. The confidence of that time looks frail today in face of the moral crisis of humanity, which is taking new and desperately urgent forms. The collapse of old religious certainties, which seventy years ago still seemed stoppable, has in the meantime to a great extent become reality. Thus the fear of a collapse of humane values, inevitably linked with this, has itself become more widespread and intense. I will simply recall the warnings of Joachim Fest, struggling with the difficult dialectic of freedom and truth, of reason and faith: "If all utopian models ... lead to dead ends, yet at the same time the Christian certainties are powerlessly ... toppling, then we have to come to terms with the fact that there are no more answers available to our demand for transcendence." [4] Yet none of the appeals addressed to man in this situation "are able to say how he is to live without the other world and with no

---

[4] J. Fest, *Die schwierige Freiheit: Über die offene Flanke der offenen Gesellschaft* [Difficult freedom: The unguarded flank of the open society] (Berlin: Siedler, 1993), p. 75.

fear of the day of judgment and yet still time after time manage to act against his own immediate interests and desires".[5] Fest reminds us in this connection of a saying of Spinoza, which in fact underlines that dialectic between subjective and objective reality, between the abdication of truth and the assertion of values, which is ultimately intolerable and which we have already met in the post-Christian bourgeois world represented by Planck: "Even if I am an atheist, I would at least like to live like a saint."

I do not want to describe further here how Heisenberg, together with his friends, both in the conversation of 1927 and in a similar one in 1952, this latter dialogue conducted in the face of the National Socialist horrors, tries to find a way out of this schizophrenia of modern culture, to work toward a central order and organization on the basis of a view of natural science that questions its own principles, an order that can become the measure and limit of our action and that belongs equally to the subjective and the objective realms.[6] I would like to try here to find another way to move toward the same goal.

But let us first try to summarize and elucidate what has become clear thus far. The Enlightenment raised the banner of "religion within the bounds of sheer reason" as an ideal. But this purely reasonable religion soon crumbled, above all because it possessed no vital force: a religion that is to serve as the fundamental force for life as a whole does no doubt need to be comprehensible to some extent. Both the collapse of the religions of antiquity and the crisis of Christianity in modern times show us this: if a religion can no longer be reconciled with the elementary certainties of a given view

[5] Ibid., p. 79.
[6] Heisenberg, *Teil und das Ganze*, pp. 288ff.

of the world, it collapses. But, on the other hand, religion also needs some authorization that reaches beyond what we can think up for ourselves, for only thus will the unconditional demand it makes upon man be acceptable. So it was that, after the end of the Enlightenment, being aware of how religion is indispensable, people sought for a new sphere for religion, within which it might be able to continue to exist, beyond the assaults of the progress of rational knowledge, upon some unattainable planet, so to speak, where this posed no threat. That is why "feeling" was assigned to it as its own domain within human existence. Schleiermacher was the great theorist of this new concept of religion: "Action is art, speculation is science, religion is the sense of and the taste for the infinite",[7] was his definition. Faust's reply to Gretchen's question about religion has become proverbial: "Feeling is all. The name is just noise and smoke." Yet religion, however necessary its separation from the plane of science may be, cannot be pigeonholed in a particular area. That is what it is there for, to integrate man in his entirety, to unite feeling, understanding, and will and to mediate between them, and to offer some answer to the demand made by everything as a whole, the demands of living and dying, of society and myself, of present and future. It should not claim to be able to solve problems in areas that work by their own laws, but it must make men capable of taking those ultimate decisions in which the whole of man and of the world is always at stake. And that is precisely what we are lacking, in that nowadays we divide the world into discrete areas and are thereby able to dominate it in our thought and action in a way that

[7] F. Schleiermacher, *Über die Religion: Reden an die Gebildeten unter ihrer Verächtern*, Philosophische Bibliothek., vol. 225 (1799; reprt., Hamburg: F. Meiner, 1958), p. 30 [English trans., *On Religion: Speeches to Its Cultured Despisers*, trans. J. Oman (1893; reprt., New York: Harper, 1958)].

could previously hardly be imagined, yet the unavoidable questions concerning truth and values, life and death, become thereby ever more unanswerable.

The present-day crisis is due to the fact that the connecting link between the subjective and objective realms has disappeared, that reason and feeling are drifting apart, and that both are ailing because of it. Reason that operates in specialized areas in fact gains enormously in strength and capability, but because it is standardized according to a single type of certainty and rationality, it no longer offers any perspective on the fundamental questions of mankind. The result is an unhealthy overdevelopment in the realm of technical and pragmatic knowledge, as against a shrinking in that of basic fundamentals, and thus the balance between them is disturbed in a way that may be fatal for man's humanity. On the other hand, religion today has by no means been made redundant. In many ways there is indeed a real boom in religion, but religion that collapses into particularism, not infrequently parting company with its sublime spiritual context, and that— instead of uplifting man—promises him greater power and the satisfaction of his needs. People look for what is irrational, superstitious, and magical; there is a danger of their falling back into an anarchic and destructive form of relationship with hidden powers and forces. We might be tempted to say that there is no crisis for religion today, but there is a crisis for Christianity. But I would disagree. For the mere spread of religious phenomena, or of those resembling religion, is not the same as a flourishing of religion. If there is a boom in defective forms of religious practice, that does indeed confirm that religion is not declining, yet it still shows that it is in a serious state of crisis. Even the illusion that in the place of a worn-out Christianity the Asiatic religions or Islam are a rising force is deceptive. It is quite obvious that in China and Japan the great traditional religions have proved incapable of resisting modern ideologies, or they do so only feebly. Yet even the religious vitality of India does not change the fact that there, too, new questions and old traditions have not as yet succeeded in coming to terms with each other. To what extent the new surge forward of the Islamic world is fuelled by truly religious forces is equally open to question. In many places, as we can see, there is the danger of a pathological development of the autonomy of feeling, which only reinforces that threat of horrifying things about which Pauli, Heisenberg, and Fest have been telling us.

There is nothing else for it: reason and religion will have to come together again, without merging into each other. It is not a matter of preserving the interests of old religious bodies. It is for the sake of man and the world. And neither of them, it is clear, can be saved unless God reappears in a convincing fashion. No one can claim to be sure of the way to deal with this emergency. That is impossible, if only because in a free society truth can find no other way to prevail, and should seek no other way, than simply by power of persuasion; yet persuasion can only be achieved with difficulty amid the multitude of pressures and demands to which people are subjected. We must venture an attempt to find the way, however, so as to make plausible once more, through various converging indications, something that for the most part lies far beyond the horizon of our own interests.

The God of Abraham

I have no intention here of taking up Heisenberg's attempt to find a way of transcending the limitations of science on the basis of the inherent logic of scientific thought, so as to

attain the "central order and organization", however reward-
ing this effort may be and however indispensable. In this lecture I shall be aiming to disentangle, so to speak, the inner
rationale of Christianity. The method will be that of asking
what it actually was that made Christianity so persuasive, amid
the collapse of the religions of antiquity, that it could, on the
one hand, absorb the decline of that world and, at the same
time, be able to pass on its answers to the new forces entering upon the stage of world history, the Germans and the
Slavs, in such a way that, despite many radical changes and
much destruction, a mode of understanding reality came into
being that lasted for over fifteen hundred years, in which the
old world and the new could form a unity. Here we meet
with a difficulty. Christian faith is not a system. It cannot be
portrayed as a complete, finished intellectual construction. It
is a path, and it is characteristic of a path that it only becomes
recognizable if you enter on it and start following it. This is
true in two senses: for any individual, Christianity only opens
up in the experiment of going along with others; and as a
whole it can only be grasped as a historical path, whose main
course I should like to sketch out in broad outline.

The path begins with Abraham. In the brief sketch I am
attempting I cannot of course plunge into the undergrowth
of multifarious hypotheses as to what may be regarded as
historical in these old stories and what cannot, nor do I wish
to do so. It is only a matter here of asking how these texts
themselves, in the form in which they eventually became
part of history, saw this path. The first thing to be said is that
Abraham was someone who knew that God was speaking to
him and who shaped his life on the basis of what was said.
For comparison we might think of Socrates, whose "daemon"
gave him a remarkable sort of inspiration—not, indeed, any
positive revelation, but something that turned him onto

another track whenever he was inclined just to follow his own ideas or to agree with the general opinion.[8] What can we make out about this God of Abraham's? He certainly does not yet appear as making the monotheistic claims of the only God of all mankind and of the whole world, yet he does have quite specific traits. He is not the God of a particular nation, of a particular country; not the God of some particular sphere or realm, of the air or of water, and so forth, which were, in the religious context of the time, among the most important manifestations of divinity. He is the God of one person, of Abraham. This peculiarity, that he did not belong to a country, a people, a sphere of life, but related himself to a person, has two consequences worthy of note.

The first consequence was that for those people who belonged to him, for those he had chosen, this God was powerful everywhere. His power is not restricted by geographical or any other boundaries; he is able to accompany the person concerned, to guard him and guide him wherever he chooses and wherever he goes. Even the promise of land does not make him just God of a particular land, which would thenceforth be his only land. It shows, rather, that he can distribute lands as he chooses. We can therefore say that the personal God has effective power without limitations of space. Then there is a second thing, that he also has power without limitations of time, indeed, his way of speaking and acting essentially bears on the future. The dimension of his existence seems, at least at first sight, to be principally that of futurity, since he gives very

---

[8] The negative character of this "voice" is made clear, for instance, in *Apologia* 31d: φωνή τις γενομένη . . . ἀεὶ ἀποτρέπει . . . προστρέπει δέ οὐδέποτε. On the form of this voice, see R. Guardini, *Der Tod des Sokrates*, 5th ed. (Mainz and Paderborn: Matthias-Grünewald-Verlag, 1987), pp. 87ff. [English trans., *The Death of Socrates: An Interpretation of the Platonic Dialogues: Euthyphro, Apology, Crito and Phaedo* (New York: Sheed and Ward, 1948)].

little that is present. All the important things are given in the category of promise of what is to come—the blessing, the land. That means that he is plainly in control of the future, of time. For the persons concerned, this involves an attitude of a quite particular kind. They always have to live outward, beyond the present moment, life in a state of reaching out toward something else, something greater. The present moment is relativized. If, finally—and this could represent a third element—we refer to the particular character of this God, his "otherness" over against other people and other things, with the concept of "holiness", then it becomes clear that this holiness, his being himself, has something to do with the dignity of man, with his moral integrity, as the story of Sodom and Gomorrah shows us. In this story there clearly appears, on one hand, the care and the kindness of this God, who is willing to spare even the wicked for the sake of a few good people; yet, on the other hand, there is at the same time the rejection of what may damage the dignity of man, which indeed takes effect in the judgment upon the two cities.

The Crisis and the Enlarging of Israel's Faith in the Exile

In the subsequent development of the league of twelve tribes, together with their taking possession of the land, the rise of the monarchy, the building of the Temple, and with the giving of a highly diversified and detailed cultic law, the religion of Israel seems to a great extent to enter the realm of the kind of religion typical of the Near East. The God of the Fathers, the God of Sinai, has now become the God of a people, the God of a country, of a particular ordered way of life. That that was not all, and that in all the to-and-fro of religious life in Israel the particular and distinctive elements of its faith in God survived, and indeed developed further, can be seen at the time of the Exile. In the normal way of things, a God who loses his land, who leaves his people defeated and is unable to protect his sanctuary, is a God who has been overthrown. He has no more say in things. He vanishes from history. When Israel went into exile, quite astonishingly, the opposite happened. The stature of this God, the way he was completely different from the other divinities in the religions of the world, was now apparent, and the faith of Israel at last took on its true form and stature. This God could afford to let others have his land because he was not tied down to any country. He could allow his people to be defeated so as to awaken it thereby from its false religious dream. He was not dependent on this people, yet nevertheless he did not abandon them in their hour of defeat. He was not dependent upon the Temple or on the cult celebrated there, as was then commonly supposed: people gave nourishment to the gods, and the gods maintained the world. No, he did not need this cult, which to some extent had concealed his real being. Thus, together with a more profound concept of God, a new idea of worship developed. Certainly, since the time of Solomon the personal God of the Fathers had been identified with the high god, the Creator, who is known to all religions, but in general this latter had been excluded from worship, as not being responsible for one's individual needs. This identification, which had been made in principle, although it had probably hitherto impinged little upon people's consciousness, now became the driving force for survival of the faith: Israel has no particular God at all but simply worships the one single God. This God spoke to Abraham and chose Israel, but he is in reality the God of all peoples, the universal God who guides the course of all history. The purifying of the idea of worship belongs with this. God needs no sacrifice; he does not have to be nourished by men, because everything belongs to him. The true sacrifice is the man who has become worthy of God. Three hundred years after the Exile, in the similarly severe crisis of the Hellenistic suppression of the Temple cult, the Book of Daniel expressed it thus: "At this time there is no prince, or prophet, or leader, no burnt offering, or sacrifice, or oblation, . . . no place to make an offering before thee or to find mercy. Yet with a contrite heart and a humble spirit may we be accepted" (Dan 3:38 = Prayer of Azariah 15–16). At the same time, given the failure of the present time to match up to the power and the goodness of God, the future aspect of Israel's faith emerges with correspondingly greater emphasis; or, better, we might say that the present is made relative to a wider horizon that runs far beyond the moment, indeed beyond the whole world, so that the present can be properly dealt with and understood.

The Path to a Universal Religion, after the Exile

There are above all two new factors that characterize the five hundred years following the Exile, up to the appearance of Christ. There is first of all the rise of the so-called wisdom literature and the spiritual movement that underpins it. Alongside the law and the prophets, on the basis of whose books a canon of Scripture gradually began to be built up, as a yardstick for the religion of Israel, there appears a third pillar—that is, wisdom.[9] This is at first especially influenced

[9] G. von Rad, *Weisheit in Israel* (Neukirchen: Neukirchener Verlag, 1970) [English trans., *Wisdom in Israel*, trans. James D. Marton (London: S.C.M. Press, 1972)], still remains basic for understanding the wisdom literature of the Old Testament; see also L. Bouyer, *Cosmos* (Paris: Cerf, 1982), pp. 99–128 [English trans., *Cosmos: The World and the Glory of God*, trans. Pierre de Fontnouvelle (Petersham, Mass.: St. Bede's, 1988)].

by the Egyptian wisdom tradition, but subsequently it shows more and more evidence of contact with Greek thought. Here the faith in a single God is developed and given greater depth, and the criticism of the other gods, which already appears in the prophets, becomes more radical. The meaning of monotheism is further elucidated, and, associated with an attempt to understand the world in rational fashion, it becomes more rationally persuasive. It is the concept of wisdom that enables the idea of God and the interpretation of the world to be bracketed together. The rationality that is to be seen in the structure of the world is understood as a reflection of the creative wisdom that has produced it. The view of reality that now develops corresponds to some extent to the question Heisenberg formulated in the conversation we referred to in our introduction, when he said: "Is it completely meaningless to imagine, behind the ordering structures and principles of the world as a whole, a 'consciousness' whose 'intention' these would express?" [10] In the present-day discussion about the interplay of nature and thought, for instance in man, the question of reductibility is articulated: Can the phenomenon of thought be reduced to material terms, or is there some inexplicable element still remaining? [11] In this case, we would be able to talk rather of the opposite perspective: Thought is capable of producing material and is to be regarded as the true point of origin of reality, the starting point from which everything can be explained; the question remains of whether there is not some dark remainder that can no longer be derived in

[10] Heisenberg, *Teil und das Ganze*, p. 290.

[11] G. Beintrup, *Das Leib-Seele-Problem: Eine Einführung* [The problem of body and soul: An introduction] (Stuttgart, 1996), offers a good account of the current discussion of this subject. See also O. B. Linke and M. Kurthen, *Parallelität von Gehirn du Seele: Neurowissenschaft und Leib-Seele-Problem* [The parallel between brain and soul: Neurology and the problem of body and soul] (Stuttgart, 1988).

this way? The question has to be asked whether such a view is any less probable than the opinion expressed by Monod, which is to some extent representative of contemporary thinking, that the whole of nature's concerto has grown up and developed from a few random murmurs of noise,[12] that is to say, that rationality has been derived from the irrational. The view of the wisdom books, which links God and the world through the idea of wisdom and conceives of the world as reflecting the rationality of the Creator, also then permits the association of cosmology with anthropology, that of understanding the world with morality, because wisdom, which builds up matter and the world, is at the same time a moral wisdom, which expresses essential guidelines for living. The whole of the Torah, Israel's law for living, is now understood as wisdom's self-portrait, as the translation of wisdom into human language and human instruction. A natural consequence of all this is a similarity to Greek thought, to some themes of Platonism, on one hand, and, on the other, to the Stoic association of morality with the interpretation of the world as divinely inspired.

[12] J. Monod, *Zufall und Notwendigkeit: Philosophische Fragen der modernen Biologie*, trans. from the French [*Le Hasard et la necéssité: Essai sur la philosophie naturelle de la biologie moderne*], 5th ed. (Munich: Piper, 1973), p. 149 [English trans., *Chance and Necessity: An Essay on the Natural Philosophy of Modern Biology* (New York: Knopf, 1971)], cf. pp. 141f.: "It thus necessarily follows that only chance *alone* can be the basis of each and every innovation, every creative development in living nature. Sheer chance, nothing but chance, blind and absolute freedom as the foundation of the marvelous construction of evolution— this central insight of modern biology is today no longer merely one among various possible, or at least imaginable, hypotheses; it is the *only* conceivable hypothesis, since it is the only one that corresponds to the facts of observation and experience." Cf. J. Ratzinger, *Im Anfang schuf Gott*, 2nd ed. (Einsiedeln and Freiburg: Johannes Verlag, 1996), pp. 53–59 [English trans., *In the Beginning: A Catholic Understanding of the Story of Creation and the Fall*, trans. Boniface Ramsey (Huntington, Ind.: Our Sunday Visitor, 1990)].

The question concerning the remaining ungodly, irrational element in the world, which we touched on above, takes
on the form in the wisdom literature of a dramatic struggle
with the question of theodicy: the experience of suffering in
the world becomes a major theme—in a world in which
righteousness, goodness, and truth lose out time and again
in the face of the unscrupulousness of those who are powerful. This produces, from a quite different starting point, a
more profound understanding of morality, which is now dissociated from success and looks for significance precisely in
suffering, in the defeat of righteousness. Finally there appears,
in Job, the figure of the man from beyond the bounds of
Israel whose piety and whose suffering are both exemplary.[13]

There is then a second important step, which logically
corresponds to the closer inner relationship to the world of
Greek thought, to its enlightenment and its philosophy: the
transition of Judaism into the Greek world, which took place
above all in Alexandria, as the central meeting point of various cultures. The most important step in this process was
the translation of the Old Testament into Greek, and the
first stage—the translation of the five books of Moses—was
completed as early as the third century before Christ. From
then up to the first century there developed a Greek canon
of sacred books, which was taken over by the Christians as
their canon of the Old Testament.[14] The custom of calling

---

[13] On Job one should consult above all the great commentary of G. Ravasi,
Giobbe: Traduzione e commento, 3rd ed. (Rome: Edizioni Borla, 1993), which
also gives detailed consideration to the modern philosophical and theological
interpretations of this figure.

[14] On the question of the relationship between the Hebrew and Greek canon
and the Christian Old Testament, see C. Dohmen, "Der Biblische Kanon in
der Diskussion" [The canon of the Bible in discussion], *Theologische Revue* 91
(1995): 451–59; A. Schenker, "Septuaginta und christliche Bibel" [The Septuagint and the Christian Bible], *Theologische Revue* 91 (1995): 459–64.

this Greek translation of the Old Testament Scriptures the "Septuagint" (Book of the seventy) derives from the old legend that this translation was the work of seventy scholars. According to Deuteronomy 32:8, seventy was the number of peoples in the world. Thus this legend may signify that with this translation the Old Testament moved beyond Israel, reaching out to all the peoples of the earth. That was indeed the effect this book had, and its translation did indeed in many respects further accentuate the universalistic trait in Israel's religion—not least, in its picture of God, since the name of God, JHWH, no longer appeared as such but was replaced by the word *Kyrios*, "Lord". Thus the Old Testament's spiritual concept of God was further developed, which was for practical purposes entirely consistent with the inner tendency of the development we have mentioned.

The faith of Israel, translated into Greek, insofar as it was reflected in its sacred books, quickly became an object of fascination for the enlightened minds of the ancient world, whose religion had, since the criticisms leveled by Socrates, suffered an increasing loss of credibility. In Socratic thought, however—in contrast to that of the sophistic movement—it was not scepticism, or even cynicism or mere pragmatism, that was the decisive element; here the longing for an appropriate form of religion, which would yet go beyond the capacities of reason itself, had come into play. Thus, on the one hand, people sought after the promises of the mystery cults that were spreading from the East, and, on the other hand, the Jewish faith looked like it might offer the answer that would save them. There was a connection made between God and the world, between rational thought and revelation, which exactly answered the requirements of reason and of the deeper religious longings. There was monotheism—and not deriving from philosophical speculation, in such a way that it would have no real religious force, because one cannot worship one's own intellectual concepts, one's own philosophical hypotheses. This monotheism derived from original religious experience and thus confirmed from above, so to speak, what thought had hesitantly been groping for. For the finest circles in late antiquity, the religion of Israel must have had something of the same fascination as did the Chinese world for Western Europe in the time of the Enlightenment, when people thought (mistakenly, as we now know) that they had at last discovered a society without any revelation or any mysteries, with a religion of pure morality and reason. Thus, all across the ancient world, there developed a network of so-called "God-fearers", who attached themselves to the synagogue and its pure worship of the word, who felt sure that in attaching themselves to the faith of Israel they were coming into contact with the one God. This network of God-fearers, who believed in the faith of Israel in its Greek guise, was the precondition for the Christian mission: Christianity was that form of Judaism, with a universal dimension, in which what the Old Testament had hitherto been yet unable to give was now fully granted.

Christianity as the Synthesis of Faith and Reason

The faith of Israel, as portrayed in the Septuagint, demonstrated the harmony between God and world, between reason and mystery. It gave moral guidance, but there was still something missing: the universal God was still linked to a particular people; the universal morality was linked to most particular ways of life, which could simply not be lived at all outside of Israel; spiritual worship was still connected with Temple rituals, which one could well interpret symbolically but which had basically been rendered obsolete by the prophetic spirit and could not be appropriated by an inquiring mind. A non-Jew could only ever stand in the outer circle of this religion. He remained a "proselyte", because full membership was bound up with physical descent from Abraham, with a national community. A dilemma also remained about how far specific Jewishness was needed in order for someone to be able to serve God aright and about who should be able to draw the line between what was indispensable and what was obsolete or historically incidental, the result of chance. Full universalism was impossible, because full membership for everyone was impossible. Christianity first brought about a breakthrough here, having "broken down the dividing wall" (Eph 2:14), and it did so in a threefold sense: the blood relationship with the patriarch is no longer necessary, because being united with Jesus brings about full membership, the true relationship. Everyone can now belong to this God; all men are to be permitted and to be able to become his people. The particularist legal and moral structures are no longer binding; they have become a historical prologue, because everything has been brought together in the person of Jesus Christ, and anyone who follows him is carrying within himself, and fulfilling, the whole essence of the law. The old cult has become invalid and has been abolished in Jesus' self-offering to God and to mankind, which now appears as the true sacrifice, as the spiritual worship in which God and man embrace one another and are reconciled—something for which the Lord's Supper, the Eucharist, stands there as a concrete and evermore present assurance. Perhaps the finest and most succinct expression of this new Christian synthesis is to be found in a confession in the First Letter of Saint John: "we know and believe the love" (1 Jn 4:16). Christ had become for these people the discovery of creative love; the rational principle of the universe had revealed itself as love—as that greater reason which accepts into itself even darkness and irrationality and heals them.

Thus the spiritual development that could be perceived in Israel's path had attained its goal, the uninterrupted universality that was now a practical possibility. Reason and mystery had met together; the very fact that the whole had been brought together in one person had opened the door for everyone: through the one God, all could become brothers and sisters. And the theme of hope and the present moment took on a new form: the present was running toward the Risen One, toward a world in which God would be all in all. But precisely on that account, the present became significant and valuable as being present, permeated as it already was by the close presence of the Risen One, so that death no longer had the last word.

Seeking How to Make Truth Readily Acceptable

Can this evident truth, which at that time struck the ancient world to its depths and transformed it, be reinstated? Or is it irrevocably lost? What is standing in its way? There are many reasons for the current collapse, but I would say that the most important consists of the self-limitation of reason, which is paradoxically resting upon its laurels: the laws of method that brought it success have, through being generalized, become its prison. Natural science, which has built a new world, rests upon a philosophical foundation whose origin must be sought in Plato.[15] Copernicus, Galileo, and even

[15] On the Platonic origins of modern natural science, see N. Schiffers, *Fragen der Physik an die Theologie* [Questions posed by physics to theology] (Düsseldorf: Patmos-Verlag, 1968); W. Heisenberg, *Das Naturbild der heutigen Physik*, 7th ed. (Hamburg: Rowohlt, 1959) [English trans., *The Physicist's Conception of Nature* (New York: Harcourt, Brace, 1958)]. Cf. also Monod, *Zufall und Not-*

Newton were Platonists. Their basic assumption was that the world is mathematically and rationally structured and that, starting from this assumption, we can decipher it and by experiment can make it equally comprehensible and useful. The innovation consisted in associating Platonism and an empirical approach, ideal and experiment. The experiment is based on an existing interpretative concept, which is then tried out in a practical test, corrected, and opened up to further questions. This mathematical anticipation alone can permit subsequent generalization, the recognition of laws, which then make possible appropriate action. All our ideas about natural science and all practical applications are based on the assumption that the world is ordered according to rational, spiritual laws, is imbued with rationality that can be traced out and copied by our reason. At the same time, however, our perception of it is associated with the test of experience.

Any thinking that goes beyond this connection, that tries to look at reason in itself or to see it as preceding the present world, is contrary to the discipline of scientific method and is therefore utterly rejected as being a prescientific or unscientific way of thinking. The Logos, Wisdom, about which the Greeks spoke, on the one hand, and the Israelites, on the other, has been taken back into the material world and cannot be addressed outside of it. Within the specific path followed by natural science, this limitation is necessary and right. If, however, it is declared to be the absolute and unsurpassable

wendigkeit, e.g., p. 133, where he explicitly portrays modern biology as owing much to Platonism: The "hopes of the most convinced Platonist", he says, have been "more than fulfilled" by modern discoveries. B. d'Espagnat, "La Physique actuelle et la philosophie" [Current physics and philosophy], Revue des sciences morales et politiques, 1997, no. 3: 29–45, is also prepared to allow that modern physics resembles the ideas of Plato and Plotinus in some respects.

form of human thought, then the basis of science itself becomes contradictory; for it is both proclaiming and denying the power of reason. But above all, a self-limiting reason of that kind is an amputated reason. If man cannot use his reason to ask about the essential things in his life, where he comes from and where he is going, about what he should do and may do, about living and dying, but has to leave these decisive questions to feeling, divorced from reason, then he is not elevating reason but dishonoring it. The disintegration of man, thus brought about, results equally in a pathological form of religion and a pathological form of science. It is quite obvious today that with the detachment of religion from its responsibility to reason, pathological forms of religion are constantly increasing. But when we think of scientific projects that set no real value on man, such as cloning, the production of fetuses—that is, of people—simply in order to use their organs for developing pharmaceutical products, or indeed for any economic exploitation, or if we think of the way science is made use of to produce ever more frightful means for the destruction of men and of the world, then it is obvious that there is such a thing as science that has taken a pathological form: science becomes pathological and a threat to life when it takes leave of the moral order of human life, becomes autonomous, and no longer recognizes any standard but its own capabilities.

That means that the scope of reason must be enlarged once more. We have to come out of the prison we have built for ourselves and recognize other forms of ascertaining things, forms in which the whole of man comes into play. What we need is something like what we find in Socrates: a patient readiness, opened up and looking beyond itself. This readiness to look at things, in its time, brought together the two eyes of reason, Athens and Jerusalem, and made possible a new stage in history. We need a new readiness to seek the truth and also the humility to let ourselves be found. The strict application of methodical discipline should not mean just the pursuit of success; it should mean the pursuit of truth and the readiness to find it. That methodological strictness, which again and again lays upon us the obligation to subject ourselves to what we have found, and not just to follow our own wishes, can amount to a great school in being human and can make man capable of recognizing and appreciating truth. The humility that gives way to what has been found and does not try to manipulate it should not, however, become a false modesty that takes away our courage to recognize the truth. All the more must it oppose the pursuit of power, which is only interested in dominating the world and is no longer willing to perceive its inner logic, which sets limits to our desire to dominate. Ecological disasters could serve as a warning to us, that we may see where science is no longer at the service of truth but is destructive both of the world and of man. The ability to hear such warnings, the will to let oneself be purified by the truth, is essential. And I would add that the mystical capacity of the human mind needs to be strengthened again. The capacity to renounce oneself, a greater inner openness, the discipline to withdraw ourselves from noise and from all that presses on our attention, should once more be for all of us goals that we recognize as being among our priorities. We find Paul pleading that the inner man may be strengthened (Eph 3:16). Let us be honest about it: today there is a hypertrophy of the outer man, and his inner strength has been alarmingly weakened.

So as not to remain on too abstract a level, I should like to end by using a picture to make clear what has been said: a picture taken from history. Pope Gregory the Great (d. 604), in his *Dialogues*, tells about the last weeks in the life of Saint

Benedict. The founder of the monastic order had lain down
to sleep in the upper story of a tower, which was reached from
below by "a vertical ladder". He then got up, before the time
for night prayers, to keep a nighttime vigil; "He stood at the
window and prayed earnestly to almighty God. While he was
looking out, in the middle of the dark night, he suddenly saw
a light pouring down from above and driving all the darkness
of the night away. . . . Something quite marvelous happened in
this vision, as he himself later recounted: the whole world was
held before his eyes, as if brought together in a single ray of
sunshine." [16] Gregory's interlocutor countered this story with
the same question that springs to the mind of someone hearing it today: "What you have said, that Benedict saw the whole
world brought together before his eyes in a single ray of sunshine, is something I have never encountered, and I just cannot imagine it. How could one person ever see the whole
world?" The essential sentence in the Pope's reply is as follows: "If he . . . saw the whole world as one before him, then
it was not that heaven and earth became narrower but the
visionary's soul became so wide." [17]

Every detail is significant in this picture: the night, the tower,
the ladder, the upper room, the standing, the window. It all has,
over and beyond the topographical and biographical narra-
tion, great symbolic depth: by a long and difficult journey, which
began in a cave near Subiaco, this man has climbed up the
mountain and finally up the tower. His life has been an inner
climb, step by step, up the "vertical ladder". He has reached

---

[16] Gregory the Great, *Dialogi* 2:35:1–3; I have used the Latin-German edition of the Salzburg Conference of Abbots: Gregory the Great, *Der heilige
Benedikt: Buch II der Dialoge* (St. Ottilien: EOS-Verlag, 1995). My interpretation is heavily indebted to the excellent introduction to be found there, especially pp. 53–64.

[17] Ibid., 2:35:5 and 7.

the tower and, then, the "upper room", which from the time of the Acts of the Apostles has been understood as a symbol of being brought together and drawn up, rising up out of the world of making and doing. He is standing at the window—he has sought and found the place where he can look out, where the wall of the world has been opened up and he can gaze into the open. He is standing. In monastic tradition, someone standing represents a man who has straightened himself up from being crouched and doubled up and is thus, not only able to stare at the earth, but he has achieved upright status and the ability to look up.[18] Thus he becomes a seer. It is not the world that is narrowed down but the soul that is broadened out, being no longer absorbed in the particular, no longer looking at the trees and unable to see the wood, but now able to view the whole. Even better, he can see the whole because he is looking at it from on high, and he is able to gain this vantage point because he has grown inwardly great. We may hear an echo of the old tradition of man as a microcosm who embraces the whole world. Yet the essential point is this: man has to learn to climb up; he has to grow and broaden out. He has to stand at the window. He must gaze out. And then the light of God can touch him; he can recognize it and can gain from it the true overview. Our being planted on earth should never become so exclusive that we become incapable of ascending, of standing upright. Those great men who, by patient climbing and by the repeated purification they have received in their lives, have become seers and, therefore, pathfinders for the centuries are also relevant to us today. They show us how light may be found even in the night and how we can meet the threats that rise up from the abysses of human existence and can meet the future as men who hope.

---

[18] See the interpretation offered in ibid., pp. 60–63.

2. CHRISTIANITY—THE TRUE RELIGION?

At the close of the second Christian millenium, it is in the very area of its first great expansion, in Europe, that Christianity finds itself deep in crisis, arising from the crisis concerning its claim to truth. There are two dimensions to this crisis: First, the question is becoming ever more pressing as to whether it makes any sense to apply the concept of truth to religion at all—in other words, whether man is capable of perceiving the real truth concerning God and things divine. Today's man is more inclined to recognize himself in the Buddhist parable of the blind men and the elephant: Once, it is said, a king in northern India had all the blind people in the city brought together in one place. Then he had an elephant led out in front of them all. Some of them he allowed to feel its head, saying: That is what an elephant is like. Others were allowed to feel the ear, or the tusk, the trunk, the hindquarters, the hair at the tip of the tail. Next, the king asked them one by one, What is an elephant like? And according to what part they had felt, they answered: It is like a woven basket.... It is like a pot .... It is like a plow handle.... It is like a storeroom.... It is like a pillar.... It is like a mortar.... It is like a broom. And then, so the parable says, they began to quarrel, and, crying "an elephant is like—", they fell upon one another and struck each other with their fists, to the great delight of the king.[1] The conflict between religions seems to people today like the quarrel of those born blind in the story. For we are all born blind when it comes to the mysteries of divinity, so it seems. For the way people think today, Christianity by no means finds itself better placed

---

[1] See H. von Glasenapp, *Die fünf großen Religionen* [The five great religions] (Düsseldorf: Diederichs, 1957), 2:505; also the source (Udāna 6:4) and secondary literature given there.

than the other religions—on the contrary, with its claim to be true, it seems to be particularly blind to the limits of all our knowledge concerning what is divine, being characterized by an especially foolish fanaticism, so that it cannot be taught and insists on saying that the bit it has felt in its own experience is the whole thing.

The quite general scepticism in the face of any claim to truth where religion is concerned is then further buttressed by the questions that modern science has directed at the origins and the content of Christian teaching: the theory of creation seems to be made obsolete by that of evolution; the teaching on original sin by our knowledge of man's origins; critical exegesis relativizes the figure of Jesus and puts a question mark against his consciousness of being the Son; it seems doubtful whether the Church really originates from Jesus, and so forth. The philosophical basis of Christianity has become problematic through the "end of metaphysics"; as a result of modern historical methods its historical foundations are left in twilight. So from that viewpoint it seems an obvious step to reduce the content of Christianity to symbolism, to ascribe to it no more significance than one would to any myths from the history of religions—to regard it as one form of religious experience, which should humbly take its place alongside the others. In this sense one could then, so it seems, continue to be a Christian; one continues to make use of Christianity's forms of expression, although of course the claim they make has been radically altered: what was a power that laid an obligation upon people as being true and was a reliable promise now becomes a culturally conditioned form of expression of general religious sensibility, which simply happens, through the chances of our European descent, to be available to us.

At the beginning of the last century, Ernst Troeltsch formulated in philosophical and theological terms this inner

withdrawal of Christianity from its original claim to universality, which could only rest upon a claim to be true. He had
arrived at the view that cultures cannot be transcended and
that religion is closely associated with these cultures. Christianity is then merely the side of God's face that is turned
toward Europe. The "individual particularities of the cultural and racial areas" and the "particularities of their great
inclusive religious achievements" are accorded the status
of a court of final appeal: "Who, then, will dare to make
really decisive comparisons here in terms of values? Only
God himself, who has uttered these variations from within
himself, could do that." [2] Someone who is born blind knows
that he was not born to be blind and therefore will not
cease to ask why he is blind and to seek a way out of his
blindness. Man's resignation to the verdict that, when it comes
to what is essential, that on which his life ultimately depends,
he was born blind is merely apparent. The titanic attempt
to take possession of the whole world, to get from our life
and for our life whatever might be possible, shows—just
as much as do the outbreaks of some cult of ecstasy, of
self-transcendence and self-destruction—that man is not
content with that verdict. For if he does not know whence
he comes and whither he is going, then is he not, in all
his being, just a misshapen vessel? The apparent equanimity
of the farewell to truth about God and about the essential
nature of our selves, the seeming content at no longer

---

[2] See H. Bürkle, *Der Mensch auf der Suche nach Gott—Die Frage der Religionen* [Man in search of God—The question concerning the religions], Amateca,
no. 3 (Paderborn: Bonifatius, 1996), pp. 64–67. The quotation is taken from
Troeltsch, *Die Absolutheit des Christentums und die Religionsgeschichte*, 3rd ed.
(Tübingen: Mohr, 1929), p. 79 [English trans., *The Absoluteness of Christianity
and the History of Religions*, trans. David Reid (Richmond: John Knox Press,
1971)].

having to bother about this, is deceptive. Man cannot come to terms with being born blind, and remaining blind, where essential things are concerned. The farewell to truth can never be final.

Because that is how things stand, the old-fashioned question about the truth of Christianity has once more to be raised, however superfluous and unanswerable it may seem to many people. But how? No doubt, Christian theology will have to examine carefully the various individual authorities that have been brought to pronounce against Christianity's claim to truth in the realm of philosophy, of science, of history, and will have to engage them. It must also try, on the other hand, to reach an overall view in the question of the true nature of Christianity, of its place in the history of religions, and of its place in the life of man. I should like to take a step in this direction by throwing some light on the question of how, in the early days of Christianity, the latter itself saw its claims in the world of religion.

I know of no text from early Christianity that is so illuminating on this point as Augustine's discussion of the philosophy of religion of the "most learned of the Romans", Marcus Terentius Varro (116–27 B.C.).[3] Varro shared the Stoic picture of God and the world; he defined God as "animam motu ac ratione mundum gubernantem" (as the soul that by

[3] Seneca calls him "doctissimus romanorum" (*Helv.* 8:1); see Augustine, *De civitate Dei* (henceforth abbreviated as DcD), VI, 2 (CCL 47:167); who quotes Cicero, *Acad.* 3, who talks about Varro as "homine omnium facile acutissimo et sine ullo dubio doctissimo". On Varro, see P. L. Schmidt in *Der kleine Pauly: Lexicon der Antike* [abbreviated version of Pauly-Wissowa] 5:1131–40. In the following discussion I am turning again to the analysis of Augustine's argument with Varro, which I attempted nearly fifty years ago in my dissertation *Volk und Haus Gottes in Augustins Lehre von der Kirche* [The people of God and the house of God in Augustine's doctrine of the Church], 2nd ed. (1954; St. Ottilien: EOS-Verlag, 1997).

movement and reason directs the world),[4] in other words, as the world-soul, whom the Greeks call "cosmos": "hunc ipsum mundum esse deum".[5] No worship is of course offered to this world-soul. It is not the object of "religio". In other words, truth and religion, rational perception and cultic prescription, lie on two quite separate planes. Prescribed worship, the concrete world of religion, does not belong to the order of *res*, of "things", of reality as such, but to that of "mores"—of custom and behavior. It is not the gods who have created the state but the state that has instituted the gods, whose worship is essential for the proper ordering of the state and the proper behavior of citizens. Religion is essentially a political phenomenon. In accordance with this theory, Varro distinguishes three kinds of "theology", understanding by theology the "ratio quae de diis explicatur"— the understanding and explaining of the divine, as we may translate it. These are the "theologia mythica", the "theologia civilis" (πολιτική), and the "theologia naturalis" (φυσική).[6]

With the help of four further classifications he explains more clearly what we are to understand by these "theologies". The first classification concerns the theologians relating to the three theologies: the theologians of mythical theology are the poets, because they have composed songs about the gods and are thus singers of the gods. The theologians of physical (or natural) theology are the philosophers, that is, those learned men and thinkers who have inquired to an unusual degree into reality and truth; the theologians of civil theology are the "peoples", who by their own

---

[4] DcD IV, 31:2; CCL 47:125, lines 24ff.; Ratzinger, *Volk*, p. 267, n. 5.
[5] DcD VII, 6; CCL 47:191, lines 4f.
[6] DcD VI, 5; CCL 47:170f.

choice have not followed the philosophers (not the truth), but the poets, their poetic visions, their images and forms. The second classification concerns the place assigned to each respective theology in reality. There, the theater corresponds to mythical theology—and the theater certainly had a religious and cultic status; the prevailing opinion was that plays were instituted in Rome on the directions of the gods.[7] Political theology corresponds to the *urbs*, but the sphere of natural theology was the cosmos. The third classification specifies the content of the three theologies: mythical theology has as its content the stories about the gods that the poets have made up; civil theology has the cult; natural theology answers the question of who the gods are. Here it is worth taking the trouble to listen more carefully: "Whether—as Heraclitus says—they consist of fire, or—so says Pythagoras—of numbers, or—as Epicurus says—of atoms, and much more of that kind, one's ears can more easily bear within a schoolroom than outside on the marketplace."[8] It now becomes quite clear that this natural theology is a matter of demythologizing, or rather, of enlightenment, as it looks in critical fashion behind the mythical appearance and dissolves it by applying natural science. Worship and knowledge are thus dissociated. Worship remains necessary, as required for reasons of practical politics; knowledge becomes something that destroys religion and ought not, therefore, to be carried onto the marketplace. Finally there is the fourth classification: What kind of reality forms the content of each particular theology? Varro answers as follows: Natural theology has to do with the "nature of the gods" (who do not exist); the other two theologies deal with the "divina

[7] See Ratzinger, *Volk*, p. 269, n. 12.
[8] DcD VI, 5; CCL 47:171, lines 23–29.

instituta hominum", with the divine institutions of mankind.[9] Yet the entire distinction is thereby reduced to that between physics, in the ancient sense, and, on the other hand, cultic worship. "Civic religion does not ultimately have a god, merely 'religion'; 'natural theology' has no religion, only a divinity." [10] Well, it cannot have any religion or worship, for its god cannot be addressed in religious terms: fire, numbers, atoms. . . . Thus, *religio* (which essentially means the official cult) and reality, the rational perception of what is real, stand side by side as two separate spheres.

The *religio* derives its justification, not from the reality of the divine, but from its political function. It is an institution that is requisite for the continuing existence of the state. There is no doubt that we have before us a late phase in religious development, in which the naïve nature of religion has been destroyed and its dissolution has been initiated. Yet the essential connection between religion and civil society reaches far deeper than that. The cult is in the end a positively constituted order, which cannot as such be assessed by the question of its truth. While Varro in his time, in which the political purpose of religion was still sufficiently important to justify it as such, could still advocate a fairly crude concept of enlightenment and of the lack of truth in the politically motivated cult, very soon afterward Neoplatonism would seek another way out of the crisis, upon which the emperor Julian then built further in attempting the restoration of the Roman civil religion: What the poets say offers images that are not to be understood physically and that yet express the ineffable for those men to whom the royal road of mystical union is barred. Although the images are not true as such, they are

---

[9] DcD VCI, 5; CCL 47:172, lines 55f.
[10] Ratzinger, *Volk*, p. 270.

nonetheless justified as an approach to what must ever remain ineffable.[11]

But we have run ahead of ourselves. For the Neoplatonist position is for its own part a reaction to the position taken by Christians on the question of the authorization of Christian worship and the underlying question of the place to be assigned to Christianity in the classification of religions. Let us return to Augustine. Where does he place Christianity in Varro's threefold classification of religion? What is astonishing is that without hesitation he indicates that Christianity's place is in the sphere of "physical theology", in the sphere of philosophical enlightenment.[12] In doing so, he stands in complete continuity with the earliest theologians of Christianity, the apologists of the second century, and indeed with the place Paul assigns to Christianity in the first chapter of the Letter to the Romans, which for its part is based on Old Testament wisdom theology and reaches back beyond that to the mocking of the gods in the Psalms. According to this view, Christianity's precedents and its inner groundwork lie in philosophical enlightenment, not in religions. According to Augustine and the biblical tradition that is normative for him, Christianity is not based on mythical images and vague notions that are ultimately justified by their political usefulness; rather, it relates to that divine presence which can be perceived by the rational analysis of reality. In other words, Augustine identifies biblical monotheism with philosophical perceptions concerning the foundations of the world, as they developed in various versions in ancient philosophy. This is

[11] There is a brief review of the development of Platonism in Plotinus and his school in C. Reale and D. Antiseri, *Il pensiero occidentale dalle origini ad oggi* [Western thought from its origins to the present day], vol. 1: *Antichità e Medioevo* [Classical and medieval periods] (Brescia: La Scuola, 1985), pp. 242–68.

[12] Ratzinger, *Volk*, pp. 271–76.

what is meant when Christianity, from Paul's speech on the Areopagus onward, advances the claim to be the *religio vera*.

What that means is that Christian faith is not based on poetry and politics, the two great sources of religion; it is based on knowledge. It is the worship of that being which is the foundation of everything that exists, the "true God". In Christianity, enlightenment has become part of religion and is no longer its opponent. Because that is how it was, because Christianity saw itself as embodying the victory of demythologization, the victory of knowledge, and with that the victory of truth, it necessarily regarded itself as universal and had to be carried to all peoples: not as a specific religion that overcomes and displaces others, not on the basis of some kind of religious imperialism, but as the truth that renders mere appearance superfluous. And for that very reason it necessarily appears, within the broad tolerance of polytheistic religions, as intolerable, indeed, as being opposed to religion, as "atheistic": it refused to accept the relativism and the interchangeability of the images, and thereby, above all, it obstructed the political purpose of those religions and thus endangered the foundations of the state, in that it insisted that it was not one religion among others but represented the victory of perception and knowledge over the world of religions.

Connected with this place of Christianity in the sphere of religion and philosophy, on the other hand, is Christianity's power to assert and establish itself. Even before the appearance of the Christian missions, people in educated circles in the ancient world had sought to associate themselves with the Jewish faith in the persons of the "God-fearers", because that Jewish faith seemed to them the religious form of philosophical monotheism and, thus, corresponded both to the demands of reason and to the religious needs of man, for which philosophy alone had no answer—one does not pray to a god who has simply been thought up. But if the God who has been discovered by thinking appears within a religion, as a God who speaks and who acts, then thought and faith have been reconciled.[13] When people associated themselves with the synagogue in this way, there was one unsatisfactory element not accommodated: the non-Jew could only ever be an outsider and could never truly belong. In Christianity this shackle was broken by the figure of Jesus, as interpreted by Paul. Now at last the monotheism of Judaism had become universal, and thereby the unity of thought and faith, the *religio vera*, had become accessible to all. Justin the philosopher, Justin Martyr (d. 167) may be taken as representative for this accessibility of Christianity: he had studied all the philosophers and had finally recognized in Christianity the *vera philosophia*. In becoming a Christian, he had had, in his view, not laid aside what he believed as a philosopher, but become for the first time a true philosopher in the full sense.[14] The view that Christianity is a philosophy, the perfect philosophy, that is, the philosophy that has attained to the truth, was held for long after the patristic period. It is still present and regarded as self-evident in Byzantine theology in the fourteenth century in the work of Nicholas Cabasilas.[15]

[13] On the phenomenon of the "God-fearer", see M. Simon, "Gottesfürchtiger", in *Reallexikon für Antike und Christentum*, 11:1060–70; L.H. Feldman, *Jew and Gentile in the Ancient World* (Princeton, N.J.: Princeton University Press, 1993), pp. 342–82.

[14] On Justin, see H. Bürkle, *Mensch auf der Suche nach Gott*, pp. 45f.; C.P. Vetten, "Justin der Märtyrer", in S. Döpp and W. Geerlings, *Lexikon der antiken christlichen Literatur* (Herder, 1998), pp. 365–69 [English trans., *Dictionary of Early Christian Literature*, trans. Matthew O'Connell (New York: Crossroad, 2000)]; *Justin Martyr, Œuvres Complètes*, Bibliothèque Migne (Brépols, 1994).

[15] In his book on *The Life in Christ*, the view of Christianity as the true philosophy is a theme that runs right through.

Philosophy, in this view, was of course understood, not as an academic discipline of a purely theoretical nature, but above all as being at the same time practical, as the art of living and dying aright, something that can after all only be successfully done by the light of the truth.

The uniting of enlightenment and faith that was achieved when the Christian mission was developed and the Christian theology was built up did of course involve far-reaching corrections to the picture of God offered by philosophy, two of which should especially be mentioned. The first is that the God in whom the Christians believe and whom they worship is—in contrast to the mythical and political gods— truly *natura Deus* ("by his very nature"); that is in line with the ideas of the philosophical enlightenment. Yet at the same time it is the case that "non tamen omnis natura est Deus"— not everything that is nature is God.[16] God is God by his very nature, but it is not nature as such that is God. A distinction is made between all-embracing nature and the being that gives it life, gives it its origin. Thus for the first time physics and metaphysics clearly diverge. Only the true God, whom we may perceive in nature by thinking things out, is worshipped. But he is more than nature. He comes before it, and it is his creation. Besides this distinction between God and nature there appears another, even more far-reaching perception: No one had been able to pray to the god who is nature, the world-soul, or whatever he may have been; he was, as we saw, not a "religious god". Yet this God who was there before nature, as the faith of the Old Testament already said and, even more so, that of the New Testament, had now turned toward man. Precisely because he is not merely nature, he is not a silent God. He has entered into history, has come

[16]DcD VI, 8; CCL 47:176, line 6; Ratzinger, *Volk*, p. 272.

to meet man, and thus man can now go to meet him. He can unite himself with God, because God has united himself with man. The two sides of religion, which are forever separating from each other, eternally working nature and the need for salvation of suffering and struggling man, have been united. The enlightenment can become part of religion, because the God of the enlightenment has himself entered into religion. That thing which makes a real demand for faith, the historical utterance of God, is the presupposition of religion's now being able to turn to the God of philosophy, who is no longer merely a philosophical God and who nonetheless does not reject the perceptions of philosophy but assumes them. Something quite astonishing appears here: the two apparently contradictory fundamental principles of Christianity—the link with metaphysics and the link with history—are mutually determinative and belong together; between them, they constitute the apology of Christianity as *religio vera*.[17]

If, accordingly, we may say that the victory of Christianity over the pagan religions was rendered possible not least by the claim of its rational nature, then we should add that a second theme of equal weight is associated with this. Speaking quite generally, this consists in the moral seriousness of Christianity, which of course Paul, yet again, had connected with the rational character of Christianity: What the law really means, those essential demands of the one God upon human life that have been illuminated by the Christian faith, is identical with what is written in the heart of man, of every man, so that he can recognize the good when he meets it. It is identical with "what is good by nature" (cf. Rom 2:14f.). The allusion to Stoic morality, and to its ethical interpretation of nature, is just as obvious here as in other Pauline texts

[17] More fully explained in Ratzinger, *Volk*, pp. 274f.

such as the Letter to the Philippians: "Whatever is true, whatever is honorable, whatever is just, whatever is pure, whatever is lovely, whatever is gracious, if there is any excellence, if there is anything worthy of praise, think about these things" (4:8). The fundamental agreement (albeit a critical agreement) concerning the concept of God with philosophical enlightenment is here reinforced and embodied in a similarly critical agreement with philosophical morality. Just as, in the realm of religion, Christianity went beyond the limits of the wisdom of the philosophical schools in that the notional God was met as a living God, so here also it went beyond ethical theory to a moral practice that was embodied and lived out in community, which went one better than the philosophical view, especially in concentrating all morality on the twofold commandment of loving God and loving one's neighbor and translating this into practical action.

We could simplify by saying that Christianity was convincing because of the connection of faith with reason and by directing behavior by *caritas*, by loving care for the suffering, the poor, and the weak, across any boundaries of class or status. We can see that this gave Christianity its inner power perhaps most clearly in the way that the emperor Julian went about trying to restore paganism in a new form. He, the Pontifex Maximus of the restored religion of the old gods, now set up something that had never before existed, a pagan hierarchy with priests and metropolitans. The priests were supposed to give a moral example; they were to practice the love of God (the high god over all the gods) and of their neighbors. It was their duty to practice deeds of love toward the poor; they were no longer allowed to read lascivious comedies or erotic novels, and on festivals they were to preach on a philosophical theme, so as to teach and to edify the people. Teresio Bosco quite rightly remarks about this that in reality the emperor was seeking, not to restore paganism, but to reform it in a Christian sense—in a synthesis of enlightenment and religion within which the cult of the gods was enfolded.[18]

Looking back, we may say that the power of Christianity, which made it into a world religion, consisted in its synthesis of reason, faith, and life; and it is precisely this synthesis that is summed up and expressed in the term *religio vera*. All the more forcefully the question arises: Why is this synthesis no longer convincing today? Why, on the contrary, are enlightenment and Christianity regarded today as contradicting each other or even as mutually exclusive? What has changed in enlightenment, or in Christianity, that it should be so? In those days, Neoplatonism, and especially Porphyry, offered another interpretation of the relationship between philosophy and religion, in opposition to the Christian synthesis, which was meant to be a new philosophical basis for the religion of the gods. It was on this that Julian was building and failed. Today, however, it is just this alternative form of balancing religion with enlightenment that seems to be prevailing, as the kind of religious sensibility more in keeping with modern consciousness. Its first principle is thus formulated by Porphyry: "Latet omne verum"—the truth is hidden.[19] Let us recall the parable of the elephant, which is animated by this very idea, in which Buddhism and Neoplatonism are agreed. In this view there is no certainty about truth or concerning God: there are only opinions.

[18] T. Bosco, *Eusebio di Vercelli nel suo tempo pagano e cristiano* [Eusebius of Vercelli in his age, both Christian and pagan] (Turin: Elle Di Ci, 1995), pp. 206ff.

[19] Quoted by Macrobius, *Somn.* I, 3:18; see C. Gnilka, *Chrēsis: Die Methode der Kirchenväter im Umgang mit der antiken Kultur* [Chrēsis: The method of the Church Fathers in dealing with classical culture], vol. 2: *Kultur und Conversion* (Basel: Schwabe, 1993), p. 23.

In the Roman crisis of the late fourth century the senator Symmachus—the contemporary who reflected Varro's theory of religion—reduced the Neoplatonic conception to simple pragmatic formulae, which are to be found in his oration of 384 before Emperor Valentinian II, in defense of paganism and advocating the restoration of the statue of the goddess "Victoria" in the Roman senate. I quote only the decisive sentence, which has become famous: "It is the same thing that we all worship; we all think the same; we look up to the same stars; there is one sky above us, one world around us; what difference does it make with what kind of method the individual seeks the truth? We cannot all follow the same path to reach so great a mystery." [20] This is exactly what enlightenment is saying today: We do not know truth as such; yet in a variety of images, we all express the same thing. So great a mystery as the Divinity cannot be fixed in *one* image, which would exclude all others—to *one* path obligatory for all. There are many paths; there are many images; all reflect something of the whole, and none is itself the whole. He is practicing the ethic of tolerance who recognizes in each one a little of the truth, who does not set his own above what is strange to him, and who peacefully takes his place in the multiform symphony of the eternally unattainable that hides itself in symbols, symbols that yet seem to be the only way we have to grasp in some sense the Divinity.

Has the claim of Christianity to be *religio vera*, then, been overtaken by the progress of enlightenment? Is it bound to step down from its claim and take its place in the Neoplatonic or Buddhist or Hindu view of truth and symbol, to content itself—as Troeltsch suggested—with showing the side

---

[20] Quoted from Gnilka, *Chrēsis*. On pp. 19–26, Gnilka offers a detailed analysis of the text.

of God's face that is turned toward Europeans? Will it even have to go a step farther than Troeltsch, who still thought that Christianity was the appropriate form of religion for Europe, whereas today it is precisely Europe that is doubting this appropriateness? This is the real question that the Church and theology have to ask themselves. All the internal crises in Christianity we can observe at present arise only in a quite secondary sense from institutional problems. The difficulties with institutions and with personalities in the Church ultimately arise from the enormous impact of this question. No one will expect this question, which is making such fundamental demands on us at the end of the second millenium, to be answered here in any way conclusively. It cannot be answered in purely theoretical fashion at all, just as religion, as the ultimate attitude of man, is never just theoretical. It demands that interplay of perception and action on which the Christianity of the Fathers founded its power to convince people.

This by no means signifies that one can avoid the intellectual claims of the difficulty by referring to its necessary relation to actual practice. To close, I will just try a perspective that might give some direction. We have seen how the original unified relation between enlightenment and faith, which was of course never quite beyond dispute and which had finally been brought into a systematic form by Thomas Aquinas, was torn apart less by the development of the faith than by the new steps taken by enlightenment. We could suggest that Descartes, Spinoza, and Kant are points along the way in this process of separation. The attempt at a new comprehensive synthesis by Hegel did not give faith back its proper place in philosophy but tried to transform it completely into reason and to do away with it as faith. To this giving absolute status to the spirit, Marx opposed a system of solely material values; philosophy was now to be based upon exact science. Only exact scientific knowledge was knowledge at all. Any idea about God was thereby made redundant. Auguste Comte's proclamation that one day there would be a "physics of man", and that those great questions hitherto left to metaphysics could in the future be dealt with in just as "positive" a way as everything that now constitutes science, left an impressive echo in our own century in the social sciences. The separation of physics from metaphysics achieved by Christian thinking is being steadily canceled. Everything is to become "physics" again.[21] The theory of evolution has increasingly emerged as the way to make metaphysics disappear, to make "the hypothesis of God" (Laplace) superfluous, and to formulate a strictly "scientific" explanation of the world. A comprehensive theory of evolution, intended to explain the whole of reality, has become a kind of "first philosophy", which represents, as it were, the true foundation for an enlightened understanding of the world.[22] Any attempt to involve any basic elements other than those worked out within the terms of such a "positive" theory, any attempt at "metaphysics", necessarily appears as a relapse from the standards of enlightenment, as abandoning the universal claims of science. Thus the Christian idea of God is necessarily regarded as unscientific. There is no longer any

[21] On Comte, see H. de Lubac, *Le Drame de l'humanisme athée*, 7th ed. (Paris: Cerf, 1983) [English trans., *The Drama of Atheist Humanism* (San Francisco: Ignatius Press, 1995)].

[22] J. Monod, *Le Hasard et la nécessité: Essai sur la philosophie naturelle de la biologie moderne*, 5th ed. (Paris: Éd. du Seuil, 1970), remains a classic instance of this attempt [English trans., *Chance and Necessity: An Essay on the Natural Philosophy of Modern Biology* (New York: Knopf, 1971)]. For a discussion of the whole subject, see R. Chandebois, *Pour en finir avec le darwinisme: Une nouvelle logique du vivant* [Doing away with Darwinism: A new logic of life] (Montpellier: Éd. Espaces, 1993).

theologia physica (θεολογία φυσική) that corresponds to it: in this view, the doctrine of evolution is the only *theologia naturalis*, and that knows of no God, either a creator in the Christian (or Jewish or Islamic) sense or a world-soul or moving spirit in the Stoic sense. One could, at any rate, regard this whole world as mere appearance and nothingness as the true reality and, thus, justify some forms of mystical religion, which are at least not in direct competition with enlightenment.

Has the last word been spoken? Have Christianity and reason permanently parted company? There is at any rate no getting around the dispute about the extent of the claims of the doctrine of evolution as a fundamental philosophy and about the exclusive validity of the positive method as the sole indicator of systematic knowledge and of rationality. This dispute has therefore to be approached objectively and with a willingness to listen, by both sides—something that has hitherto been undertaken only to a limited extent. No one will be able to cast serious doubt upon the scientific evidence for micro-evolutionary processes. R. Junker and S. Scherer, in their "critical reader" on evolution, have this to say: "Many examples of such developmental steps [microevolutionary processes] are known to us from natural processes of variation and development. The research done on them by evolutionary biologists produced significant knowledge of the adaptive capacity of living systems, which seems marvelous." [23] They tell us, accordingly, that one would therefore be quite justified in describing the research of early development as the reigning monarch among biological disciplines. It is not toward that point, therefore, that a believer will direct

[23] R. Junker and S. Scherer, *Evolution: Ein kritisches Lesebuch* [Evolution: A critical reader], 4th ed. (Gießen: Weyel, 1998), p. 5.

the questions he puts to modern rationality but rather toward the development of evolutionary theory into a generalized *philosophia universalis*, which claims to constitute a universal explanation of reality and is unwilling to allow the continuing existence of any other level of thinking. Within the teaching about evolution itself, the problem emerges at the point of transition from micro- to macro-evolution, on which point Szathmáry and Maynard Smith, both convinced supporters of an all-embracing theory of evolution, nonetheless declare that: "There is no theoretical basis for believing that evolutionary lines become more complex with time; and there is also no empirical evidence that this happens." [24]

The question that has now to be put certainly delves deeper: it is whether the theory of evolution can be presented as a universal theory concerning all reality, beyond which further questions about the origin and the nature of things are no longer admissible and indeed no longer necessary, or whether such ultimate questions do not after all go beyond the realm of what can be entirely the object of research and knowledge by natural science. I should like to put the question in still more concrete form. Has everything been said with the kind of answer that we find thus formulated by Popper: "Life as we know it consists of physical 'bodies' (more precisely, structures) which are problem solving. This the various species have 'learned' by natural selection, that is to say by the method of reproduction plus variation, which itself has been learned by the same method. This regress is not necessarily infinite." [25] I do not think so. In the end this concerns a choice that can no longer be

[24] Ibid. Szathmáry and J. M. Smith, "The Major Evolutionary Transitions", *Nature* 374:227–32, quoted in Junker and Scherer, *Evolution*, p. 5.

[25] K. Popper, *Unended Quest: An Intellectual Autobiography* (La Salle, Ill.: Open Court, 1976), 179.

made on purely scientific grounds or basically on philosophical grounds. The question is whether reason, or rationality, stands at the beginning of all things and is grounded
in the basis of all things or not. The question is whether
reality originated on the basis of chance and necessity (or,
as Popper says, in agreement with Butler, on the basis of
luck and cunning)[26] and, thus, from what is irrational; that
is, whether reason, being a chance by-product of irrationality and floating in an ocean of irrationality, is ultimately
just as meaningless; or whether the principle that represents
the fundamental conviction of Christian faith and of its philosophy remains true: "In principio erat Verbum"—at the
beginning of all things stands the creative power of reason.
Now as then, Christian faith represents the choice in favor
of the priority of reason and of rationality. This ultimate
question, as we have already said, can no longer be decided
by arguments from natural science, and even philosophical
thought reaches its limits here. In that sense, there is no
ultimate demonstration that the basic choice involved in
Christianity is correct. Yet, can reason really renounce its
claim to the priority of what is rational over the irrational,
the claim that the Logos is at the ultimate origin of things,
without abolishing itself? The explanatory model presented by Popper, which reappears in different variations in
the various accounts of the "basic philosophy", shows that
reason cannot do other than to think of irrationality according to its own standards, that is, those of reason (solving
problems, learning methods!), so that it implicitly reintro-
duces nonetheless the primacy of reason, which has just
been denied. Even today, by reason of its choosing to assert
the primacy of reason, Christianity remains "enlightened",

[26] Ibid., p. 180.

and I think that any enlightenment that cancels this choice must, contrary to all appearances, mean, not an evolution, but an involution, a shrinking, of enlightenment.

We saw before that in the way early Christianity saw things, the concepts of nature, man, God, ethics, and religion were indissolubly linked together and that this very interlinking contributed to make Christianity appear the obvious choice in the crisis concerning the gods and in the crisis concerning the enlightenment of the ancient world. The orientation of religion toward a rational view of reality as a whole, ethics as a part of this vision, and its concrete application under the primacy of love became closely associated. The primacy of the Logos and the primacy of love proved to be identical. The Logos was seen to be, not merely a mathematical reason at the basis of all things, but a creative love taken to the point of becoming sympathy, suffering with the creature. The cosmic aspect of religion, which reverences the Creator in the power of being, and its existential aspect, the question of redemption, merged together and became one. Every explanation of reality that cannot at the same time provide a meaningful and comprehensible basis for ethics necessarily remains inadequate. Now the theory of evolution, in the cases where people have tried to extend it to a *philosophia universalis*, has in fact been used for an attempt at a new ethos based on evolution. Yet this evolutionary ethic that inevitably takes as its key concept the model of selectivity, that is, the struggle for survival, the victory of the fittest, successful adaptation, has little comfort to offer. Even when people try to make it more attractive in various ways, it ultimately remains a bloodthirsty ethic. Here, the attempt to distill rationality out of what is in itself irrational quite visibly fails. All this is of very little use for an ethic of universal peace, of practical love of one's neighbor, and of the necessary overcoming of oneself, which is what we need.

The attempt, in this crisis for mankind, to give back an obvious meaning and significance to the concept of Christianity as the *religio vera*, must, so to speak, be based in equal measure upon orthopraxy and orthodoxy. At the most profound level its content will necessarily consist—in the final analysis, just as it did then—in love and reason coming together as the two pillars of reality: the true reason is love, and love is the true reason. They are in their unity the true basis and the goal of all reality.

3. FAITH, TRUTH AND CULTURE

REFLECTIONS PROMPTED BY THE ENCYCLICAL
FIDES ET RATIO

What is the encyclical *Fides et Ratio* really about? Is it a document intended only for specialists, an attempt from a Christian perspective at restoring philosophy, a discipline that is in a state of crisis and thus of interest only to philosophers, or is it putting a question that matters to us all? We could also put it another way: Does faith really need philosophy, or is faith—which, according to a saying of Saint Ambrose, was given into the keeping of fishermen and not dialecticians— quite independent of the existence of a philosophy that is open to faith? If we regard philosophy as just one academic discipline among others, then faith is in fact independent of it. But the Pope understands philosophy in a far broader sense, and one far more in keeping with its origins. This philosophy puts the question of whether man can know truth, know the fundamental truths about himself, about his origin and his future, or whether he lives in a twilight that cannot be illuminated and must finally restrict himself to the question of what is useful. It is the peculiarity of Christianity, in the realm of religions, that it claims to tell us the truth about God, the world, and man and lays claim to being the *religio vera*, the religion of truth. "I am the way, and the truth, and the life": this saying of Jesus from the Gospel of John (14:6) expresses the basic claim of the Christian faith. The missionary tendency of this faith is based on that claim: Only if the Christian faith is truth does it concern all men; if it is merely a cultural variant of the religious experience of mankind that is locked up in symbols and can never be deciphered, then it has to remain within its own culture and leave others in theirs.

That, however, means that the question about the truth is the essential question of the Christian faith as such, and in that sense it inevitably has to do with philosophy. If I had briefly to sketch the main intention of the encyclical, I would say that it is trying to rehabilitate the question of truth in a world characterized by relativism; it is trying to reinstate it as a rational and scientific task in the situation of modern science, which does indeed look for truths but which to a great extent disqualifies the search for the truth as being unscientific; it is attempting this, because otherwise faith loses the air it breathes. The encyclical is quite simply attempting to give us courage for the adventure of truth. It is thereby speaking far beyond the sphere of faith yet also into the heart of the world of faith.

1. *Words, the Word, and the Truth*

In his best-seller, *The Screwtape Letters*, which appeared in the forties, the English writer and philosopher C. S. Lewis depicted very wittily how unmodern it is to ask about truth

today. This book consists of fictional letters from a senior
devil who is giving advice on how best to proceed to one
beginning in the work of leading men astray. The younger
devil has expressed concern to his superior that especially
intelligent people, in particular, might read the books of
wisdom of the ancients and might thus come upon the track
of the truth. Screwtape calms him by pointing out that the
"Historical point of View", with which the intellectuals of
the Western world have fortunately been inculcated by the
devils, means in fact that "when a learned man is presented
with any statement in an ancient author, the one question
he never asks is whether it is true. He asks who influenced
the ancient writer, and how far the statement is consistent
with what he said in other books, and what phase in the
writer's development, or in the general history of thought, it
illustrates, and how it affected other writers", and so on.[1]
Josef Pieper, who quotes this passage from C. S. Lewis in his
essay on interpretation, points out in this connection that
the editions of Plato, for instance, or Dante produced in Communist countries always gave an introduction to the works
being reprinted, which gave the reader a "historical" understanding of them and were meant thus to preclude the question of truth.[2]

Scholarly activity carried on in such a manner will have the
effect of immunizing against the truth. The question of whether,
and how far, something an author says is true is supposed to be
an unscholarly question; it would indeed lead us beyond
the realm of what can be demonstrated and supported by

[1] C. S. Lewis, *The Screwtape Letters* (1942; Glasgow: Collins, 1955), pp. 139f.
Quoted by J. Pieper in "Was heißt Interpretation?" [What does interpretation
mean], in his *Schriften zum Philosophiebegriff* [Writings on the concept of phi-
losophy], vol. 3 of his *Werke*, ed. B. Wald (Hamburg: Meiner, 1995), pp. 226f.
[2] Ibid., p. 227.

quotation, would be a relapse into the naïveté of a precritical world. In this way even the reading of the Bible is neutralized: we can say when, and in what conditions, some statement originated, and we have thus placed it in its historical setting, which does not ultimately concern us. Behind this kind of "historical interpretation" stands a philosophy, a basic attitude toward reality, which tells us that it is meaningless to ask about what is; we can only ask about what we are able to do with things. It is a matter, not of truth, but of action, of dominating things to our own advantage. As against such an apparently obvious restriction of human thought, the question of course arises: What is to our advantage? And in what way to our advantage? What are we here for? For anyone who looks below the surface, a false humility and a false pride at once become apparent in this fundamental attitude of modernity: false humility, which denies man the capacity to know and recognize truth, and false pride, with which he sets himself above things, above truth itself, by setting the expansion of his power, the domination of all things, as the goal of all his thinking.

We can today find presented in scientific form in the study of literature what appears in Lewis' writing in ironical form. There, the question of truth is quite openly excluded as unscholarly. The German exegete Marius Reiser recently referred to the words of Umberto Eco in his best-selling novel *The Name of the Rose*, where he says: "The only truth lies in learning to free ourselves from the insane passion for the truth." [3] The essential basis for this unmistakable renunciation of truth consists of what people call nowadays the "linguistic turning point": No one can get back behind

[3] M. Reiser, "Bibel und Kirche: Eine Antwort an U. Luz" [Bible and Church: A reply to U. Luz], *Trierer Theologischer Zeitschrift* 108 (1999): 62–81, this point on p. 72; U. Eco, *The Name of the Rose*, trans. William Weaver (1983; London: Picador, 1984), p. 491.

language and its images; reason is conditioned by language and restricted to language.[4] As early as 1901, F. Mauthner had coined the phrase, "what people call thinking is only empty words."[5] In this connection, M. Reiser talks of a "surrender of the belief" that one could relate "by linguistic means to nonlinguistic things".[6] The eminent Protestant exegete U. Luz observes that—just as we heard Screwtape saying to start with—historical criticism has in modern times renounced any approach to the question of truth. He believes himself bound to accept this capitulation and to admit that truth is not to be found today beyond the texts themselves; rather, there are only competing truth constructs, offers of truth, which have to be presented and justified in public discourse in the marketplace of all the views of life.[7]

Anyone reflecting on these views will almost inevitably feel reminded of a very profound passage from Plato's *Phaedrus*. Socrates is telling Phaedrus a story he had from the ancients who knew about truth. Thoth, the "father of letters" and the "god of time" once came to the Egyptian king Thutmose of Thebes. He taught this ruler about various arts he had invented and especially about the art of writing that he had thought up. In praise of his invention, he said to the

[4] Reiser, "Bibel und Kirche", p. 63, with a reference to O. Tracy, *Theologie als Gespräch: Eine postmoderne Hermeneutik* [Theology as conversation: A postmodern hermeneutic] (Mainz: Matthias-Grünewald-Verlag, 1993), pp. 73–97.

[5] F. Mauthner, *Beiträge zu einer Kritik der Sprache* [Contributions to a criticism of language], 3 vols., 2nd ed. (1923; reprt., Frankfurt, 1982); the quotation is from 3:635. See Reiser, "Bibel und Kirche", p. 73.

[6] Quoted by Reiser, "Bibel und Kirche", pp. 73f.

[7] See ibid., pp. 63f. U. Luz, "Kann die Bibel heute noch Grundlage für die Kirche sein? Über die Aufgabe der Exegese in einer religiös pluralistischen Gesellschaft" [Can the Bible still be the basis of the Church? On the task of exegesis in a society of religious pluralism], *New Testament Studies* 44 (1998): 317–39.

king: "This knowledge, O King, will make the Egyptians more wise and better able to remember things; for it has been invented as an aid to the memory as well as for wisdom." But the king was not impressed. On the contrary, he foresaw as the result of the art of writing that:

> This will bring forgetfulness into men's souls ... through the neglect of remembering, in that by trusting in writing they will draw remembrance from without ... and not from within, from their own selves. You have not, therefore, invented a means of remembering but of recording, and you pass on to your pupils only the appearance of wisdom, not the thing itself. For they are people who hear much without learning anything and will therefore think themselves very knowledgeable, since in general they are ignorant, and they are people who are difficult to deal with, in that they are apparently wise but not truly so.[8]

Anyone who thinks of the way television programs from all over the world overwhelm people with information and thus make them apparently knowledgeable; anyone who thinks about the further possibilities of computers and the Internet, which make available, for instance, to anyone searching, all the texts of some Church Father containing some particular word, yet without the person's having worked his way into his thinking, will not consider these warnings to be exaggerated. Plato is not rejecting writing as such, just as we do not reject the new information media but rather give thanks and make use of them; but he sets up a warning sign, the seriousness of which is demonstrated every day by the consequences of the "linguistic turning point" and by many

---

[8] *Phaedrus* 274d–275b. Cf. on this H. Schade, *Lamm Gottes und Zeichen des Widders* [The Lamb of God and the sign of the ram] (Freiburg: Herder, 1998), pp. 27f.

developments of which we are all currently aware. H. Schade points out the essence of what Plato has to say to us today in this text: "What Plato was warning us about was the domination of a philological method and the accompanying loss of reality."[9]

When writing, when what has been written, becomes a barrier to the content, then it has itself become an anti-art that does not make man more wise but sentences him to a sick appearance of wisdom. A. Kreiner is thus right when he remarks, about the linguistic turning point, that "the surrender of the belief that one can relate by linguistic means to nonlinguistic contents amounts to much the same thing as surrendering the possibility of any meaningful discourse at all."[10] On the same point, the Pope in his encyclical makes the following remark: "The interpretation of this word [= the word of God] cannot merely keep referring us to one interpretation after another, without ever leading us to a statement that is simply true."[11] Man is not caught in a hall of mirrors of interpretation; he can and must look for the way out to the reality that stands behind the words and manifests itself to him in and through the words.

This brings us to the heart of the Christian faith's struggle with a certain type of modern culture, which would like to be seen as modern culture as such, but which—praise God—is only one variety of it. That is, for instance, glaringly obvious in the criticism leveled at the encyclical by the Italian philosopher Paolo Flores d'Arcais. Precisely because the encyclical insists on the need to put the question of truth, he declares that "the official Catholic culture

[9] Schade, *Lamm Gottes*, p. 27.

[10] A. Kreiner, *Ende der Wahrheit?* [The end of truth?] (Freiburg: Herder, 1992), p. 116, quoted by Reiser, "Bibel und Kirche", p. 74.

[11] No. 84.

[that is, that of the encyclical] has no more to say to 'culture *tout court* [as such]'." [12] Yet that also means that the question of truth stands outside "culture *tout court*"; And is not then this "culture *tout court*" rather an anticulture? And is not then its presuming to be culture itself, as such, an arrogant presumption showing how it despises people?

That this is the main point becomes clear when Flores d'Arcais accuses the Pope's encyclicals of having "murderous consequences for democracy" and identifies his teaching with the "fundamentalist" version of Islam. He indicates as the basis for his charge the Pope's having described laws that permit abortion and euthanasia as being beyond the pale of authentic legal validity. [13] Anyone setting himself against an elected Parliament in that way and trying to exercise worldly power on the basis of ecclesiastical claims shows, he says, that his thinking still bears the watermark of Catholic dogmatism. Such assertions assume that there can be no appeal from the decisions of a majority. The chance occurrence of a majority becomes an absolute. For there is still such a thing as something absolute, beyond which there is no appeal. We have been handed over to the rule of positivism and of the

[12] P. Flores d'Arcais, "Die Frage ist die Antwort: Zur Enzyklika *Fides et Ratio*" [The question is the answer: On the encyclical *Fides et Ratio*], *Frankfurter Allgemeine Zeitung*, no. 51 (March 2, 1999): 47.

[13] In nos. 68–74 of the encyclical *Evangelium Vitae*, the Pope deals in detail with the thesis that the lawgiving of any society should restrict itself to registering and giving established status to the convictions of the majority and that private conscience and public order should be strictly separate, and he argues against this (no. 69). As against this, the Pope asserts that democracy cannot become a surrogate for morality; the value of democracy, he says, stands and falls with the values it embodies (no. 70). This fundamental exposition of the principles of politics and the state cannot be set aside by brashly referring to them as "fundamentalism"; they do at least deserve a fresh examination and discussion. In this connection I might refer the reader to my book *A Turning Point for Europe?* trans. Brian McNeil (San Francisco: Ignatius Press, 1994).

erection of what is accidental, what can indeed be manipulated, into an absolute value. When man is shut out from the truth, he can only be dominated by what is accidental and arbitrary. That is why it is, not "fundamentalism", but a duty of humanity to protect man from the dictatorship of what is accidental and to restore to him his dignity, which consists precisely in the fact that no human institution can ultimately dominate him, because he is open to the truth. In its very insistence on our capacity to know and recognize the truth, the encyclical is a most necessary apology for the stature of man against everything that would like to be seen as "culture *tout court*".

It is of course difficult, in view of the canon of methodology that has established itself today as bearing the "watermark of scholarly seriousness", to get a further hearing in public debate on the question of truth. It is therefore necessary to clear the ground through an argument about the nature of science and scholarly work, about truth and method, about the task of philosophy and its possible paths. The Pope did not see it as his task to tackle in the encyclical the quite practical question of whether, and how, truth can once more become "scientific" or "scholarly". But he does show why we have to set ourselves this task. He did not want to carry out the philosophers' task himself, but he was aware of the task of raising an objection to a self-destructive tendency in "culture *tout court*". Raising this objection is itself a genuinely philosophical step, conjures up the presence of the Socratic origins of philosophy, and thereby witnesses to the philosophical potentiality that lies in the biblical faith.

There is a kind of scientific attitude that is contrary to philosophy, that forbids it to deal with the question of the truth or makes the question impossible. Such a self-circumscription, such a contraction of reason cannot constitute the yardstick for philosophy, and science as a whole cannot end by rendering impossible man's real questions, without which it would itself remain an empty, and ultimately dangerous, bustle of activity. It cannot be the task of philosophy to submit itself to a methodological canon that in particular sectors of thought may be correct. Its particular task must be to reflect on science and scholarship as a whole, to achieve a critical comprehension of its nature, and at the same time to transcend it in a manner that can be rationally justified in an approach to what gives meaning to science and scholarship. Philosophy has always to ask about man himself and must therefore always be seeking its way toward life and death, toward God and eternity. To this end it will today have to handle right at the start a problem with that type of scientific and academic attitude that cuts men off from such questions, and starting from those problems, which our society sets right in front of our eyes, will have to try to open up a way to what is necessary and what answers our needs. In the history of modern philosophy there has never been a lack of such attempts, and even today there are sufficient heartening approaches being made toward opening the door to the question of truth, the door that leads out of the circle of language turning around on itself.[14] There is no doubt that the call uttered by the encyclical is in this sense critical of our current conception of culture, yet it is at the same time in a profound unity with essential elements of the spiritual struggle of

[14] In this respect, the list of names mentioned in no. 74 of the encyclical is certainly too modestly framed. One need only think, in our own century, of the importance of the phenomenological school, from Husserl to Scheler, and of the great movement of personalism, with names such as F. Ebner, E. Mounier, and G. Marcel, or to recall such great Jewish thinkers as Bergson, Buber, and Lévinas, to see that philosophy in the sense in which the encyclical is speaking is possible even today and is indeed at work in many and various forms.

the modern age. The confidence to seek for the truth and to find it is never anachronistic: it is precisely this that maintains the dignity of man, that breaks down particularism, and that leads men toward one another beyond the bounds of their cultural settings on the basis of their common dignity.

2. Culture and Truth

a. On the Nature of Culture

What we have reflected on thus far might be described as the disputation between the Christian faith as it finds expression in the encyclical and a certain type of modern culture, from which we have left out of consideration the side of culture associated with natural science and technology. Our attention was directed to the side of culture to do with humane studies. It would not be difficult to show that their helplessness in the face of the question of truth, which has in the meantime developed into a quite angry reaction to it, rests in the final analysis on the fact that these disciplines would like to use the same methodology, and to attain the same measure of certainty, as is available in empirical spheres. The methodological restriction of natural science to what can be tested by experiment has become a real certificate of scholarly seriousness, indeed, of being rational at all. The methodological renunciation that makes sense, and is, indeed, necessary, within the framework of empirical science thus becomes a barrier before the question of truth: this is fundamentally a question of truth and method and concerns the universality of a strictly empirical canon of methodology. As against this, the Pope is defending the multiplicity of paths followed by the human mind and, likewise, the breadth of rationality, which has to use varying methods in accordance with the nature of its object. Immaterial things cannot be approached with methods appropriate to what is material; we might thus very roughly summarize the Pope's objection to a one-sided form of rationality.

The dispute with modern culture, the dispute concerning truth and method, is the one basic thread running through the encyclical. Yet the question about truth and culture is also represented under yet another aspect, which essentially refers to the realm of religion as such. People nowadays often like to put forward the relativity of cultures to counter the universal claims of Christianity—which are grounded on the universal nature of truth. We can hear this as early as the eighteenth century in the writings of Gotthold Ephraim Lessing, who represented the three great religions in the parable of the three rings, of which one is the genuine and true ring, though there is no longer any way to establish this genuineness: the question of truth is insoluble and is replaced by the question of the healing and purifying effects of religion. At the beginning of our own century, Ernst Troeltsch then explicitly formulated the themes of the question concerning religion and culture, truth and culture. If at the outset he still posited Christianity as "the most concentrated revelation of personalist religious sensibility and practice, the only one that makes a complete break with the limitations and conditional forms of natural religion", in the course of his reflections the perception of the cultural determination of religion increasingly overlaid his view of the truth and left all religions subject to a cultural relativity. The validity of Christianity ended by becoming for him an "affair of Europeans": Christianity was for him the appropriate form of religion for Europe, whilst he recognized Buddhism and Brahmanism as having "absolute independence". For practical purposes, the question of truth has been rendered redundant, and cultural boundaries can no longer be transcended.[15]

An encyclical that is entirely directed toward the adventure of truth had therefore necessarily to put the question concerning truth and culture. It had to ask whether there can ever be a communion of cultures in the one truth—whether truth can be expressed for all men, beyond its cultural forms, or whether it is ultimately to be only dimly perceived as a convergence behind varying or even contradictory cultural forms.

In his encyclical, the Pope has contrasted a dynamic and communicative understanding of culture as against a static concept of culture that assumes set forms that merely stand side by side together and remain constant, being unable to transpose and merge into one another. He emphasizes that, if they "are deeply rooted in experience, cultures show forth the human being's characteristic openness to the universal and the transcendent".[16] Hence cultures, as the form of expression of the one being, man, are marked by the dynamics of man, which transcend all boundaries. Cultures are not therefore fixed once and for all in one single form; they have the inherent capacity for progression and metamorphosis, though also of course the risk of decadence. They are concerned with encounter and with mutual fertilization. Because the inner openness of man to God is more influential in them, the greater and more pure they are, the inward readiness for the revelation of God is written into them. Revelation is not something alien to them; rather, it corresponds to an inner expectation in the cultures themselves.

[15] See on this point H. Bürkle, *Der Mensch auf der Suche nach Gott—Die Frage der Religionen* [Man in search of God—The question concerning the religions], Amateca, no. 3 (Paderborn: Bonifatius, 1996), pp. 60–67.

[16] No. 70.

Theodore Haecker spoke in this connection about the advent character of the pre-Christian cultures,[17] and many and various studies in the history of religions have meanwhile been able to show quite clearly this progression of cultures toward the Logos of God, who became flesh in Jesus Christ.[18] In this context the Pope turns to the list of peoples in the story of Pentecost, in the Acts of the Apostles (2:7–11), which tells us how the witness to Jesus Christ can be heard through the medium of all languages and in all languages, that is, in all the cultures that present themselves in language. In all of them, the words of men become bearers of God's own utterance, of his own Logos. The encyclical says about this: "While it demands of all who hear it the adherence of faith, the proclamation of the Gospel in different cultures allows people to preserve their own cultural identity. This in no way creates division, because the community of the baptized is marked by a universality that can embrace every culture." [19]

On this basis, and taking as his example Indian culture, the Pope develops criteria which, in the general relationship of the Christian faith with pre-Christian cultures, should be observed whenever these cultures encounter the faith. He first briefly refers to the great spiritual striving for higher realms in Indian thought, which struggles to free mind and spirit from the limitations of time and space and thus effects that metaphysical opening up of man that has then also been given form in the thought of several important philosophical systems.[20] These few references show the universal tendency of great cultures, their transcending of time and space, and

---

[17] T. Haecker, *Vergil: Vater des Abendlandes* [Virgil: Father of the West], 5th ed. (Munich: Kösel, 1947), e.g., pp. 117f.

[18] See, e.g., Bürkle, *Mensch auf der Suche nach Gott*, pp. 14–40.

[19] No. 71.

[20] No. 72.

thus the forward impetus they impart to man's being and to his highest capacities. Therein exists the capacity of cultures to enter into dialogue with one another—in this case, dialogue between Indian cultures and the cultures that have developed on the basis of Christian faith. Thus, out of the inner contact with Indian culture, the first criterion arises, as it were, of itself: this consists in "the universality of the human spirit, whose basic needs are the same in the most disparate cultures".[21] From that a second criterion follows directly: "In engaging great cultures for the first time, the Church cannot abandon what she has gained from her inculturation in the world of Graeco-Latin thought. To reject this heritage would be to deny the providential plan of God."[22] Finally, the encyclical specifies a third criterion, which follows from the previous reflections on the nature of culture: One should take care "lest, contrary to the very nature of the human spirit, the legitimate defense of the uniqueness and originality of Indian thought be confused with the idea that a particular cultural tradition should remain closed in its difference and affirm itself by opposing other traditions."[23]

b. The Transcending of Cultures in the Bible and in the History of Faith

If the Pope insists that the particular cultural heritage that has once been won and has become a vehicle for the truth shared by God and man is then irreplaceable, the question then naturally arises of whether this is not then a Eurocentric character of the faith that is being canonized, a

[21] Ibid.
[22] Ibid.
[23] Ibid.

characteristic that does not seem to be eliminated even when in the continuing history of the faith new elements of heritage can enter, and indeed have entered, into the persisting identity, that which concerns us all, of the faith. There is no avoiding the question of how "Greek", and how "Latin", the faith actually is that originated, not in the Greek or the Latin world, but in the Semitic world of the Near East, within which Asia, Africa, and Europe have always rubbed shoulders and still do. The encyclical takes a definite view of this question, especially in its second chapter, on the development of philosophical thought within the Bible, and in the fourth chapter, on the fateful encounter of this wisdom of reason, which had developed within the faith, with the Greek philosophical wisdom. This is a question we meet in this book from various angles, again and again, and a few indications concerning it may be helpful at this stage.

Even within the Bible itself the intellectual material, both religious and philosophical, drawn from a variety of cultural worlds, is being worked into new form. The word of God reveals itself gradually in a process of encounters, in the course of man's search for answers to his ultimate questions. It did not simply fall directly down from heaven, but it is a real synthesis of cultures. Yet looking more deeply into it, we are able to perceive a process in which God struggles with man and gradually opens him up for his most profound Word, for himself: for the Son, who is the Logos. The Bible is not simply the expression of the culture of the people of Israel; rather, it is ever at odds with the natural temptation these people have simply to be themselves, to make themselves at home in their own culture. Faith in God and an assent to God's will are forever being wrung from this people against their own wishes and their own ideas. This faith is in continual opposition to Israel's own religious inclinations and to its own religious culture, which is inclined to express itself in the cult of high places, in worship of the queen of heaven, and in the claims to power of its own kingdom. From the anger of God and of Moses against the worship of the golden calf on Sinai, right down to the late postexilic prophets, it is always a matter of tearing Israel out of its cultural identity, contrary to its own religious wishes, so that it has, so to speak, to leave off the worship of its own nationality, the cult of "blood and soil", to bow down before the wholly other, the God who is not their own, who has created heaven and earth and who is the God of all peoples. The faith of Israel signifies a continual transcending of the limits of its own culture into the wide-open spaces of truth that is common to all.

The books of the Old Testament may in many respects seem less pious, less poetic, less inspired, than important passages in the holy books of other peoples. Yet the feature peculiar to them is this struggle of faith against what is Israel's own, in this leaving behind of one's own, which starts with the wandering of Abraham. Paul's struggle to break out from the limits of the law, which he wages on the basis of his encounter with the risen Jesus Christ, takes this fundamental movement of the Old Testament to its logical goal. This signifies the complete universalizing of the faith, which is freed from being proper to the social order of a particular people. All peoples are now invited to participate in this process of transcending their own heritage that first began in Israel; they are invited to turn to the God who, for his part, transcended his own limits in Jesus Christ, who has broken down "the dividing wall of hostility" between us (Eph 2:14) and in the self-deprivation of the Cross has led us toward one another. Faith in Jesus Christ is, therefore, of its nature, a continual opening of oneself, God's action of breaking into the human world and in response to this man's breaking out toward God, which at the same time leads men toward one another. Everything anyone possesses now belongs to everyone, and everything else becomes at the same time our own, this whole comprehended in the Father's words to the elder son: "All that is mine is yours" (Lk 15:31), which returns again in the high-priestly prayer of Jesus, as the Son addresses the Father: "All mine are thine, and thine are mine" (Jn 17:10).

This basic model likewise determines the encounter of the Christian message with Greek culture—which, of course, did not begin with the Christian mission but had already developed within the writings of the Old Testament, especially through its translation into Greek, and on the basis of that within early Judaism. This encounter was made possible because within the Greek world a similar process of self-transcendence had started to get underway. The Fathers did not just mix into the gospel a static and self-contained Greek culture. They could take up a dialogue with Greek philosophy and could make it an instrument of the gospel, wherever in the Hellenistic world the search for God had brought into being a self-criticism of that world's own culture and its own thought. Faith links the various peoples—beginning with the Germans and the Slavs, who came into contact with the Christian message in the era of tribal migrations, and right up to the peoples of Asia, Africa, and America—not with Hellenistic culture as such, but with Hellenistic culture in the form in which it transcended itself, which was the true point of contact for the interpretation of the Christian message. From that starting point, faith drew these peoples into the process of self-transcendence. Quite recently, Richard Schäffler aptly remarked that from the beginning, the Christian preaching "had demanded" of the peoples of Europe (which, in any case, did not exist as such before Christian missionary activity) "that they take leave . . . of every native god of Europe long before they set their sights on any cultures beyond Europe".[24] That helps us to understand why it was that the Christian proclamation sought points of contact with philosophy, not with religions. Where people did make this latter attempt, where for instance people tried to interpret Christ as the true Dionysius, the true Asclepius or Heracles, these attempts were soon rendered obsolete.[25] The fact that they sought points of contact, not with the religions, but with philosophy is connected with the fact that they were not canonizing a culture but did find it possible to enter into it at those points where it had itself begun to move out of its own framework, had started to take the path toward the wide spaces of truth that is common to all, and had left behind its comfortable place in what belonged to it. That is even today a fundamental indicator of the answer to the question concerning points of contact and transitions to other cultures and peoples. Faith cannot of course find points of contact with philosophies that exclude questions concerning the truth, but it can do so with movements that are trying to break out of the relativist prison. It can certainly not take over the old religions directly. Yet these religions can prepare such forms and usages, especially attitudes—reverence, humility, readiness to make sacrifices, kindness, love of one's neighbor, the hope of everlasting life.[26] Let me add that this seems to me to be also of some importance for the question of the significance of the religions for salvation. They do not save people, so to speak, as closed systems and through faithfulness to

---

[24] R. Schäffler, "Ent-europäisierung des Christentums?" [De-Europeanizing Christianity?], *Theologie und Glaube* 86 (1996): 121–31; quoted from p. 131.

[25] Cf. ibid., p. 125.

[26] These connections, with acceptance and transformation, the making of distinctions and rejection, are very well portrayed by Bürkle, *Mensch auf der Suche nach Gott*, pp. 18–40.

the system; rather, they bring redemption only when they bring men to the point of "asking after God" (as the Old Testament puts it), "seeking his face", "seeking the kingdom of God and his righteousness".

3. Religion, Truth, and Salvation

Let me pause for a moment here, because this touches on a fundamental question of human existence that is quite rightly one of the main questions in the current theological debate. For it is a matter of the true underlying motive that is the starting point of philosophy and to which it must always return; if they remain true to their tasks, philosophy and theology necessarily touch upon this question. It is the question: How is man healed? How does he become righteous? In facing this question, the ancient world thought mainly of death and of what comes after death; the contemporary world, which sees as uncertain the existence of the world beyond and, therefore, to a great extent leaves it out of the questions it asks, has nonetheless to seek after righteousness within time and, in doing so, cannot leave the problem to one side of how to get the better of death. In the debate about Christianity and world religions, of course, the real point at issue has remained, quite remarkably, that of how religions relate to eternal salvation. The question of how men can be saved still tends to be put in the classical manner. And then the theory has been fairly generally accepted that the religions are paths of salvation. Perhaps not the proper, ordinary path of salvation, but—if at all, then "extraordinary paths of salvation": one attains salvation through all the religions, that has become the current view.

This answer corresponds not only to the idea of tolerance and of respect for others, which so thrusts itself upon us these days. It also corresponds to the modern idea of God: God cannot reject people just because they know nothing of Christianity and happen to have grown up in other religions. He will accept their worship and religion just as he does ours. However obvious this theory seems to be at first sight—and it is meanwhile underpinned with many other arguments—it does still raise questions. For what each of these religions demands of people is, not just different from, but contrary to what is demanded by others. Meanwhile, in the face of the rising number of people who are not committed to any religion, this theory of universal salvation is even being extended to include nonreligious ways of life that are lived out seriously. Then it becomes quite true that things that contradict each other are seen as leading to the same goal—in other words, that we are once more facing the question of relativism. It is being silently assumed that all contents are basically of equal use. What is actually of any use, we do not know. Everyone just has to go his own way—to become happy in his own "façon", as Frederick II of Prussia used to say. Thus, by way of the various theories of salvation, relativism slips in through the back door again: the question of truth is excised from the question concerning religions and the matter of salvation. Truth is replaced by good intentions; religion remains in the subjective realm, because we cannot know what is objectively good and true.

a. The Inequality of Religions and Their Dangers

Do we just have to put up with this? Is there an inevitable choice to be made between dogmatic rigorism and a humane, kindly relativism? I think that in the theories we have just been talking about, there are three things people have not thought through carefully enough. First of all, religions (and, nowadays, also agnosticism and atheism) are seen as being all of the same kind. But that is by no means the case. There are in fact sick and degenerate forms of religion, which do not edify people but alienate them: the Marxist criticism of religions was not entirely based on delusions. And even religions whose moral value we must recognize, and which are on their way toward the truth, may become diseased here and there. In Hinduism (which is actually a collective name for a whole multitude of religions) there are some marvelous elements—but there are also negative aspects: involvement with the caste system; suttee [self immolation] for widows, which developed from beginnings that were merely symbolic; offshoots of the cult of the goddess Sakti—all these might be mentioned, to give just a little idea. Yet even Islam, with all the greatness it represents, is always in danger of losing balance, letting violence have a place and letting religion slide away into mere outward observance and ritualism. And there are of course, as we all know but too well, diseased forms of Christianity—such as when the crusaders, on capturing the holy city of Jerusalem, where Christ died for all men, for their part indulged in a bloodbath of Moslems and Jews. What that means is that religion demands the making of distinctions, distinctions between different forms of religion and distinctions within a religion itself, so as to find the way to its higher points. By treating all content as comparably valid and with the idea that all religions are different and yet actually the same, you get nowhere. Relativism is dangerous in quite particular ways: for the shape of human existence at an individual level and in society. The renunciation of truth does not heal man. How much evil has been done in history in the name of good opinions and good intentions is something no one can overlook.

b. The Question of Salvation

That brings us already to the second point, which is generally neglected. When people talk about the significance of religions for salvation, it is quite astonishing that they for the most part think only that all of them make eternal life possible and when they think like that, the concept of eternal life is neutralized, since everyone gets there in any case. But that sells the question of salvation short, in most inappropriate fashion. Heaven begins on earth. Salvation in the world to come presumes a righteous life in this world. Thus one cannot simply ask who will get to heaven and suppose that this disposes of the matter of heaven. We have to ask what heaven is and how it comes upon earth. Future salvation must make its mark in a way of life that makes a person "human" here and thus capable of relating to God. That in turn means that when we are concerned with the question of salvation, we must look beyond religions themselves and that this involves standards of right living that one cannot just relativize at will. I would say, therefore, that salvation begins with man becoming righteous in this world— something that always includes the twin poles of the individual and society. There are kinds of behavior that can never serve man's growth in righteousness and others that are always a part of man's righteousness. That means that salvation does not lie in religions as such, but it is connected to them, inasmuch as, and to the extent that, they lead man toward the one good, toward the search for God, for truth, and for love. The question of salvation therefore always carries within it an element of the criticism of religion, just as, contrariwise, it can build a positive relationship to religions. It has in any case to do with the unity of the good, with the unity of what is true—with the unity of God and man.

c. Conscience and Man's Capacity to Know the Truth

This statement leads to the third point I wish to address here. The unity and integrity of man has an organ: the conscience. It was Saint Paul who was daring enough to maintain that all men were capable of listening to their consciences and, thus, to separate the question of salvation from the matter of knowing and keeping the Torah and setting it on the common ground of the demands of conscience, in which the one God is speaking, and declaring to each one what is truly essential in the Torah: "When Gentiles who have not the law do by nature what the law requires, they are a law to themselves, even though they do not have the law. They show that what the law requires is written on their hearts, while their conscience also bears witness" (Rom 2:14–15). Paul does not say, If the pagans keep their own religion, that is good before the judgment-seat of God. On the contrary, he condemns the majority of the religious practices of his time. He points to another source—to what is written in everyone's hearts, the one good, from the one God. There are in any case two opposing concepts of the conscience here, although they are most often simply lumped together. For Paul, the conscience is the organ within all men— who are *one* man—which makes transparent the one God. In current thinking, on the other hand, the conscience appears as an expression of the absolute value of the subjective self, above and beyond which there can be no further judgment in the moral realm. What is good as such cannot be known. The one God cannot be known. As far as morality and religion are concerned, the self is the final arbiter. That is logical, if we have no access to the truth as such. Thus, in the modern concept of the conscience, the conscience represents the canonizing of relativism, of the impossibility of establishing common moral and religious standards; just as for Paul and for the Christian tradition it had been, on the contrary, the guarantee of the unity of man and the possibility of knowing God, of the common and binding character of one and the same good.[27] The fact that in every age there have been, and still are, "pagan saints" is because everywhere and in every age—albeit often with difficulty and in fragmentary fashion—the speech of the "heart" can be heard, because God's Torah may be heard within ourselves, in our creaturely being, as the call of duty, and it is thus possible for us to transcend what is merely subjective in order to turn toward each other and toward God; And that is salvation. Beyond that, what God makes of the poor broken pieces of our attempts at good, at approaching him, remains his secret, which we ought not to presume to try to work out.

Final Reflections

At the close of these reflections I should like to draw your attention to a methodological suggestion the Pope offers concerning the relationship between theology and philosophy, between faith and reason, because it addresses the practical question of how a renewal of theological and philosophical thinking, as the encyclical conceives it, might start to come about. The encyclical talks about a "circular movement" between theology and philosophy, understood in the sense that theology must always start from the word of God; but since this word is truth, theology will set it in relation with man's search for truth, with the struggle of reason for the truth, and will thus bring it into dialogue with philosophy. The believer's search for the truth will accordingly take place

[27] For the question of the conscience, I may refer the reader to my little book *Wahrheit, Werte, Macht* [Truth, values, power], new ed. (Frankfurt: Knecht, 1999), pp. 25–62.

through a movement in which listening to the word that has gone forth will continually be meeting with the seekings of reason. Thereby, on the one hand, faith becomes purer and more profound, while, on the other hand, thought is also enriched, because new horizons are opened up for it.

It seems to me that this idea of circularity could be taken a little farther: Philosophy, too, ought not to shut itself in within its own material, within what it has itself thought up. Just as it has to pay heed to empirical perceptions that emerge within the various scientific disciplines, so also it ought to regard the holy traditions of religions and espe-cially the message of the Bible as a source of perception and let itself be made more fertile by this. There is in fact no great philosophy that has not received illumination and guidance from religious tradition, whether we are thinking of the philosophy of Greece and that of India or of the philosophy that developed within Christianity or even of the modern philosophies that were persuaded of the auton-omy of reason and held this autonomy of reason to be the ultimate criterion of thought—but that still remained indebted for the great themes of thought that biblical faith had given to philosophy on the way: Kant, Fichte, Hegel, Schelling would be unthinkable without all that faith had already given, and even Marx, in the midst of his radical reinterpretation, drew his life from the horizon of hope, which he had taken from the Jewish tradition. When phi-losophy completely blanks out this dialogue with the thought of faith, it ends—as Jaspers once expressed it—in a "seri-ousness that is becoming empty".[28] In the end, it finds itself

---

[28] Quoted by J. Pieper, in "Die mögliche Zukunft der Philosophie" [The possible future of philosophy], in his *Schriften zum Philosophiebegriff*, pp. 315–23; quoted on p. 323.

forced to renounce the question of truth, that is, forced to give up itself. For a philosophy that no longer asks who we are, what we are here for, whether there is a God and an eternal life, has abdicated its role as a philosophy.

Finally, it may be helpful to refer to a commentary on the encyclical that appeared in the German newspaper *Die Zeit*, which has otherwise been somewhat distant from the Church. The commentator, Jan Ross, grasps the essence of this papal teaching document quite precisely when he says that the dethroning of theology and metaphysics has made thought "not just more free, but also more narrow"; indeed, he does not shy away from talking about people "rendered stupid by lack of faith". "Reason, in turning away from the ultimate questions, has rendered itself indifferent and boring, has resigned its competence where the keys to life are concerned: good and evil, death and immortality." The voice of the Pope, he says, "has given courage to many people and to entire nations and has sounded hard and piercingly in many people's ears and has even aroused hatred; but when it falls silent, that will be a moment of frightful silence." And indeed, if no one talks about God and man, about sin and grace, about death and eternal life, any more, then all the shouting and all the noise there is will only be a vain attempt to deceive ourselves about the voice of true humanity falling silent. With his candor, with the fearless frankness of faith, the Pope has stood up against the danger of such a silence, and in doing so he renders a service, not only to the Church, but to mankind. We should be grateful to him for that.

TRUTH—TOLERANCE—FREEDOM

1. FAITH—TRUTH—TOLERANCE

Are tolerance and belief in revealed truth opposites? Putting it another way: Are Christian faith and modernity compatible? If tolerance is one of the foundations of the modern age, then is not the claim to have recognized the essential truth an obsolete piece of presumption that has to be rejected if the spiral of violence that runs through the history of religions is to be broken? Today, in the encounter of Christianity with the world, this question arises ever more dramatically, and ever more widespread becomes the persuasion that renouncing the claim to truth in the Christian faith is the fundamental condition for a new universal peace, the fundamental condition for any reconciliation of Christianity with modernity.

The "Mosaic Distinction"—Or, Does the Question of Truth Belong in Religion?

The Egyptologist Jan Assmann recently reformulated this whole complex of questions and reinforced them with further argument, on the basis of a contrast drawn between biblical religion and Egyptian religion—indeed, polytheistic religion in general—and has expounded them in such a way that their whole historical and philosophical foundation is made clear.[1] It is worthwhile listening to what Assmann has to say, and it seems to me that his conception can be summed up in three theories. Assmann leaves the question of the historical Moses open, as also that of the original formulation of monotheistic faith in Israel, and he regards "Moses" as a placeholder for a memory, for the way that memory has shaped historical consciousness. It is in this sense that he talks about the "Mosaic distinction", which he sees as the true watershed in the history of religion as a whole. What he means by that is expressed as follows: "By the 'Mosaic distinction', I mean the introduction of a distinction between true and false in the realm of religion. Hitherto, religion had been based on the distinction between pure and impure, or between sacred and profane, and had no place at all for the idea of 'false gods' . . . , whom one should not worship."[2] The gods of the polytheistic religions, he says, are ranged in a functional equivalence one to another and have therefore always been able to be transposed or interchanged with each other. Religions, he says, always used to function as a medium of intercultural translation and transposition. "The divinities were international, because they were cosmic. . . . No one disputed the reality of foreign gods or the legitimacy of foreign ways of worshipping them. The concept of a religion being untrue was wholly alien to the ancient polytheistic

---

[1] J. Assmann, *Moses der Ägypter: Entzifferung einer Gedächtnisspur* (Munich and Vienna: Hanser, 1998) (Eng. ed.: *Moses the Egyptian: The Memory of Egypt in Western Monotheism*).

[2] See E. Zenger, "Was ist der Preis des Monotheismus? Die heilsame Provokation von J. Assmann" [At what price monotheism? The healthy provocation of J. Assmann], *Herder-Korrespondenz* 55 (2001): 186–91; quoted here, p. 187; cf. Assmann, *Moses der Ägypter*, pp. 17–23.

religions."[3] With the introduction of belief in a single god, something completely new and revolutionary occurred accordingly: this new kind of religion was of its nature an "anti-religion", which excluded everything that came before as "paganism" and was a medium, not of intercultural translation, but of intercultural alienation. From now on, the concept of "idolatry" as being the greatest of all sins began to develop: "In the portrayal of the golden calf, the biblical 'original sin' of monotheistic iconoclasm, ... the potential for hate and for violence was set down in writing, and in the history of monotheistic religions this has ever and again taken concrete form."[4] With this potential for violence, the story of the Exodus appears as the foundation myth of monotheistic religion and is at the same time an enduring depiction of the way it works.

The conclusion to be drawn is clear: the Exodus must be reversed; we must go back to "Egypt"—that is to say, the distinction between true and untrue in the realm of religion must be done away with; we must return to the realm of the gods, which are an expression of all the wealth and the variety of the cosmos and thus do not ever exclude one another but rather facilitate mutual understanding. The demand to reverse the Exodus runs through the whole of the Old Testament, in any case. It breaks out again and again in the story of the wanderings in the wilderness and is once more present, in dramatic fashion, at the end of the Old Testament literature, in the First Book of the Maccabees. There we are told about "lawless men", who suggested making "a covenant with the Gentiles", "for since we separated from them many evils have come upon us". They decide to live no longer

[3] Assmann, *Moses der Ägypter*, p. 19.
[4] Ibid., p. 20; cf. Zenger, "Was ist der Preis", p. 188.

according to the law of Moses but "to observe the ordinances of the Gentiles" (1 Macc 1:11–15).

For his part, Assmann depicts in detail the longing for Egypt, for a return to the time before the Mosaic distinction, from the Renaissance with its reverence for the *Corpus Hermeticum* as a primeval theology to the Enlightenment's Egyptian dreams, with Mozart's *Magic Flute* as the wonderful artistic embodiment of this longing. He demonstrates quite impressively how the religious and political conflicts of that age gave rise to this new interest in Egypt, the age that had lived through "the frightful experience of the wars of religion and, following the work of Thomas Hobbes and Baruch Spinoza, the religious controversies concerning atheism, polytheism, deism, and free-thinkers". As the "source of all religions", Egypt stood for the "ultimate convergence of reason and revelation, or nature and scripture." [5] There is no doubt that, in his own way, Assmann takes his place in this movement to get back behind the Exodus, simply because he sees the "Mosaic distinction", which is what the Exodus is for him, as the source of the evil, distorting religion and bringing intolerance into the world. If I have rightly understood him, Spinoza's formula "Deus sive natura" [God, that is, nature; God and nature are indistinguishable] is at the same time the summary of what is meant by this return, by his notion of "Egypt": the distinction between true and false can be removed from religion if the distinction between God and cosmos disappears, if the divine and the "world" are once more seen as an undivided whole. The distinction between true and false in religion is indissolubly linked with the distinction between God and the world. The return to Egypt is the return to the gods, inasmuch as it rejects a God who

[5] Assmann, *Moses der Ägypter*, p. 40.

stands over against the world but regards the gods merely as symbolical forms of expression for nature, which is divine.

At the end of Assmann's book, however, yet a third dimension of the Mosaic distinction becomes apparent, which affects the existential aspect of religion, so to speak, and which speaks from the heart to modern man: With the Mosaic distinction, so Assmann tells us, there appears inevitably "the consciousness of sin and the longing for redemption". Assmann further says that "sin and redemption are not themes of Egyptian religion".[6] What is characteristic for Egypt, he says, is rather the "moral optimism to 'eat your bread with enjoyment', conscious that 'God has already approved what you do'— one of the Egyptian verses in the Bible" (Eccles 9:7–10).[7] "It looks", writes Assmann, "as though sin came into the world with the Mosaic distinction. Perhaps that is the most serious reason for questioning the Mosaic distinction."[8] One thing in all this has certainly been correctly perceived: The question of truth and the question of what is good cannot be separated from each other. If we can no longer recognize what is true and can no longer distinguish it from what is false, then it becomes impossible to recognize what is good; the distinction between good and evil loses its basis.

It is quite clear that in the theories here briefly outlined, the essential contents of the crisis of Christianity, which is at present becoming ever more acute, have been quite precisely formulated, and that any effort to understand and to renew Christianity must face up to the questions they pose. For here the fundamental problem of our time, the question of truth and toleration and, likewise, the whole area of

[6] Ibid., p. 281.
[7] Ibid., p. 282.
[8] Ibid.

questions concerning Christianity's place in the history of religions and, likewise again, the existential problem of guilt and redemption, has been laid bare in one single great interconnected context. Obviously, no satisfactory answer to all this can be given within the limits of one lecture; I can only try to suggest some lines along which the conversation, so it seems to me, will have to move.

Perhaps it will be useful, before we enter into the discussion about these problems, to indicate one more variant of the renunciation of truth in religion, which arises this time, not from history, but from philosophical thought—the theses Wittgenstein posed concerning our subject. G. Elizabeth M. Anscombe has summarized the views of her teacher, Wittgenstein, on this question in two theses: "1. There is no such thing as being true for a religion. This is perhaps suggested when someone says: 'This religious statement is not the same as a statement of natural science.' 2. Religious faith may be compared rather to a person's being in love than to his being persuaded that something is true or false."[9] In accordance with this logic, Wittgenstein noted, in one of his many notebooks, that it would make no difference to the Christian religion whether or not Christ had actually done some of the things recounted concerning him or whether indeed he had existed at all. This corresponds to the thesis of Bultmann that believing in a God who is the Creator of heaven and earth does not mean that

[9] I am relying here on what J. Seifert has said. Seifert refers to Elizabeth M. Anscombe, *Paganism, Superstition and Philosophy*, in Mariano Crespo, ed., *Menschenwürde und Ethik* [Human dignity and ethics] (Heidelberg: Winter, 1998), pp. 93–105; L. Wittgenstein, *Vermischte Bemerkungen / Culture and Value*, p. 32; L. Wittgenstein, *Über Gewißheit*, ed. G. E. M. Anscombe and G. H. von Wright (Frankfurt: Suhrkamp, 1969), p. 29 [English trans., *On Certainty*, trans. Denis Paul and G. E. M. Anscombe (Oxford: Blackwell, 1969)].

we believe that God *really* created heaven and earth but only that we understand ourselves as being his creatures and thereby live a more meaningful life. Similar concepts have in the meantime become widespread in Catholic theology and may be heard, more or less clearly enunciated, in preaching.[10]

The faithful sense this and are asking themselves whether they have been being made fools of. Living in beautiful fictions may be something that people who hold theories about religion can do; for the person who is asking himself how he can live and die, and for what, they are not enough. Renouncing the claim to truth, which would be a renunciation of the Christian faith itself, is here being sugared over by allowing faith to go on existing as a kind of being-in-love, with its lovely subjective consolations or as a kind of make-believe world side by side with the real world. Faith is transposed onto the plane of play, of make-believe, whereas hitherto it had mattered on the plane of life itself.[11] Faith that is make-believe is at any rate something fundamentally different from faith that is believed and lived out. It does not show us the way but is merely decorative. It does not help us in living or in dying; at most it provides us with a little change, a little

[10] This approach has been worked out consistently by G. Hasenhüttl, *Glaube ohne Mythos* [Faith without myth], 2 vols., 2nd ed. (Mainz: Matthias-Grünewald-Verlag, 2001).

[11] In the article to which we have referred, Seifert remarks that "For Wittgenstein, the religious person and the nonreligious live, as it were, in two make-believe worlds and move upon different planes without contradicting one another." According to Wittgenstein, in religious statements nothing is basically being said ... "just as little as would be said in a game of chess or of checkers about the people represented by the pieces outside of these games. Religion must there be interpreted, he said, not in the same way as meaningful sentences with some claim to truth, but in a purely anthropological and entirely subjective sense, like a game that is simply someone's personal preference."

fine appearance—but only the appearance, and that is not enough for living and for dying.

Interchangeability and War between the Gods

Now let us turn back to Assmann. What about the "Deus sive natura", the good-natured and tolerant gods who do not inquire about truth, what about being set free from the distinction between sin and what is good? How is that lived? How "true" is it? For Assmann proposes his theses as a serious scholar, and thus the question of whether they are true must at any rate be directed to them. He also recommends a way. So we will also have to ask whether and how we can follow that way. When we look into the actual history of polytheistic religions, then the picture he sketches—a rather vague one, by the way—appears itself as a myth. In the first place, polytheistic religions differ considerably among themselves. In not a few of them, there is an awareness in the background, in some shape or form, of the one God who is truly God. In Buddhism, and in some parts of Hinduism, as also in late forms of Platonism, the gods appear as the powers belonging to a world that is only appearance, or at any rate is not the ultimate one, and should be left behind if one really wishes to attain full salvation. The theory that polytheistic gods are completely interchangeable and are hence a medium for cultural interchange and greater understanding can claim the support of the religious policy of the Imperium Romanum but by no means corresponds to the history of polytheism in general.[12] Reading Homer is quite enough for us to remember

[12] According to Assmann, *Moses der Ägypter*, pp. 74ff., the tradition of translating the foreign names of gods goes back to the Mesopotamian "literary

the wars between the gods and to remember that human wars were regarded as reflecting and resulting from the wars of the gods. It is illuminating to read what Athanasius of Alexandria—who was an Egyptian and had himself lived in the age of the gods—has to say about this:

> Once, when people still gave worship to the gods, the Greeks and barbarians went to war and showed themselves without mercy toward their fellowmen. It was practically impossible to travel by land or by sea without taking a sword in one's hand, in view of their endless fighting with one another. They spent their entire lives under arms; the sword took the place of the staff and was the only way to get through life. Although they sacrificed to the gods, as we have said, their reverence for the gods in no way helped to correct this attitude.[13]

In the conversion of the peoples to Christ, Athanasius sees the fulfillment of the prophecy of Isaiah the prophet that swords would be beaten into ploughshares (Is 2:4), and he says:

> This prophecy has nothing incredible about it. For as long as the barbarians, with their naturally uncivilized behavior, offered sacrifice to their gods, they became enraged with one another and could not pass one hour without their swords. Yet when they accepted the teaching of Christ, they left off

studies" of the third century before Christ. He then refers us to the Akkadian assimilation of the Sumerian pantheon and sees in this a process that developed into a "general technique of culture". His great example of this universalistic concept of divinity, then, is Isis, as she was understood and invoked in the "Graeco-Egyptian" cult of Isis. It is undisputed that such processes of translation and transposition took place amid the cultural amalgamations in great empires that included various peoples and cultures, above all on account of political motivations, but the problem of polytheism goes far beyond these processes.

[13] Athanasius of Alexandria, *De incarnationi verbi* 51:4; *Sources chrétiennes*, vol. 199, ed. C. Kannengiesser (Paris, 1973), p. 450.

war straightaway and turned to cultivation, and, instead of
arming themselves with sword in hand, they lifted their hands
in prayer—in brief, instead of waging war among themselves, they arm themselves against the devil and against the
demons and are victorious through their moderation and the
virtues of their souls.[14]

Certainly, this picture is stylized and schematic, in accordance with apologetic purposes. Yet Athanasius certainly had
to reckon that some readers had lived in the time before the
Christian mission and could not simply let his fancy have
free reign. What he says is quite enough to demythologize
the picture of the oh-so-peaceful world of the gods, however one might judge its historical content in detail.

We can note this: the gods were by no means always peaceful and interchangeable. They were just as often, indeed more
often, the reason for people using violence against each other;
and we also know of the phenomenon of the gods of one
religion becoming the demons of another. Besides that, the
Bible sets the reality of Egypt side by side with the dreams of
Egypt in the most realistic fashion: the real Egypt had been,
not a land of lovely freedom and peace, but a "house of slavery", a land of oppression and of wars. And now we must go
one step farther. Polytheistic religions are not a static reality
that once existed as an essentially identical entity, which we
can restore whenever we wish. They are entirely subject to
historical processes, which we can observe with particular
clarity in late antiquity. Those myths that initially express
men's experience of the world and of living, which are lived
out in worship and given form in poetry, increasingly—in
the very process of being given concrete shape—lose their
credibility. The way things developed in Graeco-Roman

[14] Ibid., 52:2–3, p. 452.

antiquity shows us in exemplary fashion how people's growing awareness of wider realms inevitably, and with increasing urgency, raises the question of whether the whole of this is actually true. The question concerning the truth was not invented by "Moses". It inevitably appears wherever people's consciousness attains a certain maturity.

Something like Wittgenstein's fiction (if I may so term the theory concerning "games", which relativizes all religions) then automatically offers itself as an approach to the problem. Graeco-Roman antiquity provides some classic instances of this. In his important book *Chrēsis*, Christian Gnilka has given a detailed picture of the way the question of truth broke into the world of the ancient gods and of Christianity's encounter with this situation. Characteristic of this process is the figure of the Roman Pontifex Maximus, C. Aurelius Cotta, who is described by Cicero; in his functions as augur and as head of the Collegium Pontificum, Cotta represented the pagan religion of that era. In conformity with his office, Cotta insisted on the conscientious observation of the rites of the public cult and declared that he would defend the "views" (*opiniones*) concerning the gods inherited from the forefathers and would never let himself be diverted from this.[15] Yet at home, among friends, the same Cotta showed himself to be an academic sceptic who raised the question of truth. He would have liked to be persuaded by the truth, rather than by mere acceptance, and concluded from his reflections that it was to be feared that the gods did not exist at all. "The criterion of truth, when introduced into the world of the ancient gods, had the effect of an explosive device", Gnilka

---

[15] C. Gnilka, *Chrēsis: Die Methode der Kirchenväter im Umgang mit der antiken Kultur* [Chrēsis: The method of the Church Fathers in dealing with classical culture], vol. 2: *Kultur und Conversion* (Basel: Schwabe, 1993), p. 15.

observes.[16] Assmann himself showed how this schizophrenia led to a fiction defended by the state: for the uninitiated the gods remained as entities necessary to maintain the state, while the initiated could see through them as nonentities.[17]

The question concerning the truth had arisen among the pre-Socratic thinkers and had found its most sublime form in the thought of Socrates. It may be helpful, in order to perceive the whole depth of the question, to give at least a quick glance at Socrates. For the entry of the question of truth into the realm of the gods, the short dialogue with Eutyphron seems to me especially helpful, with the priest who is still entirely caught up in the myths and their careful observance in the cult but who in conversation with Socrates becomes ever more entangled in contradictions. Finally, Eutyphron has to admit, in the face of Socrates' penetrating questions, that the same thing is both loved and hated by the gods. To the question, "So along these lines, what is pious and what is impious would be the same, Eutyphron?" he has to answer, "That is how it is." [18] This brings us to a very important point. Socrates had referred to war among the gods. Guardini comments here: "Everything is divine. There are powers everywhere, and each one is a part of existence. . . . All powers are swallowed up in the unity of the world, which is itself the ultimate divinity and comprehends all contradictions. . . . The fact that they have to fight represents the necessary tragedy." [19] That means that the equation "Deus sive

[16] Ibid., p. 16.

[17] Assmann, *Moses der Ägypter*, pp. 272ff.

[18] *Eutyphron* 8a (Oxford ed., vol. 1).

[19] R. Guardini, *Der Tod des Sokrates*, 5th ed. (Mainz and Paderborn: Matthias-Grünewald-Verlag, 1987), p. 38 [English trans., *The Death of Socrates: An Interpretation of the Platonic Dialogues: Euthyphro, Apology, Crito and Phaedo* (New York: Sheed and Ward, 1948).

natura", the renunciation of the Mosaic distinction, does not mean universal reconciliation but that the universe is irreconcilable. For being itself is now contradictory; war derives from existence itself; good and evil are ultimately indistinguishable. Ancient tragedy is the interpretation of existence on the basis of men's experience of the contradictory world, which inevitably brings forth guilt and failure. In his system of the ideal, which develops itself in dialectical steps, Hegel was basically taking up this view of the world again and, of course, trying to portray its reconciliation in the totally comprehensive synthesis as a hope for the future and thus, at the same time, as a solution of the tragedy. The Christian eschatological direction has here been amalgamated with the ancient vision of the unity of being and now appears to "assume" them both and thus to explain everything. Yet the dialectic remains dreadfully cruel, and the reconciliation merely apparent. At the moment when Marx transformed Hegel's speculation into a concrete conception for the shaping of history, this cruelty became visible, and we have become witnesses of all its cruelty. For, quite simply, it is the case that the dialectic of progress, speaking in practical terms, requires its sacrificial victims: in order for the progress brought about by the French Revolution to be made, people had to accept the sacrifices it demanded—that is what we are told. And in order for Marxism to set up the reconciled society, the mass sacrifice of human beings was necessary; there was no other way: There we see the mythological dialectic translated into facts. Man becomes the plaything of progress; as an individual, he does not count; here he is merely fodder for the cruel god, "Deus sive natura". The theory of evolution teaches us something similar: Progress has its price. And the present-day experiments with man, who is being turned into an "organ bank", show us the entirely practical application of such ideas, in which man himself takes further evolution in hand.

The Inevitability of the Question of Truth and the Alternatives in the History of Religions

Let us return to our theme. The notion that the gods are peacefully interchangeable will not stand up to reality. They have, rather, a profoundly irreconcilable aspect, which is founded in the contradictions of being itself. The second point we have noted is even more important in this connection: The question concerning truth cannot be avoided. It is necessary to man and particularly concerns the ultimate decisions in his life: Is there a God? Is there such a thing as truth? Is there such a thing as good? We may say that the "Mosaic distinction" is the same as the Socratic distinction. At this point, the inner basis—and the inner necessity—of the historical encounter of Hellas and the Bible becomes apparent. What unites the two is precisely the question of truth, and of good as such, which they put to religion, the Mosaic-Socratic distinction, as we may now call it. This encounter began to take place long before the beginning of the synthesis between biblical faith and Greek thought, which was the work of the Church Fathers. It was already happening in the middle of the Old Testament, above all in the wisdom literature and in the memorable step of translating the Old Testament Scriptures into Greek, a step in the process of intercultural encounter with the widest possible implications. Certainly, in the ancient world the issue of the Socratic question remained open, different in Plato from what it is in Aristotle. In that sense, there remained an expectation within the Greek world, to which the Christian message appeared to be the longed-for answer. This open expectation, seen in

Greek thought as an outward-looking attitude, was one of the main reasons for the success of the Christian mission.[20]

Let us reiterate that the polytheism of the "nature religions" is not a static entity to which one could return at any time. Religious development, so far as we can see, goes through three stages—leaving open the question of whether there were other forms of worship that came before polytheism. If here, for the sake of simplicity, we regard polytheism as the first stage, it then becomes increasingly subjected to the criticism of enlightenment, that is, to questions concerning its truth, which gradually dissolve it and, after a phase of division of truth (the useful fiction and the knowledge of the initiated), then cause its collapse. At this point, in the Mediterranean world, and later in the sphere of Arabia and in parts of Asia, monotheism offers a reconciliation between enlightenment and religion: the Divinity toward which reason is moving is the same as the Divinity who shows himself in revelation. Revelation and reason correspond to one another. There is the "true religion"; the question concerning truth and the question of God have been reconciled.[21] Yet the ancient world does show us another possible outcome, which today is once more of immediate interest. On the one hand, there is the Christian interpretation of Plato, the amalgamation of the Greek expectation and its question concerning truth with the Christian answer and its claim to truth, in which the basic Greek material is taken up and at the same time fundamentally reshaped. There is, on the other

[20] For more on this point, and on what follows, see the section: "The Truth of Christianity?" in this book.

[21] This synthesis of rational religion and biblical revelation, of which the foundations were laid in the Old Testament, is the central theme of the Church Fathers; Augustine, in his arguments with Plotinus and Porphyry in *De civitate Dei*, gave it its final systematic form.

hand, also the late Platonism of Porphyry and Proclus, which aims to refute the Christian claims and to offer a new foundation for polytheism—the other face of Platonic thought. Now it is the sceptical position itself that becomes the foundation of polytheism: Because one cannot know the divine, one can only worship it in place holders of many forms, in which the mystery of the cosmos and its multiplicity, too great to be comprehended in any name, is expressed.[22] In late antiquity, this attempted restoration of a polytheism that was given a philosophical justification and the appearance of rationality could not endure. It remained an academic construction, from which the necessary power of hope and truth did not emanate. This was the more so, since its originators could not quite renounce the division of truth. The polytheistic dedications and rituals were seen as the way for the many, those who were incapable of higher things, while the philosophers intended for themselves, as the "chosen spirits", the "royal way", which climbed up above all this in mystical union into the ineffable sphere. Here again it was Christianity's luck that it opened up the way of the simple ones, as the true "royal way" in fellowship with him who lived in the bosom of God and who saw God.

Present-day attempts to offer a way of getting back to Egypt, a "redemption" from Christianity and from its teaching about sin, will fare the same. For here too everything remains in the sphere of fiction, in what can be thought out academically but is not enough for living. Certainly, the flight from

---

[22] See on this point Gnilka, *Chrēsis*, 2:9–55. Yet another stage in the encounter between Christianity and Platonism occurred at the end of the fifth or the beginning of the sixth century, when Pseudo-Dionysius reinterpreted the world view of Proclus in a Christian sense, transformed his polytheism into the teaching about choirs of angels, and became, with his negative theology, one of the fathers of Christian mysticism.

the one God and his claims will continue. And scepticism will continue, for there seem to be stronger grounds for this than in the ancient world. Christianity's claim to be true cannot correspond to the standard of certainty posed by modern science, because the form of verification here is of a quite different kind from the realm of testing by experiment; because the kind of experiment demanded—pledging one's life for this—is of a quite different kind. The saints, who have undergone the experiment, can stand as guarantors of its truth, but the possibility of disregarding this strong evidence remains. And thus people will continue to look for other solutions, to seek them in the form of mystical union, for the attainment of which advice and techniques are, and will be, available. In that sense, what late Platonism has to offer remains on the menu for the day; I would assign what Assmann says to this category.

Yet does not Asia show us a way out? Religion that works without having to raise any claim to be true? This question will, without doubt, form the theme for other future dialogues. Just a suggestion here. Even Buddhism has its own way of raising the question of truth. It asks about redemption from the suffering that arises from the thirst for life. Where is the place of salvation? Buddhism comes to the conclusion that it is not to be found in the world, in the whole of apparent being. This is in its entirety suffering, a circle of rebirth and ever-new entanglement. The way of enlightenment is the way out of the thirst for being into what seems to us to be nonbeing, Nirvana. That means that in the world itself there is no truth. Truth comes by leaving the world. In that sense, the question of truth is swallowed up in the question of redemption—or perhaps abolished in it. There are gods, but they belong in the world of what is temporary, not to the ultimate salvation. Only in the Hinayana version is this view strictly adhered to. Mahayana Buddhism has a much stronger social dimension, help toward the redemption of others and for the helper. Yet the basic expectation of the annihilation of existence and of the person of the individual remains intact, if far removed into the future.[23] There can be no talk of "Deus sive natura" here. The world in itself is suffering—and is thereby also void of truth—and only removal from the world can in the end be salvation. This is a matter of existential attitudes, which include a view of the world that is far removed from the Western vision and also from that of "Egyptian" polytheism and which stands as an alternative over against the Christian view of the world, with its fundamental affirmation of the world as creation. This way, of all others, does not of course dispense us from facing the question of truth.

Christian Tolerance

One final reflection is needed. Assmann praises the way that the gods may be transposed one into another, since it appears as a path of intercultural and interreligious peace. The "intolerance" of the First Commandment and the condemnation of idolatry as a fundamental sin are opposed to this. This, in turn, looks like a canonization of intolerance, as we have seen. Now, it is true that the one God is a "jealous God", as the Old Testament calls him. He unmasks the gods, for in his light it becomes clear that the "gods" are not God, that the plural of "God" is as such a lie. But a lie always means a lack of freedom, and it is no mere chance, above all no

[23] See H. Bürkle, *Der Mensch auf der Suche nach Gott—Die Frage der Religionen* [Man in search of God—The question concerning the religions], Amateca, no. 3 (Paderborn: Bonifatius, 1996), pp. 143–60.

untruth, that in Israel's memory Egypt appears as the house of slavery, as the place of lack of freedom. Only the truth makes us free. Wherever usefulness is set above truth, as happens in the case of the division of truth we were talking about earlier, then man becomes a slave to practical purposes and to those who make the decisions about what is useful and practical. In this sense the "demythologizing" is necessary, to strip the gods of their false glamor and thereby of their false power, so that the "truth" of them may stand out, that is, to explain which worldly powers and real entities stand behind them. To put it another way: when this "demythologization", this unmasking, has taken place, their relative truth can and must appear.

There are, accordingly, two phases in the Christian relationship with "pagan" religions, which of course are interconnected and inwardly involved with each other and cannot be assigned places in a purely temporal sequence. The first phase is the alliance of the Christian faith with enlightenment, which dominates Christian literature from Justin to Augustine and beyond: those who are propagating Christianity put themselves on the side of philosophy, of enlightenment, against religion, against the divided truth of those such as C. Aurelius Cotta. They see the seeds of the Logos, of divine rationality, not in the religions, but in the movement toward rationality that destroyed these religions. But a second point of view becomes ever clearer, in which the connection with the religions and the limits of enlightenment emerge. Gregory the Great's thought seems to me quite clearly characteristic of this. In a first letter of his—still in the phase of enlightenment—he writes to the English King Ethelbert: "Therefore, my most illustrious son, carefully preserve the grace you have received from God. . . . Inflame your noble zeal. . . . Suppress the worship of idols; destroy their

temples and altars. Uplift the virtues of your subjects by out-
standing behavior and morality." [24]

Yet Gregory reflects further on the question within himself, and just a month after that letter he writes quite differently to a group of missionaries who have just departed and
to a certain Mellitus:

> But when, with the grace of almighty God, you reach our
> most reverend brother, Bishop Augustine, then tell him that
> I have been reflecting at length about one matter concern-
> ing the Englishmen. That is, one should by no means destroy
> the temples of this people's idols; rather, simply destroy the
> idols to be found within them. . . . When the people see that
> we are not destroying their temples, then they will nonethe-
> less abandon their errors and will that much more joyfully
> turn to the knowledge and the worship of the true God in
> their accustomed places. [25]

Gregory also suggests that the ceremonies and animal sacrifices at the festivals should be transformed in honor of the
saints and martyrs and that the animals that are slaughtered as
sacrifices should be eaten on those occasions. This shows
what we call continuity in worship. The holy place remains
holy, and the intentions and petitions of prayer, and the worship of the divine, which formerly took place, are taken up
and transformed, given a new significance. In Rome you can
study that all over the place. In a name like Santa Maria sopra
Minerva transformation and continuity are equally demonstrated. The gods are no longer gods. As such, they have

[24] *Ep.* XI, 37. See on this point J. Richards, *Consul of God: The Life and
Times of Gregory the Great* (London: RKP, 1980); German trans., *Gregor der
Große: Sein Leben—seine Zeit* (Graz: Verlag Styria, 1983); ref. to pp. 235–56,
especially p. 250f., in the German edition.

[25] *Ep.* XI, 56. See Richards, *Gregor der Große*, pp. 251f.

been overthrown: the question of truth has itself deprived them of divinity and brought about their downfall. Yet at the same time their truth has emerged: that they were a reflection of divinity, a presentiment of figures in which their hidden significance was purified and fulfilled. In that sense, there is such a thing as the "transposition" of the gods, who, as intimations, as steps in the search for the true God and for his reflection in creation, may become messengers of the one God.

Finally we must once more return to Assmann's closing theory, that with the Mosaic distinction the concept of sin also entered the world. "Sin and redemption are not Egyptian themes", was what we heard. Yet they certainly are themes of most world religions, which sought with multitudes of sacrifices—including human sacrifices—to reconcile the divinities and to find expiation. But we cannot take this dispute farther here. One thing seems to me important for the question we are facing: the themes of what is true and what is good cannot in fact be separated one from another. Plato was right when he identified the highest divinity with the idea of good. To put it the other way round: if we cannot know the truth about God, then the truth about what is good and what is bad remains equally inaccessible. Then there is no good and evil; only the reckoning up of consequences remains: ethics is replaced by calculation. To put it still more clearly: the three questions, concerning truth and good and God, are but one single question. And if there is no answer, then as far as the essential things in our life are concerned, we are groping around in the dark. Then human existence is truly "tragic"—and then, of course, we understand what redemption really means. The Bible's concept of God recognizes God as good, as the One who is Good (see Mk 10:18). This concept of God attains its climax in the Johannine declaration: God is love (1 Jn 4:8). Truth and love are identical. This sentence—if the whole of its demand is understood—is the surest guarantee of tolerance; of an association with truth, whose only weapon is itself and, thereby, love.

2. FREEDOM AND TRUTH

1. *The Question*

In the consciousness of mankind today, freedom is largely regarded as the greatest good there is, after which all other good things have to take their place. In legislation, artistic freedom and freedom of speech take precedence over every other moral value. Values that conflict with freedom, that could lead to its being restricted, appear as shackles, as "taboos", that is to say, as relics of archaic prohibitions and anxieties. Political action has to demonstrate that it furthers freedom. Even religion can make an impression only by depicting itself as a force for freedom for man and for mankind. In the scale of values with which man is concerned, to live a life worthy of humanity, freedom seems to be the truly fundamental value and to be the really basic human right of them all. The concept of truth, on the other hand, we greet rather with some suspicion: we recall how many opinions and systems have already laid claim to the concept of truth; how often the claim to truth in that way has been the means of limiting freedom. In addition there is the scepticism fostered by natural science regarding anything that cannot be precisely explained or demonstrated: that all seems in the final analysis to be just subjective judgment, which cannot claim to be obligatory for people in general. The modern attitude to truth shows itself most succinctly in Pilate's words:

What is truth? Anyone who claims to be serving truth with his life, and with his words and actions, must be prepared to be regarded as an enthusiast or a fanatic. For "Our line of sight to all above is blocked"; this quotation from Goethe's *Faust* sums up the way we all feel about it.

There is no doubt that we have reason enough, in the face of a sentimental and all-too-confident claim to truth, to ask: What is truth? Yet we have just as much reason to put the question: What is freedom? What do we actually mean when we praise freedom and set it on the highest level of our scale of values? I believe that the content generally associated with the demand for freedom is most accurately described in the words Karl Marx once used to express his dream of freedom. The state of affairs in the future Communist society will make it possible "to do one thing today, another tomorrow, to go shooting in the morning and fishing in the afternoon and in the evening look after the cattle, to indulge in criticism after dinner, just as the fancy takes me".[1] It is just in this way that the average attitude, without thinking about it, understands by "freedom" the right, and the practical possibility, of doing everything we wish and not having to do anything we do not wish to do. Putting it another way, freedom would mean that our own will was the only criterion for our action and that this will would be able to want to do anything and also be able to put into practice anything it wanted. At this point the question arises, of course: How free in fact is our will? And how rational is it?—And, is an irrational will truly a free will? Is irrational freedom truly freedom? Is it really a good thing? Does not the definition of freedom, as being

---

[1] K. Marx and F. Engels, *Werke* in 39 vols. (Berlin, 1961–1971), 3:33; quoted by K. Löw, *Warum fasziniert der Kommunismus?* [Why does Communism fascinate us?] (Cologne: Deutscher Instituts-Verlag, 1980), p. 65.

able to decide to do anything and being able to do what we
decide, have to be expanded to include the connection with
reason, with mankind as a whole, in order to avoid becoming tyranny and unreason? And will not seeking for the common reason of all men, and thus the mutual compatibility of
freedoms, be a part of the interplay of reason and the will? It
is obvious that the question of truth is concealed within the
question of the rationality of the will and its relation to reason.

We are brought up against such questions, not merely by
abstract philosophical reflections, but also by our quite concrete situation in a society in which the demand for freedom
is indeed unbroken yet doubts concerning all previous forms
of movements for freedom and systems for ensuring freedom appear in ever more dramatic form. Let us not forget
that Marxism, as the one great political force of our twentieth century, made its appearance with the claim to be bringing a new world of freedom and of free people. This very
promise of knowing the scientifically guaranteed way to freedom, and of creating the new world, drew to it many of the
boldest spirits of our age; ultimately, it even appeared as the
force through which the Christian teaching of redemption
could be transformed into a realistic practical means for
liberation—as the force that could bring the Kingdom of
God as the true kingdom of men. The collapse of realist
socialism in the East European states has not quite laid aside
all such hopes, and here and there they still subsist, silently
awaiting some new form. There was no real spiritual defeat
corresponding to the political and economic collapse, and
to that extent the questions raised by Marxism have by no
means been solved. Even so, the fact that his system did not
work in the way that had been promised is quite clear. No
one can any longer seriously deny that what was supposed to
be a movement to bring freedom was, along with National

Socialism, the greatest system of slavery in modern history: the extent of the cynical destruction of human beings and of the world is very often passed over in shame and silence, but no one can deny it any longer.

The moral superiority of the liberal system in politics and the economy that thus emerged arouses no enthusiasm, even so. The number of those who have no share in the fruits of this freedom is too great—those, indeed, who lose every kind of freedom: being out of work has once more become a mass phenomenon; the feeling of not being needed, of being superfluous, torments people no less than material poverty. Unscrupulous exploitation is becoming widespread; organized crime is making use of the opportunities of the free world; and in the midst of it all the ghost of meaninglessness is wandering around. At the Salzburg Further Education sessions in 1995, the Polish philosopher Andrej Szczypiorski described in pitiless clarity the dilemma of freedom that came into being with the fall of the wall; it is worthwhile listening to him at some length:

> No doubt can remain that capitalism was a great step forward. And equally, no doubt can remain that it failed to fulfill expectations. In capitalism, the cry of the great masses is always to be heard, the masses whose cravings are unfulfilled.... The decline of the Soviet conception of the world and of man embodied in its political and social practice meant the liberation of millions of human lives out of serfdom. But in terms of the heritage of European thought, in the light of the tradition of the last two hundred years, the anti-Communist revolution also means the end of the illusions of the Enlightenment, that is, the destruction of the intellectual concept that formed the basis of the development of early Europe.... A remarkable age of growing uniformity in development, hitherto unknown anywhere, has

begun. And suddenly it has appeared—probably for the first time in history—as if there were only a single recipe, a single way forward, one single model, and just one way of shaping the future. And people lost their belief in the sense of the transformations that were taking place. They lost hope in the possibility of changing the world at all and in its being worth the effort to change the world.... Yet the current lack of any alternative induces people to ask entirely new questions. The first question is: Perhaps the West was not right, after all? The second question: If the West was not right, then who was right? Because no doubt remains, for everyone in Europe, that Communism was not right, then the third question arises: Perhaps there is no such thing as being right? But if that is the case, then the entire intellectual heritage of the Enlightenment is worthless.... Perhaps the veteran Enlightenment steam engine, after two hundred years of useful and undisturbed work, has stopped before our eyes and with our cooperation. And the steam is just going up into the air. If that is in fact so, then the outlook is indeed dark.[2]

However much one might put counterquestions here, the realism and the logic of Szczypiorski's fundamental questions cannot be set aside; yet at the same time, the diagnosis is so oppressive that one cannot just stand still in the face of it. Was no one right? Perhaps there is no such thing as being right? Are the foundations of the European Enlightenment, upon which our path to freedom is built, false—or at least, defective? The question, "What is freedom?" is ultimately no less complicated than the question, "What is truth?" The dilemma of the Enlightenment, into which we have undeniably fallen, obliges us to put these two questions anew and

[2] I am quoting from the manuscript that was available at the Further Education sessions.

also to renew our search for the relation between the two. To find a way forward, we have therefore to reconsider the starting point of the modern path to freedom; the correction to our course, which we obviously need so that paths may become visible once more in the darkness before us, must be made on the basis of the starting points themselves and be worked out from there. Here, of course, I can only try to highlight a couple of points, to hint at some of the strong points and the dangers of the modern way, so as to prompt new reflections.

2. *The Problems Associated with the Modern History of Freedom and with Its Conception of Freedom*

There is no doubt: the era we call modern times has been determined from the beginning by the theme of freedom; the striving for new forms of freedom is the only basis upon which to justify such a division into periods. Luther's controversial polemic "The Freedom of the Christian Man" immediately strikes the note of this theme in strong tones.[3] It was the call of freedom that caught men's ear, that set off a real avalanche and brought into being, from the writings of a monk, a mass movement that completely changed the face of the medieval world. It was a matter of the freedom of conscience as against ecclesiastical authority, that is, of the inmost freedom man has. It is not social institutions that save man, but his own personal faith in Christ. The fact that, suddenly, the whole institutional system of the medieval Church no longer ultimately counted for anything was felt to be an enormous liberating thrust. The institutions that

[3] On this whole subject, see, e.g., E. Lohse, *Martin Luther* (Munich: Beck, 1981), pp. 60f., 86ff.

were actually supposed to support and save people appeared to be a burden; they were no longer obligatory, which meant they no longer had any significance for redemption. Redemption is liberation, being liberated from the yoke of supra-individual institutions. Even if one ought not to talk about the individualism of the Reformation, this new significance of the individual and the transposition of the relationship between the individual conscience and authority is nonetheless a characteristic trait. This movement for liberation did of course remain limited to the religious realm. Wherever it became a political program, as in the peasants' wars and in the Baptists' movement, Luther vigorously opposed it. In the political sphere, quite to the contrary, with the creation of state churches and provincial churches, worldly authority was increased and strengthened. In the Anglo-Saxon sphere, the Free Churches then broke out of the mold of this amalgamation of religious and political power structures and thus became heralds of a new historical structure, which then in the second phase of the modern period, the Enlightenment, took clear shape.

What the whole Enlightenment has in common is the desire for emancipation, first of all in the sense of Kant's *sapere aude*—dare to use your reason for yourself. It is a matter of the individual reason breaking free of the constraints of authority, which should in every case be subjected to critical examination. Only what can be rationally comprehended should be allowed to continue. This philosophical program is of its nature also a political program: reason alone should rule; there should ultimately be no authority other than reason. Only what can be readily understood should be allowed. What is not "rational", that is, able to be readily understood, cannot be obligatory either. This basic trend of the Enlightenment is, however, presented in various, indeed contradictory, social philosophies and political programs. It seems to me we may distinguish two main tendencies: the Anglo-Saxon trend, which is more inclined to natural law and tends toward constitutional democracy as being the only system realistically ensuring freedom; over against that, the radical direction launched by Rousseau, which ultimately aims at complete freedom from any rule. The natural law school of thought criticizes positive law and concrete forms of rule by the standard of the inherent rights of human existence, which are prior to all legal ordinances and constitute their standard and their basis. "Man is created free, is free even if he is born in chains", is what Friedrich Schiller said to the same effect. That is not a statement to comfort slaves with metaphysical thoughts; rather, it is a polemical assertion, a principle for action. Legal systems that create slavery are systems of injustice. Man has rights on the basis of his creation, rights that must be brought into effect, that justice may prevail. Freedom is not granted to man from without; he has rights because he was created free. The idea of human rights developed from this way of thinking, as the Magna Carta of the movement for freedom.

If "nature" is being talked about here, then what is meant is not just a system of biological processes. Rather, what is being said is that prior to all systems of order, within man himself, on the basis of his nature, there are rights. In that sense, the idea of human rights is in the first instance a revolutionary idea: it stands against the absolutism of the state, against the arbitrary will of positive legislation. Yet it is also a metaphysical idea: inherent in being itself there is an ethical and legal claim. Being is not blindly material, so that one might shape it in accordance with sheer utilitarian aims. Nature bears spirit within it, bears ethical value and dignity, and thus at the same time constitutes the legal claim to our liberation and the standard for this. What we have here is in principle identical with the concept of nature in Romans 2, which was inspired by Stoic teaching transformed by the theology of creation: the pagans know the law "from nature" and are thus a law for themselves (Rom 2:14).

What we may regard as specifically enlightened and modern in this line of thought is that the legal claims of nature against the existing institutions of government take the form above all of calling for the rights of the individual over against the state and against institutions. It is seen as being the nature of man, above all, that he has rights against society, rights that have to be protected from society: the institution appears as the opposite pole to freedom; the individual appears as supporting freedom and as its goal, the emancipation of the individual.

Therein this tendency joins forces with the second movement, which was from the start more radical: for Rousseau, everything created by reason and the will is contrary to nature, is a corruption and a contradiction of it. The concept of nature is not so much itself shaped here by the idea of justice, so that the natural law is prior to all of our institutions. Rousseau's concept of nature is antimetaphysical, directed toward the dream of a complete freedom unregulated by anything.[4] Something similar again makes its appearance with Nietzsche, who sets the intoxicating Dionysiac element in opposition to the ordered Apollonian, conjuring up primeval oppositions from the history of religion: the ordering

[4] See D. Wyss, "Zur Psychologie und Psychopathologie der Verblendung: J.J. Rousseau und M. Robespierre, die Begründer des Sozialismus" [On the psychology and psycho-pathology of blindness: J.J Rousseau and M. Robespierre, the founders of socialism], *Jahres- und Tagungsbericht der Görres-Gesellschaft*, 1992, pp. 33–45; R. Spaemann, *Rousseau—Bürger ohne Vaterland: Von der Polis zur Natur* [Rousseau—A citizen without a country: From the polis to nature] (Munich: Piper, 1980).

activity of reason that Apollo stands for spoils the free and untrammeled intoxication of nature.[5] Klages took up the same theme, with the idea of spirit as that which opposes the soul: The spirit is not the great new gift that alone brings freedom for the first time; rather, it is the factor that undermines our original self with its passion and freedom.[6] In a certain sense this attack on the spirit is anti-Enlightenment, and to that extent National Socialism, with its hostility to the Enlightenment and its adoration of "blood and soil", could claim support from such tendencies. Yet the basic theme of the Enlightenment, the cry for freedom, is not just at work here; rather, it has been taken to its most extreme form. In the political radicalism of the last century, as of the present one, in contrast to the domesticated democratic form of freedom, such movements have broken out again and again, in many different forms. The French Revolution, which had started with an idea of constitutional democracy, quickly threw off these shackles and set out on the road of Rousseau and of anarchic concepts of freedom; and in doing so it inevitably turned into a bloodthirsty dictatorship.

Marxism, too, continues this radical line: it has always criticized democratic freedom as merely apparent freedom and has promised a better and more radical freedom. Indeed, its fascination derived from the fact that it promised a greater and more daring freedom than is ever realized in democracies. Two aspects of the Marxist system seem to me to be of

---

[5] See P. Köster, *Der sterbliche Gott: Nietzsches Entwurf übermenschlicher Größe* [The dying God: Nietzsche's sketch for superhuman greatness] (Meisenheim: Hein, 1972); R. Löw, *Nietzsche Sophist und Erzieher* [Nietzsche as sophist and educator] (Weinheim: Acta humaniora, 1984).

[6] See T. Steinbüchel, *Die philosophische Grundlegung der christlichen Sittenlehre* [The philosophical basis of Christian moral teaching], 3rd ed., vol. I, pt. I (Düsseldorf: Mosella-Verlag, 1947), pp. 118–32.

particular importance for the whole problem of freedom in the modern era and for the question of freedom and truth:

a. Marxism makes the assumption that freedom is indivisible, that is, that it only exists as such when it is the freedom of everyone. Freedom is linked to equality: in order for freedom to exist, equality must first be restored. That means that in pursuit of the goal of complete freedom, some renunciation of freedom is required. The solidarity of those who are fighting for the common freedom of all must precede the establishment of individual freedoms. The quotation from Marx with which we started shows that the end is once more nonetheless the idea of the limitless freedom of the individual, but for the present the social aspect takes priority; equality takes priority over freedom, and therefore the rights of society as against the individual.

b. Associated with that is the assumption that the freedom of the individual is dependent upon the structure of the whole and that the struggle for freedom must for the moment be waged, not as a struggle for the rights of the individual, but as the struggle for a changed social structure in the world. As to the question of what this structure would look like and, hence, what the rational means to achieve it would be, Marxism runs out of breath at that point. For a blind man could see that none of the structures that have been constructed, for the sake of which the renunciation of freedom is demanded, truly render freedom possible. But intellectuals are blind where their mental constructs are concerned. That is why they could dispense with any realism and continue to struggle for a system whose promises just could not be kept. People took refuge in mythology: the new structures would produce a new man—for indeed, the promises could only work with new men, with quite different men. If the moral character of Marxism lies in promoting solidarity and in the idea of the indivisibility of freedom, in its heralding of a new man a lie could be seen that also paralyzed the initial moral effort. Partial truths are made subordinate to a lie, and thus the whole thing comes to grief: the lies about freedom cancel out the elements of truth. Freedom without truth is no freedom.

That is where we are standing now. We have come back again to the problems that Szczypiorski formulated in such drastic fashion in Salzburg. We now know what is a lie—at least in relation to the forms Marxism has hitherto taken. But we are still a long way from knowing what is true. Indeed, our fear is growing: Perhaps there is no such thing as truth? Perhaps there is no such thing as being right or the right thing to do? Perhaps we have to be satisfied with a minimum of absolutely necessary institutions? Yet perhaps even those may not work, as the most recent developments in the Balkans and in so many other parts of the world show us? Scepticism is growing, and the reasons for it are becoming stronger, yet the desire for the absolute is not to be set aside.

The feeling that democracy is still not the right form of freedom is fairly general and is steadily becoming more widespread. One cannot simply push aside the Marxist criticism of democracy: How free are elections? To what extent is the people's will manipulated by publicity, that is, by capital, by the agency of a few people who dominate public opinion? Is there not a new oligarchy of the people who decide what is modern and progressive, what somebody enlightened has to think? How fearsome this oligarchy is, the way they can publicly execute people, is well enough known. Anyone who gets in their way is an enemy of freedom because he is preventing freedom of expression. And what about the way public opinion is shaped in democratically representative councils and committees? Who can still believe that the general good is what really determines their decisions? Who can doubt the power of interests whose dirty hands are being seen more and more often? And is this system of majority and minority really a system of freedom at all? Are not alliances in this or that interest, of every kind, becoming visibly stronger than the actual political representation in Parliament? In this confusion of forces the problem of society becoming ungovernable is an ever greater threat: the desire of opposing groups for domination blocks the freedom of the whole.

There is, no doubt, flirtation with authoritarian solutions, a flight from uncontrolled freedom. But this attitude is not yet characteristic of the spirit of this century. The radical tendency of the Enlightenment has not lost its effectiveness; indeed, it is growing stronger. Precisely in view of the limitations of democracy, the call for total freedom is growing louder. Now as ever—indeed, quite noticeably—"law and order" is seen as the opposite of freedom. Now as ever, institutions, tradition, authority as such appear as the opposite pole from freedom. The anarchistic trait in the demand for freedom is growing stronger, because people are not satisfied with the ordered forms of social freedom. The great promises of the dawn of the modern era were not redeemed, yet their fascination is unbroken. Nowadays the democratically ordered form of freedom can no longer be defended just by this or that reform of the law. The foundations are being called into question. It is a matter of what man is and of how he, as an individual and as a whole, can live the right life.

One can see it: the political, the philosophical, and the religious problems of freedom have become an indissoluble whole; anyone looking for ways forward into the future must

keep the whole of this in view and cannot make do with
superficial pragmatic action. Before I attempt to give a few
indications, in the final section, as to the ways forward that
seem to me to be open to us, I should like to glance at what
is perhaps the most radical philosophy of freedom in this past
century, that of J. P. Sartre, where the whole seriousness and
stature of the question become clear. Sartre regards the freedom of man as being his damnation. In contrast to animals,
man has no "nature". An animal lives its life according to
the pattern of law that it has inbuilt within it; it does not
need to consider what to do with its life. But the being of
man is undetermined. It is an open question. I have to decide
for myself what I understand by "being a man", what I can
do about it, what shape I can give it. Man has no nature but
is simply freedom. He has to live his life in some direction or
other, yet it runs out into nothingness even so. His meaningless freedom is man's hell. What is exciting about this
proposition is that the separation of freedom and truth is
carried through quite radically here: there is no truth. Freedom is without direction or measure.[7] Yet this complete
absence of truth, the complete absence also of any kind of
moral or metaphysical restraint, the absolute anarchic freedom of man constituted by his self-determination, is revealed,
for anyone who tries to live it out, not as the most sublime
exaltation of existence, but as a life of nothingness, as absolute emptiness, as the definition of damnation. In this extrap-
olation of a radical concept of freedom, which was for Sartre

[7] See J. Pieper, "Kreatürlichkeit und menschliche Natur: Anmerkungen zum
philosophischen Ansatz von J. P. Sartre" [Being a creature and human nature:
Notes on J. P. Sartre's attempt at philosophy], in his *Über die Schwierigkeit, heute
zu glauben* (Munich: Kösel, 1974), pp. 304–21 [English trans., *Problems of Modern Faith: Essays and Addresses*, trans. Jan van Heurck (Chicago: Franciscan Herald Press, 1984)].

his experience of life, it becomes clear that being freed from truth does not engender pure freedom; rather, it abolishes it. The anarchistic freedom, taken to a radical conclusion, does not redeem man; rather, it makes him into a faulty creation, living without meaning.

3. Freedom and Truth

3.1 On the Nature of Human Freedom

Following this attempt to understand the origins of our problems, and thus to bring their inner impulse before us, it is now time to look for an answer. It must have become clear that the crisis in the history of freedom in which we find ourselves arises from an unclarified and one-sided conception of freedom. On the one hand, people have isolated the concept of freedom and have thereby distorted it: freedom is good, but it is only good in association with other good things, with which it constitutes an indissoluble whole. On the other hand, people have narrowed down the concept of freedom to individual rights and freedoms and have thus robbed it of its human verity. I should like to make clear the problem of this understanding of freedom with one concrete example, which can at the same time open up for us the way toward a more appropriate conception of freedom. I mean the question of abortion. In the radical version of the Enlightenment's individualistic tendency, abortion appears to be one of the rights of freedom: a woman must be able to have total control over herself. She must have the freedom to bring a child into the world or to rid herself of it. She must be able to make decisions concerning herself, and nobody else—so we are told—can impose upon her, from without, any ultimately binding norm. It is a matter of the right of self-determination. But, in an abortion, is the woman actually making a decision that concerns herself? Is she not in fact making a decision about someone else—deciding that this other person should be allowed no freedom, that the sphere of freedom—his life—should be taken away from him because it is in competition with her own freedom? And thus we should ask: What kind of a freedom is this that numbers among its rights that of abolishing someone else's freedom right from the start?

Now people should not say that the problem of abortion touches on a specific special case and does not help to clarify the problem of freedom as a whole. On the contrary, in this particular example the basic shape of human freedom, its typically human character, becomes clear. For what is at issue here? The being of another person is so closely interwoven with the being of this first person, the mother, that for the moment it can only exist at all in bodily association with the mother, in a physical union with her, which nonetheless does not abolish its otherness and does not permit us to dispute its being itself. Of course, this being itself is, in quite radical fashion, a being from the other person, through the other person; conversely, the being of the other person—the mother—is forced through this coexistence into an existence-for-someone that contradicts its own self-will and is thus experienced as the contrary of its own freedom. Now, we have to add that the child, even when he is born and the outward form of being-from and of coexistence changes, remains even so just as dependent, just as much in need of someone being there for it. Of course, you can push it away into a home and assign someone else to be there for it, but the anthropological figure stays the same; it remains the derived being, demanding someone be there for it, meaning an assumption of the limits of my freedom, or rather the living of my freedom, not in competition, but in mutual support.

If we open our eyes, we see that this is not only true of a child, that the child in its mother's womb just makes us most vividly aware of the nature of human existence as a whole: it is also true of the adult that he can exist only with the other person and from him and is thus forever dependent on this being for that he would most of all like to eliminate. Let us put it more precisely: Man presumes completely of his own accord that others will be there for him, as has been arranged today in the network of services provided, yet for his own part he would prefer not to be included in the constraint of such a "from" and "for" others; rather, he would prefer to become entirely independent, to be able to do and allow only just what he wants. The radical demand for freedom that arose with ever greater clarity in the path of the Enlightenment, especially along the line established by Rousseau, and that today is largely determinative of general consciousness, wishes to be neither "coming from" nor "going toward", wishes to exist neither from nor for another, but just to be completely free. That is to say, it regards the real basic shape of human existence itself as an attack on freedom that is prior to every individual life and activity; it would like to be freed from its own human nature and existence itself to become a "new man": in the new society, these dependencies that restrict the self and this obligation to give of oneself should not be allowed to exist.

Basically, what clearly stands behind the modern era's radical demand for freedom is the promise: You will be like God. Even if Ernst Topitsch believed he could establish that no rational man still wanted nowadays to be like God or equal to God, if we look more closely we have to maintain the very opposite: The implicit goal of all modern freedom movements is, in the end, to be like a god, dependent on nothing and nobody, with one's own freedom not restricted by anyone else's. When we first take a look at this hidden theological core in the radical desire for freedom, then the fundamental error also becomes clear, which is having an effect even where such radical programs are not specifically desired, where they are even rejected. Being completely free, without the competition of any other freedom, without any "from" and "for"—behind that stands, not an image of God, but the image of an idol. The primeval error of such a radically developed desire for freedom lies in the idea of a divinity that is conceived as being purely egotistical. The god thus conceived of is, not God, but an idol, indeed, the image of what the Christian tradition would call the devil, the anti-god, because therein lies the radical opposite of the true God: the true God is, of his own nature, being-for (Father), being-from (Son), and being-with (Holy Spirit). Yet man is in the image of God precisely because the being for, from, and with constitute the basic anthropological shape. Whenever people try to free themselves from this, they are moving, not toward divinity, but toward dehumanizing, toward the destruction of being itself through the destruction of truth. The Jacobin variant of the idea of liberation (let us just use that term for modern forms of radicalism) is a rebellion against being human in itself, rebellion against truth, and that is why it leads people—as Sartre percipiently observed—into a self-contradictory existence that we call hell.

It has thus become fairly clear that freedom is linked to a yardstick, the yardstick of reality—to truth. Freedom to destroy one-self or to destroy others is not freedom but a diabolical parody. The freedom of man is a shared freedom, freedom in a coexistence of other freedoms, which are mutually limiting and thus mutually supportive: freedom must be measured according to what I am, what we are—otherwise it abolishes itself. Now, however, we come to a substantial correction to the superficial present-day picture of freedom that has hitherto been largely dominant: If the freedom of man can only continue to exist within an ordered coexistence of freedoms, then this means that order—law—is, not the concept contrary to that of freedom, but its condition, indeed, a constitutive element of freedom itself. Law is not the obstacle to freedom; rather, it constitutes freedom. The absence of law is the absence of freedom.

3.2 *Freedom and Responsibility*

When we recognize this, of course, a new question also arises: What kind of law is consonant with freedom? How must the law be constituted in order for it to be a law of freedom, for there is definitely a pseudo-law that is a law of slaves and is therefore, not a law at all, but a regulated form of injustice. Our criticism should not be directed against law itself, which belongs to the essence of freedom; it should serve to convict merely pseudo-law as such and should serve the emergence of true law—of that law which is consonant with the truth and, therefore, with freedom.

But how do we find it? That is the big question, the question that is at least correctly put, concerning the real history of liberation. Let us proceed here, as we have done up to now, not with abstract philosophical considerations, but let us try instead to feel our way toward an answer, starting from the given realities of history. Let us start with a small community we can view as a whole, so that from its capabilities and limitations it may to some extent be possible to fathom what form of order best serves the life together of all its members, so that a common shape of freedom arises from their coexistence. But no small community exists of itself; it is sheltered and its nature partially determined by the greater institutions to which it belongs. In the era of nation-states, people assumed that their own nation was the unity that set the standards—that its common good was the accurate yard-stick of common freedom. The developments in our own twentieth century have made it clear that this point of view is inadequate. On this subject, Augustine said that a state that measured itself only by the common interests of that state, and not by justice itself, by true justice, was not struc-turally differentiated from a well-organized band of robbers. It is characteristic of such a band that it takes as its standard the good of the band, independent of the good of others. Looking back on the colonial period, and the damage it left behind it in the world, we can see today that, however well-ordered and civilized states may have been, in some way or other they resembled robber bands, because they only thought from the point of view of their own good, and not from that of good in itself. A freedom guaranteed in that way does have something of the freedom of robbers about it. It is not true, genuine human freedom. In seeking the true yardstick of freedom, the whole of mankind must be kept in view, and—as we see more and more clearly—again, not just today's mankind, but also tomorrow's.

The yardstick of true justice, that which can really be called justice and, therefore, a law of freedom, can thus only be the good of the whole, good itself. Starting from this perception, Hans Jonas explained how the concept of responsibility should be the central concept of ethics.[8] That means that freedom, in order to be properly understood, must always be thought of

---

[8] H. Jonas, *Das Prinzip Verantwortung* [The principle of responsibility] (Frank-furt am Main: Insel-Verlag, 1979).

together with responsibility. The history of liberation can, accordingly, only ever take place as the history of growing responsibility. The growth of freedom can no longer consist simply in the demolishing of barriers to individual rights ever more widely—something that leads to absurdity and to the destruction of those very individual rights. The growth of freedom must consist in the growth of responsibility. That includes the acceptance of ever greater ties, as demanded by the claims of human coexistence, by what is appropriate for the essence of being human. If responsibility means answers to the truth of human existence, then we can say that a constant purification in the direction of truth is a part of the true history of liberation. This true history of freedom consists of the purification of the individual and of institutions by this truth.

The principle of responsibility establishes a framework that needs to be filled with some content. It is in this context that the suggestion of developing a universal ethic, to which Hans Küng is above all passionately committed, needs to be seen. No doubt it makes sense, and indeed in our present position it is necessary, to search for the basic elements held in common by the ethical traditions in the various religions and cultures; in that sense, such activity is certainly both important and appropriate. On the other hand, the limits of such an attempt are obvious, and Joachim Fest has pointed them out in an analysis that is entirely supportive of Küng yet also very pessimistic and moves in the same direction as the scepticism of Szczypiorski.[9] For such an ethical minimum,

[9] J. Fest, *Die schwierige Freiheit* [Difficult freedom] (Berlin: Siedler, 1993), especially pp. 47–81; on p. 80 he summarizes his comments on Küng's "universal ethic" in these terms: "The farther we push such elements of agreement, which cannot be achieved without concessions, the more flexible—and, consequently, the less powerful—the ethical norms will then necessarily become, until the whole project is directed toward merely strengthening that

distilled out of the world religions, would in the first place lack any binding character, that inner authority which any ethic needs. And despite all efforts toward understanding, it lacks also the rational evidence that, in the opinion of the authors, could and should probably replace authority; it lacks also the concrete character that alone makes any ethic effective.

One thought, which is probably associated with this attempt, seems to me correct: Reason needs to listen to the great religious traditions if it does not wish to become deaf, blind, and mute concerning the most essential elements of human existence. There is no great philosophy that does not draw its life from listening to and accepting religious tradition. Wherever this relationship is cut off, then philosophical thinking withers and becomes a mere game of concepts.[10] It is precisely in connection with this theme of responsibility, that is, with the question of freedom's being rooted in the truth of what is good, in the truth of man and of the world, that the need for listening is most clearly seen. For however appropriate the principle of responsibility may be, as an approach to the matter, the question remains: How shall we gain an overall view of what is good for everyone and of what is good not only for today but for tomorrow? There is a twofold danger lurking here: on the one hand, we risk slipping off into "consequentialism", which is something the Pope quite rightly criticized in his encyclical on morality.[11] Man is quite simply taking on too much

---

non-obligatory moral behavior that is in fact, not our aim, but the problem from which we start."

[10] There are some penetrating comments on this in J. Pieper, *Schriften zum Philosophiebegriff* [Writings on the concept of philosophy], vol. 3 of his *Werke*, ed. B. Wald (Hamburg: Meiner, 1995), pp. 300–323; likewise pp. 15–70, especially pp. 59ff.

[11] *Veritatis splendor*, nos. 71–83.

if he believes he can work out the all-around consequences of his actions and take these as the norm for his freedom. Then the present is straightaway being sacrificed to the future, and yet not even the future is being built up. On the other hand, the question is there: Who, then, will decide what our responsibility demands? If truth is no longer seen as understanding and appropriating the great traditions of faith, then it is replaced by consensus. But again, we must ask: The consensus of whom? Then it is said that this should be the consensus of those who are capable of reasoning. Because no one can then overlook the elitist presumption of such an intellectual dictatorship, it is then said that those who are capable of reasoning must stand in for those who are supposedly incapable of rational discourse, as their "advocates". All that can hardly inspire much confidence. We can all see with our own eyes how fragile any consensus is and how easily and quickly, in a certain intellectual climate, parties and interest groups can impose themselves as the only legitimate representatives of progress and responsibility. It is only too easy here to drive out the devil with the help of Beelzebub; all too easy for our house to be occupied, in the place of the devil of past spiritual combinations, by seven new and worse devils.

3.3 The Truth of Our Human Existence

The question of how to set responsibility and freedom in the right relationship cannot simply be decided by calculating the effects. We must look back to our previous notion, that human freedom is a freedom in a coexistence of freedoms; only thus is it true—that is, appropriate to the true reality of man. That means that I have no need at all to seek corrective factors for the freedom of the individual from without; if that were so, then freedom and responsibility, freedom and truth would remain forever opposites, and they are not. Correctly perceived, the reality of the individual carries in it an element of reference to the whole, to others. Accordingly, we shall say that there is such a thing as the common truth of the one human existence within every man, what is referred to in tradition as the "nature" of man. We can formulate this more clearly on the basis of our belief in creation: There is one divine idea of man, and our task is to correspond to this. In this idea, freedom and community, order and being turned toward the future, are all one thing.

Responsibility would then mean living our existence as a response—as a response to what we are in truth. This one truth of man, in which the good of all and freedom are indissolubly related to each other, is expressed most centrally in the biblical tradition in the Ten Commandments, which in many respects correspond to the great ethical traditions of other religions, besides. In the Ten Commandments God presents himself, depicts himself, and at the same time interprets human existence, so that its truth is made manifest, as it becomes visible in the mirror of God's nature, because man can only rightly be understood from the viewpoint of God. Living out the Ten Commandments means living out our own resemblance to God, responding to the truth of our nature, and thus doing good. To say it again, another way: Living out the Ten Commandments means living out the divinity of man, and exactly that is freedom: the fusing of our being with the Divine Being and the resulting harmony of all with all.[12]

So that this proposition may be properly understood, one further remark must be added. Every great human utterance

[12] See the *Cathechism of the Catholic Church*, nos. 2052–82.

reaches beyond what was consciously said into greater, more profound depths; there is always, hidden in what is said, a surplus of what is not said, which lets the words grow with the passing of time. If this is true of human speech, then it is certainly true of the word that comes from the depths of God. The Ten Commandments can never simply be completely understood. In the circumstances and situations of historical responsibility that follow one another and change each other, the Ten Commandments appear in ever-new perspectives, and ever-new dimensions of their meaning open up. What is occurring is a process of being guided into the whole of truth, into the truth that absolutely cannot be carried within one historical moment alone (see Jn 16:12f.). For the Christian, the interpretation that was completed in the words and the life and the death and the Resurrection of Christ represents the ultimate interpretative authority, wherein emerges a depth that could not previously have been foreseen. Because that is so, human listening to the message of faith is no passive reception of hitherto unknown information; rather, it is the awakening of our submerged conscience and the opening up of the powers of understanding that are awaiting the light of truth within us. Thus, such understanding is a highly active process, in which the quite rational search for the standards of our responsibility really gains in strength. This rational search is not stifled but is rather freed from helpless circling around what is unfathomable and brought onto the right track. If the Ten Commandments, as expounded by rational understanding, are the answer to the inner demands of our nature, then they are not at the opposite pole to our freedom but are rather the concrete form it takes. They are then the foundation for every law of freedom and are the one truly liberating power in human history.

4. *Summary of Conclusions*

"Perhaps the veteran Enlightenment steam engine, after two hundred years of useful and undisturbed work, has stopped before our eyes and with our cooperation. And the steam is just going up into the air." That is Szczypiorski's pessimistic diagnosis, which at the start challenged us to reflect on our path. Now, I should say that this machine had never worked without disturbance—think of the two world wars in our own twentieth century and of the dictatorships we have lived through. But I would add that we do not by any means need to bid adieu to the heritage of the Enlightenment as such and, as a whole, to regard it as a superannuated steam engine. What we do of course need is to correct our course in three essential points, in which I should like to summarize the results of my reflections.

1.   An understanding of freedom is wrong if it would see as liberating simply an ever-wider loosening of norms and the constant extension of individual freedoms in the direction of a total liberation from all order. Unless it is to lead to lying and self-destruction, freedom must relate to the truth, that is to say, to what we actually are, and must correspond to this nature of ours. Since man is a being who exists in being-from, being-with, and being-for, human freedom can only exist in an ordered coexistence of freedoms. Law is, therefore, not the opposite of freedom, but its necessary condition; it is indeed constitutive of freedom. Liberation consists, not in gradually getting rid of law and of norms of behavior, but in purifying ourselves and purifying those norms, so that they make possible that coexistence of freedoms which is appropriate to man.

2.   A second point follows, out of the true reality of our nature: Within this human history of ours the absolutely

ideal situation will never exist, and a perfected ordering of freedom will never be able to be achieved. Man is always moving on and always finite. In view of the obvious injustice of the socialist ordering of society, and in view of all the problems of the liberal order, Szczypiorski put the despairing question: Perhaps there is no such thing as being right? We now have to say to that: Indeed, an ordering of things that is simply ideal, that is all-around right and just, will never exist.[13] Wherever such a claim is made, truth is not being spoken. Belief in progress is not false in every respect. But the myth of a liberated world of the future, in which everything will be different and everything good, is false. We can only ever construct relative social orders, which can only ever be relatively right and just. Yet this very same closest possible approach to true right and justice is what we must strive to attain. Everything else, every eschatological promise within history, fails to liberate us; rather, it disappoints and therefore enslaves us. That is why the mythological glamor that has been added onto such concepts as change and revolution has to be demythologized. Change is not good in itself. Whether it is good or bad depends on its particular content and how it relates to other things. The opinion that the main task in the struggle for freedom is that of changing the world is, I repeat, a myth. There will always be ups and downs in history. In relation to the actual moral nature of man, it does not run in a straight line; rather, it repeats itself. It is our task always to struggle for the relatively best possible framework of human coexistence in our own present day and, in doing so, to preserve anything good that has already been achieved, to overcome anything bad that exists at the time, and to guard against the outbreak of destructive forces.

[13] See the Vatican II constitution *Gaudium et spes*, no. 78: ". . . numquam pax pro semper acquisita est. . . ."

3. We must also bid farewell to the dream of the absolute autonomy of reason and of its self-sufficiency. Human reason needs a hint from the great religious traditions of mankind. It will certainly look at the individual traditions in a critical light. The pathology of religion is the most dangerous sickness of the human spirit. It exists within the religions, yet it exists also precisely where religion as such is rejected and relative goods are assigned an absolute value: the atheistic systems of modern times are the most frightful examples of passionate religious enthusiasm alienated from its proper identity, and that means a sickness of the human spirit that may be mortal. When the existence of God is denied, freedom is, not enhanced, but deprived of its basis and thus distorted.[14] When the purest and most profound religious traditions are set aside, man is separating himself from his truth; he is living contrary to that truth, and he loses his freedom. Nor can philosophical ethics be simply autonomous. It cannot dispense with the concept of God or dispense with the concept of a truth of being that is of an ethical nature.[15] If there is no truth about man, then he has no freedom. Only the truth makes us free.

---

[14] See Fest, *Schwierige Freiheit*, p. 79: "None of the appeals made on man's behalf is able to say how he can live without a life beyond this, and without any fear of a final judgment, and nonetheless act, time and time again, contrary to his own interests and desires." See also L. Kolakowski, *Falls es keinen Gott gibt* [If there is no God] (Munich: Piper, 1982).

[15] See Pieper, *Schriften zum Philosophiebegriff.*

INDIVIDUAL CHAPTERS
PREVIOUSLY PUBLISHED

PART ONE

Chapter 1: The Unity and Diversity of Religions: The Place of Christianity in the History of Religions

Appeared in *Gott in Welt: Festgabe für Karl Rahner zum 60. Geburtstag* [God in world: Essays presented to Karl Rahner on his sixtieth birthday], edited by H. Vorgrimler (Freiburg, 1964), 2: 287–305; and again in Joseph Cardinal Ratzinger, *Vom Wiederauffinden der Mitte: Grundorientierungen: Texte aus vier Jahrzehnten* [Rediscovering the center: Basic outlines: Texts from four decades], published by his former students, edited by Stephan Horn, Vinzenz Pfnür, Vincent Twomey, Siegfried Wiedenhofer, and Josef Zöhrer (Freiburg, Basel, and Vienna: Herder, 1997; 2nd ed., 1998), pp. 60–82.

Chapter 2: Faith, Religion, and Culture

Appeared as "Der christliche Glaube vor der Herausforderung der Kulturen" [The Christian faith confronting the challenge of cultures], in P. Gordan, editor, *Evangelium und Inkulturation (1492–1992): Salzburger Hochschulwochen 1992* [Gospel and inculturation (1492–1992):

Salzburg further education sessions 1992] (Graz 1993), pp. 9–26; again in: *KNA, Ökumenische Information*, no. 52/53 (December 1992): 5–15;

in Spanish, in *Ecclesia* 7 (1993): 369–86; and in *Mercurio* 1993, Santiago de Chile; revised Spanish version in *Nuova umanità* 16, no. 6 (1994): 95–118;

in English (amplified version) in *Origins: Christ, Faith and the Challenge of Cultures*, vol. 24, no. 41 (March 30, 1995): 678–86; the same version in *Communio* (Spanish), no. 18 (1996): 152–70.

PART TWO

Chapter 1: The New Questions That Arose in the Nineties—The Position of Faith and Theology Today

"On the Position of Faith and Theology Today", in *Internationale katholische Zeitschrift "Communio"* 25 (1996): 359–72; likewise in various issues of *L'Osservatore Romano*; and in M. Müller, *Stets war es der Hund, der starb* [It has always been the dog that died] (Aachen, 1998), pp. 33–53;

in Spanish, in *Ecclesia* 10 (1996): 485–502; also in *Communio* (Madrid) 19 (1997): 13–27; likewise in *Humanitas*, 1997: 280–93; an extract appeared in *Enciclopedia del Cristianesimo* (Navarra, 1997): 22–30; again in Spanish in: Consejo Episcopal Latino americano, *Fe y teología en América Latina* [Latin American Council of Bishops: Theological faith in Latin America] (Bogotá, 1997), pp. 13–36; and in *Gladius* 43 (1998): 13–27;

in Italian, in *La Civiltà cattolica* 147 (1996): 477–90;

in French, in *Communio* 22 (1997): 69–88; again in *Documentation catholique*;
in Portuguese, in *Communio Brasil* 79 (July/December 1998): 185–201.

Chapter 2: The Truth of Christianity?

1. *Faith between Reason and Feeling*

"Glaube zwischen Vernunft und Gefühl" [Faith between reason and feeling], in *Mitteilungen des Übersee-Club* (Hamburg, 1998) (Sonderdruck [one-off printing]); also in *Die neue Ordnung* 52 (1998): 164–77; and in *Konferenzblatt für Theologie und Seelsorge* (Brixen) 110 (1999): 133–44;
in Polish, in *Ethos* (Lublin) no. 44 (1998): 59–72;
in Italian, in *ArchivioTeologico Torinese* 1 (1999): 7–19.

2. *Christianity—The True Religion?*

"Vérité du Christianisme?" [The truth of Christianity?], lecture delivered on November 27, 1999, at the Sorbonne, Paris; extract in *Le Monde* (1999); extract in *La Croix* (1999); full text in *Documentation catholique*, 2000, no. 1: 29–35; in *30 Jours*, 2000, no. 1: 33–44; in Cyrille Michon, editor, *Christianisme: Héritages et destins* [Christianity: Heritages and destinies] (Paris: Librairie Générale Française, 2002), pp. 303–24;
in German, extract in *Frankfurter Allgemeine Zeitung* for January 8, 2000; full text in *30 Tage*, 2000, no. 1: 33–44; in Albert Raffelt, editor, *Weg und Weite: Festschrift für Karl Lehmann* [Path and distance: in honor of Karl Lehmann] (Freiburg: Herder, 2001), pp. 631–42;
in English, in *30 Days*, 2000, no. 1: 33–44;

in Italian, in *30 Giorni*, 2000, no. 1: 49–60; also in *Vita e Pensiero*, 2000, no. 1: 1–16; in *Nuova Umanità* 22, no. 2 (2000): 128, 187–202; *MicroMega:Almanacco di filosofia*, 2000, no. 2: 41–53;

in Portuguese, in *30 Dias*, 2000, no. 1: 33–44;

in Spanish, in *30 Dias*, 2000, no. 1: 33–44; "¿Verdad del cristianismo?" *Communio* (Santiago de Chile), 2001, no. 5: 83–98;

in Polish, in *Christianitas*, 2000, no. 3: 11–23; also in *Ethos*, no. 53–54 (2001): 79–90;

in Magyar (Hungarian), (an extract, as in FAZ of January 8, 2000) in *Mérleg*, 2000, no. 3: 292–301.

3. Faith, Truth, and Culture: Reflections Prompted by the Encyclical **Fides et Ratio**

"Culture and Truth: Reflections on the Encyclical", *Origins*, vol. 28, no. 36 (1999): 625–31; also in *Sacerdos*, no. 26 (March–April 2000): 19–28;

in German, "Die Einheit des Glaubens und die Vielfalt der Kulturen" [The unity of the faith and the multiplicity of cultures]: Reflexionen im Anschluß an die Enzyklika 'Fides et ratio', *Theologie und Glaube* 89 (1999): 141–52; in *Wahrheit, die uns trägt* [Faith that supports us] (Paderborn, 1999), pp; 24–40; and in *Internationale katholische Zeitschrift "Communio"*, 28 (1999): 289–305 (of November 17, 1998);

in Italian, "L'Enciclica Fides et Ratio: Conferenza svolta in San Giovanni in Laterano", *Per una lettura dell'Enciclica Fides et ratio* [For a reading of the encyclical "Fides et Ratio"]: *Quaderni de "L'Osservatore Romano"*, no. 45 (Vatican City, 1999), pp. 245–59; also in Rino Fisichella, editor, *Fides et ratio: Lettera enciclica di Giovanni Paolo II* (Milan: Edizioni San Paolo, Cinisello Balsamo, 1999), pp. 117–28;

in Portuguese, "Fe, verdad e cultura" [Faith, truth, and culture], part 1, *Communio* 16, no. 5 (1999): 464–72; and "Fe, verdad e cultura", part 2, *Communio* 16, no. 6 (1999): 557–68;

in Spanish, (an extensively reworked version) in: *Alfa y Omega/Documentos* (= supplement to the daily newspaper *ABC*, Madrid), no. 200 (February 17, 2000): 1–18;

in Polish, in *Analecta Cracoviensa* 32 (Concilium Editorum: Lucas Kamykowski, Stephanus Koperek, C.R., Boleslaus Kumor, Ioseph Makselon, Kazimierz Panuś Pontifica Academia Theologica Cracoviensis), Wydawnictwo Naukowe Papieskiej Akademii Teologicznej W Krakowie, 2000, pp. 231–46.

Chapter 3: Truth—Tolerance—Freedom

1. Faith—Truth—Tolerance

Not previously published.

2. Freedom and Truth

In *Internationale katholische Zeitscrift Communio* 24 (1995): 526–42; again in O. Scrinzi and J. Schwab, editors, *1848: Erbe und Auftrag* [1848: Heritage and mission] (1998), pp. 83–99;

in Italian, in *Communio*, no. 144 (1995): 9–28; also in *Studi cattolici* 40, no. 430 (1996): 820–30;

in English, in *Communio* (American edition) 23 (1996): 16–35;

in French, in *Communio* 24, no. 2 (1999): 83–101;

in Spanish, in *Humanitas* (Pontificia Universidad Católica de Chile), no. 14 (1999): 199–222.

INDEX

Abel, 96

abortion, 190, 245–47

Abraham, 20, 70, 87, 96–98, 108, 144–48, 155, 199

advent concept, 63, 63n3, 77, 79, 196

Age of Aquarius, 126–29, 127n11

Ambrose, St., 41, 183

anarchism, 243–45

"anonymous Christian", 16–17. *See also* provisional/preparatory religions

Anscombe, G. Elizabeth M., 215

Apologia David (Ambrose), 41

Areopagus speech, 20, 170

Aristotle, 223

Asiatic religions: Buddhism, 49, 68, 162, 175–76, 194, 217, 226–27; Hinduism, 24, 33, 47, 176, 194, 204, 217; Islam and, 143;

mysticism of, 33–34, 46, 84–85, 179; personalities of, 40–41; relativism of, 26, 119, 121–23, 226; ritual and, 26, 125–26

Assisi World Days of Prayer, 106–7

Assmann, Jan, 210–14, 217n12, 221–22, 226, 227, 230

Athanasius, 218–19

atheism, 82, 141, 170, 204, 213, 258. *See also* heathen

Augustine, St., 41, 86–87, 165, 169, 224n21, 229, 250

Aztecs, 74–75

Bailey, A., 127n11

Ball, H., 89n3

Bangalore conference on prayer, 100–101

baptism, 87, 89n3

Barth, Karl, 49–51, 54, 66, 80, 136

SCRIPTURE INDEX